AN ECONOMIC HISTORY OF ULSTER,

1820–1940

To the memory of
E. R. R. GREEN

AN

ECONOMIC HISTORY
OF ULSTER, 1820–1940

EDITED BY

Líam Kennedy and
Philip Ollerenshaw

Manchester
University Press

Published by
Manchester University Press
Oxford Road, Manchester M13 9PL, U.K.
and 27 South Main Street, Wolfeboro,
N.H. 03894-2069, U.S.A.

Reprinted 1987

British Library cataloguing in publication data
An economic history of Ulster, 1820–1939.
1. Northern Ireland — Economic conditions
I. Kennedy, Liam   II. Ollerenshaw, Philip
330.9416′08   HC257.N58

Library of Congress cataloging in publication data
The economic history of Ulster, 1820–1939.
Bibliography: p. 241
Includes index.
1. Ulster (Northern Ireland and Ireland) —
Economic conditions — Addresses, essays,
lectures. 2. Northern Ireland — Economic
conditions — Addresses, essays, lectures.
I. Kennedy, Liam, 1946– . II. Ollerenshaw,
Philip (Philip Gordon), 1953– .
HC260.5.Z7U474   1985   330.9416   84-26079

ISBN 0 7190 1827 7 *paperback*

Printed in Great Britain
by Bell & Bain, Glasgow

CONTENTS

TABLES AND MAPS

PREFACE

In the mid-seventeenth century Ulster was generally regarded as the poorest Irish province. From the 1680s, however, this position began to change, primarily because of the rapid growth of a domestic linen industry which exercised a major influence in Ulster throughout the eighteenth century and after. In the early nineteenth century east Ulster was probably the most prosperous area of Ireland, and retained this position throughout the period with which this book is concerned. The pace of industrialisation quickened from the 1780s and the extent of industrial development distinguished Ulster from other Irish provinces, and indeed the east of the province from the west. The experience of industrialisation in east Ulster had far more in common with similar processes in neighbouring regions of north-west Britain than with the rest of Ireland, and in fact links between Belfast, Liverpool and Glasgow became stronger as the nineteenth century progressed. Another distinctive feature of Ulster was, and remains, the presence of a substantial Protestant population. Indeed it is difficult to exaggerate the significance of Protestant influence on the economic, social and political evolution of modern Ulster.

Much has been written on the social and political history of the province, but rather less attention has been devoted to economic developments. This book is intended as an introduction to the major themes in Ulster economic history from the end of the Napoleonic wars to the eve of the Second World War. For the period 1820–1921 Ulster is here defined as the historic nine-county province outlined in Map 1. After 1921 the unit of study becomes the six-county area of Northern Ireland. The economic effects of the partition of Ireland are explored in some detail in Chapter Six.

In compiling the book we have incurred substantial debts. We are extremely grateful to Sandra Maxwell who coped calmly and efficiently with a difficult manuscript, and to Ian Alexander who drew the maps. Thanks are also due to Dr R. H. Buchanan for his encouragement and general support. The Institute of Irish Studies at Queen's University, Belfast, kindly provided financial assistance towards the cost of preparing the manuscript. Finally, the book is dedicated to the late Professor Rodney Green who, through his published work and as Director of the Institute of Irish Studies at Queen's between 1970 and 1981, made an invaluable contribution to the study of Ulster economic history.

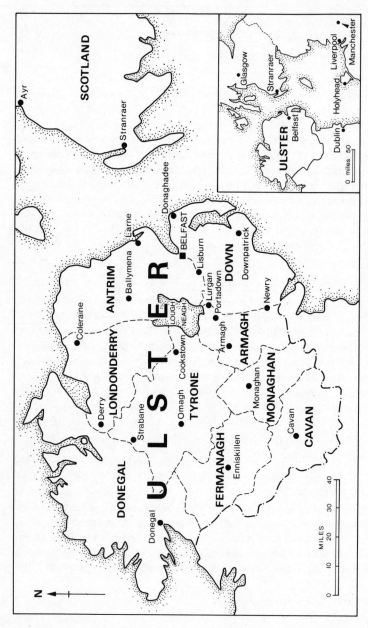

Map 1   The province of Ulster

CHAPTER ONE

THE RURAL ECONOMY, 1820–1914

Líam Kennedy

By the eve of the Great War the rural social structure had experienced a striking transformation. Ulster landlords had been effectively separated from the soil, though their political and social influence still extended, if more weakly, beyond the demesne walls. Labourers had shrunk to an almost insignificant proportion of the rural labour force. Rural industry, once such a pervasive feature of people's working lives, had either withered away or been replaced by factory-based production in urban centres, chiefly located around Belfast Lough and in the Lagan Valley. The small family farm, worked and increasingly owned by its members, dominated the rural economy. A century earlier, a much more complex pattern of work, property, and class relationships had prevailed. This chapter, using a thematic approach, traces the course of socio-economic change over this period of one hundred years or so. Industry was closely intertwined with agriculture at the beginning of our period; the focus of section one is the changing nature of this relationship over time. The second section concentrates on the technical side of farming, on patterns of land use in particular. Thus while agriculture operates within a framework imposed by soil and climatic conditions, within these broad constraints farmers can adjust production to changes in the prices of farm outputs and inputs. There follows a discussion of agricultural fluctuations, which were intimately bound up with the problem of poverty in the Ulster rural economy. Landlords make their appearance in the fourth section, where a variety of issues connected with the landlord-and-tenant system are reviewed. The final theme to be considered is the restructuring of the rural labour force in the course of the economic development of the north-east.[1]

Industry in the rural economy
Economic diversification, most notably the prevalence of rural industry, added a distinctive feature to Ulster economy and society.

1

In the eighteenth century the production of linen cloth, primarily for export to Britain, had increased enormously. In 1750 roughly eleven million yards of linen cloth, most of it produced in Ulster, were exported from Ireland. By 1815 these exports had virtually quadrupled, reaching a level of forty-three million yards in that year. Further expansion saw exports rising above the fifty million mark in the mid-1830s.[2] In addition, there was a smaller trade in hand-spun yarn; this declined steeply in the late eighteenth century, though it made a brief and unsustained recovery during the trade disruption occasioned by the Napoleonic wars.[3] To underline the significance of linen textiles to the Irish and especially the Ulster economy, it may be noted that the volume and value of linen exports from the island exceeded that of either of the two other major export commodities, cattle and corn, in the early years of the nineteenth century.[4] In terms of exports, Ulster was primarily a manufacturing rather than a food-producing region.

Originally, the industry developed as a subsidiary activity alongside agriculture, gaining increased significance and a momentum of its own over time.[5] Typically, the flax was grown on the farm. Later the women of the household, using a spinning wheel, spun the specially prepared flax into yarn. The menfolk then wove linen fabrics on handlooms located in the farmhouse or an adjoining workshop. Thus it was possible to confine the major stages of production, from the growing of the raw material through to the creation of linen cloth, within the framework of the household economy. Only the more capital-intensive finishing processes, bleaching in particular, were conducted outside the domestic system of production. There was division of labour along gender and age lines: males specialised in the heavier task of weaving, while females spun, and even quite young children would assist with such lighter tasks as winding yarn. During the busy times of the farming year the loom was abandoned for the fields; in slack periods manufacturing might be resumed again. Thus rural industry nicely complemented agriculture, which, because of its dependence on seasons and weather conditions, has a much more irregular demand for labour. This archetypal pattern did not apply throughout Ulster. Where landholdings were relatively large and fertile, there was little pressure to diversify into rural manufacturing; in geographically remote areas in the west, if textile production took place, it tended to take the form of spinning or woollen manufacture for local use. Also, by the late eighteenth century, though the independent farmer-weaver dominated, there were increasing numbers of journeymen-weavers working for wealthier weavers or for middlemen of various kinds (yarn jobbers, linen merchants, bleachers). The journeymen were essentially employees, though having accumulated some capital they might later set up as independent weavers.

This process of social differentiation assumed a more permanent form with the rise of the cottier-weaver. In south Ulster in particular, farmers and farmer-weavers frequently sublet small portions of land and a cottage to weavers, receiving payment in money, cloth, or farm work.[6] Also, because of the prosperity of the linen industry in the late eighteenth century, weaving households were able to compete effectively against farmers in bidding for land, thus extending further the lowly stratum of smallholder-weavers. The roots of the 'putting-out' system also lay in that century, though it was in the decades after 1800 that it blossomed forth on a vast scale.[7] This form of economic organisation is discussed in some detail later; we may note here that one of its primary effects was to undermine independent production and to reduce more and more weavers to an economically dependent, semi-proletarian status.

Developments in the cotton industry in Britain and Ireland had major implications for Ulster linen manufacture. Cotton spinning, which was introduced into the Belfast region on a factory basis in the 1770s, led to a greatly expanded demand for handloom weavers. Many transferred out of linen into cotton weaving. This occurred primarily in the coastal districts of the north-east: south Antrim, north and east Down, and extending inland along the valley of the Lagan. These areas formed the weaving hinterlands of the new mills, and were accessible also to cross-channel firms.[8] The earnings of cotton weavers were frequently double those of other weavers, thus explaining the rapid erosion of the traditional linen weaving trade in the north-east. Muslin weavers, for example, could earn £1 per week around 1800, and rates of pay and earnings had been higher still in the 1790s.[9] In the shorter term, competition for labour between the two major branches of the textile industry pushed up rates of pay among both cotton and linen weavers. The late eighteenth century was the golden era of the handloom weaver. In the longer term, the rapidly expanding flow of cheap, factory-produced goods from the Lancashire cotton industry meant intense competition in textile markets. Ulster linen was heavily dependent on the British market.

3

Cotton was a close substitute. Technological change, large-scale production, price cutting – characteristic features of early industrial capitalism – transformed the cotton branch of the textile industry, in the process forcing down the price of linen goods and hence the earnings of linen workers.

The competitive relationship between cotton and linen was a disagreeable fact of economic life with which linen manufacturers had to contend throughout the nineteenth century. A more immediate challenge to Ulster producers materialised within the linen industry itself. From the 1790s onwards, Scottish and English manufacturers were introducing power driven machinery into the spinning side of the linen industry (stimulated, in fact, by technical advances in the rival cotton industry).[10] The machine operator was much more productive than a hand spinner – one businessman claimed a tenfold difference in terms of *physical* output – but the cost of labour was so low in Ulster that there was no great difference initially in the cost of the two types of yarn.[11] This was about 1810, when the daily earnings of spinners were of the order of five to six pence per day.[12] Furthermore, flax-spinning machinery could only produce low counts of yarn suitable for coarse products such as canvas and sailcloth. The more complete technical breakthrough came in 1825 with the invention of wet-spinning by James Kay of Preston. This allowed the flax fibres to be drawn out and spun into fine yarn without the frequent breakages which plagued earlier attempts at machine-spinning the finer counts of yarn.[13] The way was now open, as it had been two generations earlier in cotton, to place flax spinning on a purely factory basis. The Ulster linen industry had either to incorporate the new technology or wither away in the face of competitive blasts from the mills of Dundee and Leeds. The response to this challenge was swift. Entrepreneurs who had already accumulated large amounts of capital in the textile industry – bleachers such as William Hudson of Banbridge, putters-out such as Joseph Nicholson of Bessbrook, cotton mill owners such as Andrew Mulholland of Belfast – set up large spinning mills.[14] Mulholland, who founded a massive spinning establishment at York Street in Belfast after his cotton mill burned down in 1828, is generally credited with the role of the pioneer innovator among Belfast businessmen. Significantly, his example was soon emulated by other cotton manufacturers.

The economic implications for rural industry were profound. The impact, however, was unevenly distributed over the province, depending on the type and degree of dependence on rural industry. In the 1820s, on the eve of the modernisation of the linen industry, spinning and weaving were widely diffused through the eastern and southern counties of the province. The traditional core of the industry lay in the famous 'linen triangle' formed by the towns of Lisburn, Armagh, and Dungannon. Here the finer linens such as cambric and damask were woven. Further west, in Fermanagh, there was only a weak dependence on rural industry, in part perhaps because of the relatively greater attractions of cattle rearing and jobbing. Here spinning, as distinct from weaving, was the more important manufacturing activity – a further contrast with eastern and southern Ulster. Textile production in the north-west, primarily spinning, was concentrated mainly in the eastern parts of Donegal (including the Inishowen penninsula close to Derry city) and the Strabane area of west Tyrone. But spinning was of importance also in south-west Donegal, as is evidenced by substantial linen yarn markets in Donegal town and Ardara.[15] Spinning and the weaving of coarser linen cloths were extensively developed in south Ulster.

Factory-spun yarn undermined the livelihood of tens of thousands of female spinners all over Ulster. The farming-spinning households of the north-west were particularly hard hit. But there were additional adverse effects. Homespun yarn became uneconomical, but because of the remoteness of the north-west from the sources of machine-spun yarn, weavers had difficulty in gaining access to this raw material. Their costs of production were now higher than in the east of the province, while the downward course of linen prices squeezed net earnings further. The result was that not only were spinning households forced out of work, but weavers (frequently male household heads) were also obliged to abandon their trade.[16] This process of de-industrialisation meant that household members had to fall back on farming, seasonal migration, or permanent emigration. A crucial prop of the smallholder economy had been eroded by technical and organisational change elsewhere in the regional and international economy.

The position in east and south Ulster was more complicated. Mill-spun yarn was quicker and easier to weave, with the result that women and boys were able to switch to weaving.[17] Households using two or more handlooms were able to increase their output in a harsh struggle to offset both the loss of earnings from spinning and the downward trend in rates of pay from weaving. In addition, flax growing became more concentrated in east and south Ulster in response to strong demand from mills situated locally and in Britain. Thus the rise of factory spinning, both in Ulster and elsewhere in the UK, helped shore up the rural weaving household, in the process giving rise to more specialised patterns of manufacturing and flax production.[18] The prevalence of multiple-loom households, however, should not be allowed to obscure the fact that living standards were low. And in some districts of south Ulster a crisis similar to that of the north-west must have been experienced. It is likely that a substantial decline in the numbers of weaving households occurred within the period 1815–40 in many parts of Cavan and Monaghan. These two counties accounted for only seven per cent of Ulster weavers in 1841. A total collapse of weaving ensued in the 1840s.[19]

The general decline in piece-work rates for weaving may, at first sight, appear puzzling. Other things being equal, the increase in labour productivity on the spinning side of the linen industry, as a result of mechanisation, should have boosted the demand for weavers and hence pushed up rates of pay. But an abundant supply of labour and, more importantly, a market situation where cheap cotton cloth – spun and woven in factories – competed against linen, exerted strong downward pressures on piece-rates for weaving. The application of steam power to linen weaving in England and Scotland, particularly after 1830, placed further limits on the prices at which Ulster linen goods could be sold competitively.

Accompanying mechanisation of the spinning stage of linen manufacture were far-reaching changes in work relationships and forms of business organisation in the next stage in the chain of production, that of weaving. These occurred despite the fact that weaving still operated within the limiting framework of hand technology. The crucial development was the spread of the putting-out system. This was first introduced into Ulster on a significant scale through the medium of the cotton industry at the end of the eighteenth century.[20] Virtually all cotton weaving was organised on a putting-out basis. It became widespread in the linen industry in the second quarter of the nineteenth century. This form of economic organisation – pre-factory but nonetheless capitalistic – operated as follows. A merchant distributed ('put-out') linen yarn to weavers. The yarn remained the property of the merchant, and when it was woven into finished cloth the weaver received a fixed payment which had been agreed in advance. Being craftsmen who prided themselves on their independence, weavers were reluctant to enter into such arrangements unless forced by pressing economic circumstances, preferring instead to buy yarn in the market and later to sell the finished product there.[21] As the linen industry expanded, fewer weavers were in a position to grow the flax they required; hence dependence on the market for raw materials had become more pronounced. The putting-out system also applied to yarn spinning: yarn buyers supplied the flax to spinners who lacked the resources or credit necessary to purchase their own supply; the spun yarn was then delivered to the merchant at a fixed price frequently below the market value.[22]

Some putters-out operated on a limited and local scale, being simply master weavers or middlemen on the first rung of the entrepreneurial ladder, but those who were coming to dominate employment in the weaving industry co-ordinated the productive activity of hundreds or even thousands of outworkers. In the Banbridge area, for example, large-scale enterprise and capitalistic relations of production were well advanced by the 1830s. Typical of the large employers in this sub-region was David Lindsay of Dromore, who put out work to almost a thousand weavers.[23] A merchant-organiser of this kind might be visualised as a spider at the centre of a vast web, giving out material and drawing in finished or semi-finished goods from huge numbers of spinners or weavers.[24]

The fact that manufacturers controlled the supply of mill-spun yarn, first in cotton and later in linen, ensured that the putting-out form of organisation ultimately superseded independent weaving.[25] Other relevant considerations were access to credit, problems of quality control, and changing market requirements. Many linen weavers in the 1840s still, however, had a direct connection with the land. In addition, they exercised control over the pace and duration of their work. These distinguishing features separated them from pure wage labourers. Their status, therefore, is best described as semi-proletarian.

The progress of the putting-out system was uneven. It had been most developed in cotton textiles from the beginning. A major expansion of muslin weaving after the commercial crisis of 1825–26, and of the sewn muslin trade after 1830, extended greatly the numbers of outworkers associated with the manufacture of cotton goods.[26] This, it may be noted, helped compensate for declining incomes from spinning; the census of Ireland for 1851 records the existence of a vast army of 60,000 sewn muslin workers and 40,000 embroiderers, composed almost exclusively of females. In linen in the late 1830s, however, independent producers were still firmly entrenched in north Antrim (the Ballymena area in particular), the Lurgan and Rathfriland districts, and more weakly in remoter parts of Tyrone and Londonderry.[27] It is clear, though, that by 1840 capitalistic relations of production had not only penetrated, but now dominated the rural textile industry. According to Gill, an early historian of the linen industry, 'we may mark out the east of Londonderry, the south of Antrim, the centre and west of Down, and the north of Armagh, as districts in which capitalism was the most fully developed'.[28] Accompanying these changes was the decline of open linen markets, the effect being to sever links between independent producers and the distant consumers of their goods. Only in a limited number of areas did these markets survive on any scale to mid-century – Ballymena is one of the major examples – thus allowing independent weaving to survive, but subject to poorer earnings than under the putting-out system.[29]

Changes in the earnings of handloom weavers, especially if calculated in real terms, are extremely difficult to trace in the first half of the nineteenth century. For those working directly for merchants and manufacturers, weekly real earnings depended on five factors in particular: the type of cloth being woven, piece-work rates, the productivity of the weaver (influenced not only by individual skills, but by the number of looms being used and the type of yarn available), number of hours worked, and the general price level. The size and composition of the household naturally influenced family income. Among independent producers there were further considerations: commercial acumen in purchasing raw materials and marketing the finished product had an important bearing on earnings. Available evidence on these issues is fragmentary and sometimes contradictory. Our very tentative conclusions are that, in terms of real earnings, the plight of the handloom weaver – 'crushed out with infinite misery', to quote one scholar[30] – has been exaggerated for the period before 1840. There is no doubting a major decline in the earnings of cotton weavers between 1800 and the late 1830s. By the later period it is estimated that earnings fell in the range of five to seven shillings per week, testimony of a decayed labour aristocracy. There was not, however, a comparable decline among the more numerous linen weavers. By the late 1830s their weekly earnings also appear to have been in the region of six shillings, but the fall had been from a less exalted height. Around 1800 it is likely that few, other than the most skilled of these weavers, earned in excess of ten shillings per week. A decade later there are reports of average earnings in the region of seven shillings per week. Between the early 1810s and the late 1830s the price level dropped by about a third. It is difficult therefore to detect a decline in the real value of weekly earnings, after an initial fall in the first decade or so of the nineteenth century. Indeed some rise in east Ulster (to which these data primarily refer) actually seems possible. But there is a dark side to this interpretation. The number of hours worked – twelve and thirteen hours daily was not uncommon – had increased. Given the irksome nature of work on the loom, this represented a marked decline in welfare.[31] The position of weavers in south Ulster is more difficult to assess. It is likely that the real cost of a major input into the household economy – land – rose after 1815, contributing to a decline in net earnings.[32] In relation to north-west Ulster, as we saw, a cost-price squeeze operated which greatly diminished linen weaving.

Although the earnings of cotton and linen weavers appear roughly similar in east Ulster by 1840, the position of the former was in fact weaker. Cotton weavers lived in or around towns where the cost of living was higher. Linen weavers were more firmly rooted in the rural economy:

> The weavers are small farmers and cotters, cultivating land; the loom occupies one corner of a cabin, and a pig another. In fine weather, the weaver is in the field looking after his crop of oats or potatoes; when the weather is unfavourable, he returns to his loom; or perhaps the wife, or some junior member of the family, is kept at the loom, while the husband attends to the field work. Thus when the loom pays the rent, and the farm supplies provisions, a family may live in much more favourable circumstances than one earning three times the amount in money wages, but having everything to buy.[33]

The comparison with urban wage labour is exaggerated but the underlying argument has validity.

Some contemporary observers saw the economic position of weavers as little if at all better than that of farm labourers, a lowly reference point for those who half a century earlier were acknowledged as well paid craftsmen. Greater regularity of earnings over the year was, however, an advantage, though weavers were vulnerable to severe variations in their incomes as a result of cyclical fluctuations in the UK economy. The years 1809–12, the immediate aftermath of the Napoleonic wars, 1818–19, 1826, 1837, 1839–42, and 1847–48, were troubled ones. The beginnings of a clear upward trend in earnings become apparent only at the end of the 1840s. In the decade 1845–55 there was a rise of more than 20 per cent.[34] But by then the world of the handloom weaver was about to disintegrate.

Gathering together the threads of our discussion: the outstanding developments of the linen industry to mid-century were the transition from hand-spun to mill-spun yarn, the elaboration of the putting-out system, the concentration of spinning and (to some extent) weaving in urban centres, the associated de-industrialisation of the countryside, and the process of proletarianisation and semi-proletarianisation of the labour force. The introduction of power-loom weaving, which marked the next major phase in the evolution of the industry, lagged well behind changes in Britain. The primary reason for this was the low cost of handloom weaving in Ulster. Population pressure, a cheap subsistence crop in the form of the potato, a dearth of alternative employment opportunities (particularly for the less mobile male and female weavers in the older age groups), and the dilution of skills resulting from the introduction of mill-spun yarn – all of this meant that large numbers of weavers were available and willing to work long hours for poor financial returns.

The final stage of the transition to a centralised and factory-based system – industrialisation proper – was only a matter of time. As it happened, a factor specific to Ireland but external to the industry itself hastened the process: the mid-century crisis of the Great Famine, with its associated death, migration, and emigration, reduced the supply of labour in rural Ulster and pushed up wage rates. The resulting change in the cost structure of the industry was not such as to produce a sharp transfer to power weaving. Still, in the two decades after 1850 the industry was transformed as machine technology undermined the earlier handicraft form (see Chapter Two, pp. 73–75). Handloom weavers, or rather those who survived, increasingly found refuge in using the finer threads which were not sufficiently robust to withstand the action of machinery. Gradually, however, improvements in machine technology led to further encroachment on these once-sheltered niches. By the end of the nineteenth century it is doubtful if there survived more than a few thousand weavers using the antique handcraft technology. To appreciate the massive scale of this decline, it is useful to view it in temporal perspective. One estimate suggests that there were 70,000 linen weavers in the province in the early 1820s.[35] The 1851 census shows that as many as 100,000 people then defined themselves as weavers.[36] The major collapse in handloom weaving occurred in the next censal decade, 1851–61. Both estimates should be treated with caution, but there is no doubt that the once great mass of handloom weavers had shrunk to negligible proportions by 1900. Their counterparts now congregated in the great mills of the Lagan Valley, working for low, though certainly improved wages.

The most spectacular example of an expansion of cottage industry, superimposed on the general pattern of decline, was the rise of the shirt-making industry.[37] This was founded by a Presbyterian weaver, William Scott, in Derry in the 1830s. Relying initially on the putting-out system, Scott and other entrepreneurs exploited existing local skills in 'sprigging' (a form of embroidery). Although the organisational centre of the industry was urban (Derry city), outworkers were scattered through Inishowen, east Donegal, and the Strabane area. The shirt materials were cut up in central warehouses and then distributed to workers for hand-sewing in their homes. The finished shirts were returned to the employers, payment received, and further materials collected. Technological change, in particular the invention of the sewing machine, entailed the reorganisation of the industry on a factory basis from the 1850s onwards. Scottish entrepreneurs played a prominent role in this, thus illustrating the more general point of the importance of inflows of entrepreneurs and technical knowledge in the development of Ulster industry. The rural tentacles of the shirt-making business survived, albeit in weakened form, into the twentieth century. In 1901 there were 19,000 shirtmakers in the counties of Londonderry (excluding Derry city where there were over 3,000 shirt-makers), Tyrone and Donegal. The *Londonderry Sentinel* reported in 1912 that 'this home work is a valuable asset to Donegal and Londonderry, and gives employment to several thousands in these counties and is the means of distributing annually over £40,000.' The *Sentinel* added regretfully that new techniques of production and new product requirements had 'reduced the number of out-workers more than 50 per cent in the last few years'.[38] By 1914 the rural base of the industry was in an advanced state of dissolution.

It may be helpful at this point to form a rough impression of the spatial distribution of the Ulster textile labour force at different stages in the evolution of the industry. Textile workers are defined narrowly

Table 1.1 *The spatial distribution of the Ulster textile labour force in 1821, 1851, and 1901 (expressed as the percentage share of each geographical unit in the Ulster total)*

	1821	1851	1901
Antrim	13	23	13
Down	16	21	17
Belfast	–	6	30
Armagh	12	15	11
Londonderry	11	8	8
Tyrone	13	12	8
Fermanagh	4	2	2
Monaghan	10	3	1
Cavan	8	4	1
Donegal	13	6	10
	100	100	101

Source. Calculated from occupational data in the census of Ireland, relevant years.

as spinners, weavers, textile factory workers, and (in 1901 only) shirt-makers. Table 1.1 shows the share of the Ulster textile labour force held by each county, and by Belfast after mid-century, at three different points in time.

These proportions are based on census data. Because the occupational statistics contained in the census reports are full of pitfalls, Table 1.1 needs to be interpreted with considerable caution. The principal problems revolve round issues of multiple occupations and underemployment. Since weaving and spinning were frequently combined with part-time farming or part-time labouring work (particularly in 1821), it is impossible to say how time was divided between rural industry and other activities. The degree of underemployment is also obscured since occupational status was self-defined in the census returns. Thus the label of spinner, for example, might imply only the slightest involvement with the textile industry or indicate a desire for spinning work as much as actual employment. If these problems were evenly distributed among counties, then the data in Table 1.1 would be unaffected. Although this is clearly not the case, the problems of comparability between counties at the same point in time are at least reduced by the relative form in which the data are presented. Comparisons over time are subject to additional complications. Nonetheless, Table 1.1 illustrates in crude fashion the relocation and concentration of industry and the de-industrialisation of rural Ulster. By 1901 the centres of employment were overwhelmingly situated in the east, while a county such as Monaghan, which once had an important rural textile industry, had experienced almost total decay of this form of employment. And if one examined the spatial distribution of output rather than employment at any of these three points in time, the pattern would be more heavily tilted towards the east, given the larger amounts of capital per worker there. It is interesting nonetheless that, in employment terms, the emergence of Belfast as 'Linenopolis' was post-1850.

We have managed to discuss rural industry at some length without introducing a concept much in vogue, that of proto-industry. This loose construct usually refers to peasant handicraft production, where commodities are destined for markets beyond the local and regional context, and where there is a symbiotic relationship between rural industry and commercial agriculture.[39] Though not fully coherent, the notion of proto-industry has generated numerous plausible hypotheses that are of interest to the historian of farming-manufacturing regions such as Ulster. It is asserted, for instance, that by loosening the link between landholding and household formation, rural industry promoted population growth. Manufacturing made available income opportunities that allowed earlier and more frequent marriage. Thus one authority has noted in relation to Ulster that 'on the eve of the Great Famine, County Armagh was the most densely populated county in Ireland, with 511 persons to the square mile, while another seven counties with a density of more than 400 to the square mile included the linen counties of Cavan, Monaghan, Tyrone and Down.'[40] This view, positing a direct relationship between rapid population growth and the development of rural textile industry, accords well with the theory of proto-industrialisation. It should be added, however, that the link between these two variables has recently been questioned (though not convincingly, in the view of this writer).[41]

Proto-industry is also held to promote the accumulation of capital, technical knowledge, and labour skills, thus easing the transition to modern industry. Certainly, the capital and expertise built up in the linen industry by merchants, bleachers, and putting-out manufacturers made a substantial contribution to the development of early industry in Ulster. Similarly, a background and work experience in handicraft industry (though not some of the work habits)[42] must have been of benefit to first-generation mill workers. The point is weakened of course to the extent that many mill workers were children and young adolescents. One must be careful, however, not to assign excessive significance to proto-industry. For one thing, the expansion of proto-industry was in considerable part a *response* to the development of factory textile production. There was not, therefore, a simple unilinear progression from the one to the other. More fundamentally, other factors relevant to economic growth in Ulster − inflows of entre-preneurs, capital, and technology from industrialising regions in Britain − played a strategically important role, and one which a partial theory of the transition to modern industry is in danger of obscuring. Furthermore, many sub-regions involved in rural industry − those of outer Ulster in general − did not make the transition but reverted instead to a heavy dependence on agriculture. The shirt-making industry, the narrow manufacturing base on which Derry and its hinterland were fixed in the second half of the nineteenth century, saved a part of the northwest from a similar fate. A modified but more realistic perspective would place greater emphasis on the economic nerve centres of proto-industry − the points in a region where organisational, technical, and marketing resources are concentrated, and where the major possibilities for capital accumulation exist. It is these poles of capital, rather than the vast hinterlands of lowly-paid labour over which they held sway, that are of primary importance in terms of possibilities for further industrial development.

A complementary relationship between agriculture and rural industry is a further prediction of the theory. In the northern half of Ireland the rise of manufacturing areas helped to induce regional specialisation and market-oriented agriculture. Rural industry also allowed a more intensive use of labour because it meshed with the rhythms of the farming year. But despite what is sometimes claimed for farming-manufacturing households, industry did not subsidise agriculture (though the twin sources of income were frequently essential to economic survival). Neither does it appear that commercial agriculture dominated the fertile farming areas, while proto-industry was primarily concentrated in the poorer uplands (as has been suggested in relation to proto-industry in the north of England in the eighteenth century). Lastly, a crucial defining characteristic of proto-industry is that its products are destined for markets beyond the regional one. This was clearly true of Ulster, where export markets were so important for linen manufacture, even in the eighteenth century. The growth and consolidation of the industry in the northeast of Ireland was of course part of a general tendency towards regional economic special-isation within the United Kingdom, involving closer integration of local, regional, and international markets. One may conclude that a major means whereby the rural economy contributed to industrialisation was through the medium of proto-industry.

But this is only part of the story. There was no automatic take-off from the sites of proto-industrial activity into the clear skies of self-sustaining growth. In fact, a harsh dynamic linked the industrialising centres of the Lagan Valley with the decay of rural manufacturing districts elsewhere in Ulster. (This also of course helps explain why industrialisation did not spread from its nucleus in the northeast to the rest of the island.) In addition it should be stressed that although the links between proto-industry and the modernised textile industry were strong, this was not the case for the other giant of the late nineteenth-century Ulster economy – shipbuilding and the related engineering works. The theory of proto-industrialisation sheds little if any light on the process whereby the industrial base became diversified. One might of course argue that proto-industry had a general impact on the Ulster economy by promoting population growth, increasing the supply of labour, and hence lowering wage levels. Other things being equal, a low-wage area is more attractive to industrialists than a high-wage one. The argument seems to have a certain validity for the nineteenth century; wage rates were certainly lower in Ulster than in many industrialising regions of Britain.[43] But crucial evidence on the productivity of labour, which also influences labour costs per unit of output, is lacking. One has only to reflect on the fact that Ireland as a whole was nothing if not an island of low wages, to appreciate that other major ingredients entered the stew of industrialisation.

If the rural economy was tied to the industrialisation process through proto-industry, there were other linkages as well. Most obviously perhaps, the rural economy supplied raw materials for resource-based industries: grain for brewing, milling, and distilling; flax for linen yarn. With respect to flax, in 1851 the area under this crop in Ulster was 125,000 acres. The flax acreage reached a peak at 278,000 in 1864, during the height of the linen boom, but declined to just over a 100,000 acres by 1914.[44] The phenomenal expansion in the output of the linen industry during the nineteenth century meant of course that over time the industry became increasingly dependent on imported flax. Agriculture also released factors of production, most notably labour, and to a lesser extent capital, which benefited industry. The smallholding structure of rural Ulster, as well as the

15

interpenetration of farming and proto-industry, meant that a substantial labour supply existed, which served as a drag on wage rates in the industrial sector. Lastly, the rural sector may have constituted a market for the products of industry, thus stimulating further industrial growth. But this was hardly true to any marked extent in nineteenth-century Ulster, where industry had such a strong export orientation, and where the two major sectors – agriculture and textiles – were characterised by low earnings.

Land-use patterns
Differences in natural environment give rise to different types of farming and also lay the basis for regional specialisation. There is variation in soil type, topography, even climate, within Ulster.[45] West Donegal, where the 'rocky ribs of earth break everywhere through its skin', the flooded lowlands of Fermanagh, and the fertile coastal districts of Down offer contrasts that are of deep agricultural and economic significance. Sheep raising, the production of young cattle, and cereal growing respectively distinguished these three areas in the nineteenth century. Ancient Ulster had been a primarily pastoral province. In the late eighteenth and early nineteenth centuries there was a substantial swing towards tillage farming in response to favourable grain prices and population growth. Oats, potatoes, and flax were the major components of the tillage economy of the Ulster smallholder.[46] The bulk of the population in fact subsisted on a diet of oatmeal and potatoes, with the addition of some milk.[47] Population pressure had the effect of extending the area of cultivation as waste land was brought under the spade. In Tyrone, for example, it was remarked about 1800 that small potato patches were edging upwards 'almost to the summits of the mountains'.[48] It has been plausibly argued in turn that the existence of reserves of waste land facilitated rapid population growth.[49] With the intensive development of the rural linen industry some districts became food-deficit areas, relying in part on foodstuffs imported from districts specialising in food production. Thus well before 1800 parts of east Ulster were drawing corn and potato supplies from Sligo and Mayo in years of dearth. There was also inter-regional trade in livestock. Young cattle and sheep raised in the west of the province, for example, were channelled through a network of fairs towards the better fattening lands of Londonderry and east Ulster. As the century progressed, communications improved (see Chapter

Three), transport costs declined, and a greater degree of specialisation became possible.[50] After 1813 prices fell rapidly from their inflated wartime levels, ushering in a long period of low farm prices. The movement towards tillage slackened, but it is not clear if this tendency was reversed by the early 1840s. Certainly in the decade 1841–51 there was a substantial increase in cattle numbers. Cattle (aged one year or more) increased by almost half in Ulster in this period, and on the island as a whole, by one-third.[51] Sheep numbers also expanded, the increase in Ulster again being much higher than in Ireland generally. There are also earlier hints of expanded livestock production; the increasing frequency of fairs in the early decades of the nineteenth century points towards a stronger livestock emphasis (including production of pigs, which was an integral part of the economy of the smallholder, cottier-weaver, and farm labourer).

Mean farm size fell in the decades preceding the Famine under the impact of population increase, subdivision of holdings, and colonisation of waste land. One estimate suggests that on the eve of the Famine the average size of an Ulster holding was twelve acres, which compares somewhat unfavourably with an average for Ireland of fifteen acres.[52] In south Ulster the mean size of holdings would have been considerably less than that for the province as a whole. The process of fragmentation of holdings took two main forms: division of land among two or more sons, and subletting of part of a farm to an undertenant. Though landlords increasingly opposed these practices, they survived with varying degrees of strength through much of Ulster until the catastrophe of the late 1840s. In Down in 1845, for example, it was reported that division of land among the eldest two sons was still common in some areas.[53] In remote districts in the west of the province subdivision continued well after the Famine. Here tenurial and inheritance practices were complicated by the existence of the rundale system. Each tenant, rather than having a compact farm, held small strips of ground scattered over a townland. These strips of tillage land were worked individually but were unfenced, while livestock was maintained on the rougher communal grazing lands at some distance from the human settlements (usually arranged in tight house-clusters known as *clachans*). One tenant might have several dozen different strips of land; Lord George Hill cited the extreme example in Gweedore about 1840 of a small field of roughly half an acre in which twenty-six people held land rights. In some

17

districts the strips were periodically redistributed, thus blunting the individual incentive to improve the land. M'Parlan, in his survey of Donegal in the early nineteenth century, claims that the rundale villages were 'dispersing daily into separate habitations and holdings'. It is clear, however, that in the more backward areas of the west, rundale practices persisted until mid-century, and remnants of the system survived in a few places even after 1900. The overall effect of rundale was to inhibit the introduction of improved farming techniques, though it did offer a primitive form of economic insurance to members of the *clachan*.[54]

Official agricultural statistics enable us to assess changes in land-use patterns in the second half of the nineteenth century. Such detailed information is not available for the first half of the century, but the data for 1851 may also be taken as offering some rough pointers as to the relative importance of tillage and pasture in the various regions of Ulster immediately prior to the Famine. Down, Armagh, and Monaghan had the strongest tillage orientation of the Ulster counties in 1851 and, hardly coincidentally, they also had the largest proportions of smallholdings (one to fifteen acres). By contrast, land use was heavily weighted towards pastoral pursuits in the more westerly counties of Fermanagh and Donegal. Roughly speaking, there was an east-west divide in terms of the degree of emphasis on crop husbandry, though Antrim, with two out of every three acres of its farmland under grass, was a prominent exception to this generalisation.

Surprisingly perhaps, the tillage acreage in Ireland did not change appreciably in the decade following the disastrous years of the late 1840s. This suggests that despite a major decline in the population in the 1840s and 1850s, a labour shortage was not a serious restraining factor on labour-intensive forms of agriculture. In Ulster the area devoted to tillage stood at 1·6 million acres in 1858, virtually the same level as in 1851. As in the pre-Famine decades, the dominant crops were oats and potatoes, while the smaller flax acreage maintained the historically important link between agriculture and the linen industry. In the following half-century, however, the crop area declined substantially, dipping to a level of 0·9 million acres in 1913. Ulster agriculture had reoriented itself towards a much heavier emphasis on grassland, though to a somewhat lesser extent than in the island as a whole. Cattle increased by 27 per cent and sheep by 113 per cent in Ulster between 1851 and 1913. Farmyard enterprises in the form of pig, poultry, and egg production also expanded substantially.[55]

Table 1.2 *The swing from tillage to pasture in Ulster, 1851–1913*

Year	Pasture (acres)	Tillage (acres)	Pasture-tillage ratio	Land-labour ratio
1851	2,364,000	1,592,000	1·48	10
1876	2,629,000	1,332,000	1·97	12
1913	3,061,000	915,000	3·34	16

Source. *Agricultural Statistics of Ireland*, relevant years; Kennedy, 'Ulster statistics' (see n. 51).

This shift in farming patterns came about primarily in response to changes in relative prices. From the early 1850s to the mid-1870s, the farmers enjoyed substantial gains in prosperity, as the trend in farm prices was generally upwards. Livestock products – beef, mutton, pork, butter, and eggs – experienced much sharper rises in price as compared with tillage products such as wheat and oats. The price of young store cattle, for instance, increased by almost 150 per cent between 1851 and 1876, while the price of wheat rose by a mere 20 per cent (hardly sufficient to keep pace with the rise in the general price level).[56] It is interesting to note that, before the onset of agricultural depression in the late 1870s, the movement towards a pastoral economy was markedly slower in Ulster: the fall in the tillage acreage was 16 per cent over the period 1851–76, as compared with a 27 per cent decline for Ireland as a whole. The shift out of tillage was most pronounced in the south Ulster counties of Fermanagh, Monaghan, and Cavan, which in terms of soil type, topography, and climate are naturally better suited to pastoral farming. In east Ulster and the exceptional county of Donegal, change in the balance between pasture and tillage was muted. The resilience of tillage in much of Ulster in the third quarter of the nineteenth century is largely explicable in terms of the prevalence of small farms (see Table 1.3), the integration of crop and livestock production (particularly the use of oats, maize, and potatoes as animal feedstuffs), and the availability of labour, mainly farm-family labour. The distinctive climate and soil conditions of east Down and the fertile river valleys of Londonderry meant that these areas were more favoured than most in relation to cereal growing. And flax, that peculiarly Ulster crop, covered a marginally larger area of land in 1876 as compared with 1851. The process of urbanisation, it may be added, stimulated specialised

19

forms of crop growing, most notably reflected in the market gardens of the Comber and Lagan valley districts.[57]

The bad harvests of the late 1870s ushered in a long period of agricultural depression which persisted until the mid-1890s. This downturn accelerated the swing from tillage to pasture, as livestock prices fell less heavily and also recovered more quickly. Farm prices rose after the mid-1890s, and registered moderate gains up to the eve of the Great War, but the trend in relative prices remained unfavourable to tillage products. By 1913 Down and Londonderry, the two counties with the strongest tillage orientation, had only about one-third of their farmland under crops.

Clearly there was a major diversion of land resources towards pastoral farming during the period 1851–1913.[58] But, as discussed shortly, there were also significant increases in the productivity of crops, with the result that changes in tillage output were much less than might be inferred from data on land use. Wheat production, admittedly, collapsed; the fall was from 65,000 tons in 1851 to 6,000 tons in 1913. The decline in the output of oats, however, was less than dramatic: from 577,000 tons in 1851 to 407,000 tons in 1913. Turnips registered a mild decline from 1·7 to 1·5 million tons over the same period, while the production of potatoes actually increased from 1·3 to 1·7 million tons. The continuing strength of the tillage economy, accompanied by expanded livestock production, underlines the point that intensive *mixed* farming was the key feature of Ulster agriculture during the second half of the nineteenth century.

While land use changed substantially in the second half of the nineteenth century, adjustments in farm size proceeded at a slower pace. Let us first examine the picture at mid-century. As is evident from Table 1.3, Ulster had a larger proportion of smallholdings than Ireland as a whole, a fact which probably reflected its heritage of rural industry and the reduced impact of the Great Famine there. Ulster also had a smaller proportion of large holdings. These features indicate a more equitable distribution of land resources in the northern province. Only Antrim and Donegal had in excess of 10 per cent of their holdings in the size category of fifty acres or more. Armagh had the miniscule proportion of 2 per cent of its holdings in this category. Despite some consolidation of holdings and a movement towards a larger average farm size, the distribution of holdings had not altered greatly by 1911. The Ulster countryside was still dominated by small farms, three-quarters of all holdings being less than thirty acres in size.

Table 1.3 *Landholding in Ulster and Ireland, 1851 and 1911: the percentage of holdings in each size category and the total number of holdings*

Year	No. of holdings	1–15 (acres)	15–30 (acres)	30–50 (acres)	50–100 (acres)	Above 100 (acres)
Ulster						
1851	210,000	55	27	11	5	2
1911	182,000	46	30	14	8	3
Ireland						
1851	570,000	49	25	12	9	5
1911	521,000	42	26	15	11	6

Source. Agricultural Statistics of Ireland, relevant years.

A corollary of this was fairly low farm incomes among the bulk of farmers, almost certainly less than in many of the eastern counties of Ireland – a feature which tends to be obscured by the image and the achievements of the progressive industrial North.

We cannot offer a detailed account of productivity change in Ulster farming over the century as a whole but the broad contours of change may be indicated. The key areas are: enclosure and consolidation of holdings; improvements in rotations, manuring practices, and crop yields; regional specialisation; use of better farm implements; and changes in the quality of livestock. One finds references at the opening of the nineteenth century to the 'nakedness' of the countryside and the lack of good enclosures,[59] though as trenches were sometimes used to- divide landholdings it is possible that observers were sometimes misled regarding the extent of enclosure. A recent study concludes that by 1800 there was 'an area consisting of the Lagan valley with parts of north Down, north Armagh, and north Monaghan, which was well enclosed'.[60] In the early decades of the nineteenth century there was a progressive extension of hedges and ditches in the more fertile lowland areas and on the larger farms. The north and west of the province, with important exceptions such as the Foyle basin in counties Tyrone and Donegal and the lower Bann Valley, lagged behind in terms of these changes. Rundale practices were most widespread in these regions. Yet from south Derry, a district hardly in the forefront of agricultural progress, it was reported about 1820 that 'the most remarkable recent improvement is the almost total abolition of the rundale system'. The writer, a local schoolteacher, adds: 'Farmers are becoming more sensible of the importance of enclosures, both as fences and drains. Most farms are divided into small fields, and rather well fenced'.[61] Enclosure was associated in part with the spread of the road system, a development which in turn was linked to economic expansion. In the neighbourhood of towns the impact of urbanisation and petty manufacturing was reflected in the small size of fields and holdings. Population pressure produced a similar effect, as the patchwork landscape of south Armagh eloquently testifies. Two further points need stressing. In mid and south-east Ulster, where rundale had not been widespread, the process of enclosure usually amounted to little more than fencing off an existing compact holding and dividing it internally into fields. This remaking of the landscape had been under way from the mid-eighteenth century. Elsewhere, however, enclosure frequently involved the much more complex task of breaking up communal patterns of land use and the carving out of compact farms. Lastly, the economic significance of these changes is that the clearly defined, individually controlled landholdings offered a superior framework for the adoption of improved farming practices.

A sometimes related change was the amalgamation of holdings. An analysis of testimonies from 338 areas in Ulster in the 1830s suggests that consolidation on an extensive scale was taking place in only six of these.[62] In 145 cases, or 43 per cent of the total, however, *some* consolidation was said to be under way. This was connected in particular districts with the reorganisation of the rural textile industry and the extension of the putting-out system. James Murland, a manufacturer who gave work to some 700 weavers in the Castlewellan area, claimed that the agriculture of county Down had improved since weavers had abandoned independent production and ceased 'occupying farms which were formerly necessary to them'.[63] Emigration also implied some limited opportunities for the amalgamation of holdings; significant numbers of emigrants in the 1830s appear to have been small farmers.[64] The overall impact of these tendencies on farm size, however, can only have been slight before 1845, and needs to be set alongside contrary tendencies towards subdivision of holdings.

The small size of many holdings limited the extent to which crop rotations could be practised – an instance of diseconomies in small scale production. Within these constraints there is evidence in the pre-Famine period of rudimentary rotations using various combinations of oats, potatoes, flax, and grass. Adequacy of manure supplies was a further, indeed a central problem. The main sources were animal dung, lime, and kelp in coastal districts. These inputs appear to have been diligently conserved and applied. In the later nineteenth century, increased numbers of livestock and the use by larger farmers of imported fertiliser (guano in particular) eased this constraint on soil productivity. The more widespread adoption of a five-crop rotation in this period also served to boost tillage output.[65] From the agricultural statistics of Ireland, collected annually from 1847, it is clear that cereal yields were high in Ulster at mid-century. In east Ulster in the early 1850s, wheat yields were above those registered in leading southern tillage counties such as Carlow and Wexford, while oat yields were roughly comparable. Even in south Ulster cereal yields were high but grain growing was limited and concentrated on the most suitable lands. Between the 1850s and the Great War there were substantial productivity gains: wheat yields per acre increased from 13–14 cwt to 18–19 cwt; the output of oats per acre rose from roughly 13 cwt to 17 cwt.[66] Part of these gains are of course attributable to a shift to more favoured soils in the context of a shrinking cereal acreage and increased regional specialisation. Changes in land use patterns and regional specialisation have been discussed earlier; it is sufficient to note here that such changes gave rise to productivity gains. The produce per acre of most tillage crops rose in the period 1850–1914, the most marked increases being concentrated in the final quarter-century. Potato yields dropped initially but showed substantial gains after the mid 1890s. These followed the adoption of successful spraying techniques against potato blight. By contrast with tillage production generally, hay (the 'crop' most closely associated with the swing to livestock farming) registered a decline in productivity; the acreage devoted to meadow and clover in Ulster increased from 260,000 acres in 1851 to 661,000 acres in 1913 but the output of hay per acre declined.

Extensive resort to spade cultivation before the Famine, while a source of dismay to observers who confused technical with economic efficiency, made sense in the context of a small-farm, tillage economy endowed with abundant labour. On farms whose size justified the use of ploughs and horses there are indications of the gradual substitution of the superior Scotch plough for the primitive Irish one. A further instance of the transfer of agricultural technology – part of a wider process of technological borrowing between Scotland and Ulster – was the introduction of the Scotch cart.[67] Significantly, both of these were being manufactured *locally* in the early nineteenth century. The parish of Templecorran in south-east Antrim had eight threshing machines in 1839, while in a nearby district there is evidence of scythes being used instead of the less efficient sickle from the 1830s.[68] More generally, the emergence of agricultural improvement societies as early as the first quarter of the century is indicative of a climate of opinion, at least among the gentry and larger farmers, favourable to innovation. In this, rather than their actual achievements, lies perhaps the historical significance of these societies. (The creation of the Department of Agriculture and Technical Instruction marked a further important stage in the institutionalisation and extension of activities designed to promote agricultural change, but as this did not occur until 1899 it is only marginally relevant to our discussion.)

During the second half of the century, horse husbandry, partly in reaction to rising labour costs, became increasingly important for haymaking and tillage farming. By the turn of the century a veritable revolution in the use of farm machinery had taken place. The stock of equipment and implements on Ulster farms in 1912 included 93,000 ploughs, 51,000 drills, 36,000 land rollers, 28,000 mowers and reapers, 7,000 potato diggers, 31,000 potato sprayers, 23,000 threshers and 6,000 horse hoes. The forty-three windmills, while affecting little on the ground, at least changed the skyline. There were 135,000 farm horses – a much higher number than in any of the other three provinces (an indicator, though not a conclusive one, of higher levels of investment in Ulster agriculture).

Given the eventual dominance of livestock products in Ulster farm output, it is particularly important (though difficult) to identify qualitative changes in livestock over time. Dubourdieu lamented in 1802 the indifferent approach to livestock breeding: 'the bull that is nearest the place where his interference is necessary, being, in ninety-nine instances out of a hundred, that which is preferred'.[69] Yet during the first half of the nineteenth century substantial progress was made in replacing the longhorn with the superior shorthorn cow.[70] The shorthorn cow was a dual-purpose animal: in addition to its beef characteristics (improved performance in terms of liveweight gain) it also possessed good milking qualities. The latter was important, not only in the context of the traditional buttermaking industry, but also in relation to increasing urban demand for milk. At the very end of the nineteenth century the traditional farmyard enterprise of buttermaking underwent a technological transformation. It became more economical to manufacture butter in centralised plants. Co-operative creameries, financed and controlled by farmers, spread rapidly through mid, south, and west Ulster after 1895. By contrast creameries made little headway in eastern districts dominated by Belfast and other urban centres. Here supplying milk for human consumption remained a more profitable outlet for dairy farmers. By 1914 there were 148 dairy co-operatives in the province, suggesting a satisfactory innovative response on the part of Ulster farmers.[71]

Ulster agriculture responded strongly to market forces in the nineteenth century, embodying in the process innovations that increased the productivity of both labour and land. Outside observers around mid-century were apt to comment on the extent of agricultural improvement as compared to much of the rest of the island.[72] In explaining this progress, a powerful dynamic for change has so far been insufficiently stressed – the rise of Belfast. The number of mouths to be fed increased from 37,000 in 1821 to 350,000 in 1901. Ready access to other growing urban markets reinforced this stimulus. A perceptive contemporary commentator remarks how his attention 'was most arrested by the changed face of the country, whenever I came within twenty miles of a large manufacturing or commercial town'.

> Thus, in travelling from Larne to Belfast, a distance of seventeen Irish miles, I missed the wretched cabins of the peasantry, and found instead neat lime-washed slated cottages, large farms in the place of small ones, good hedges and brick walls for fences, instead of a few loose stones piled up, merely to mark the boundary, and a state of cultivation resembling the best parts of England, rather than anything I had previously seen in Ireland. What made the difference? The secret was the vicinity of a great market for agricultural produce, and the accessibility from the same port of the two other great markets of Glasgow and Liverpool.[73]

Economic crises and fluctuations
In the first half of the nineteenth century the issue of central significance was not catholic emancipation or repeal of the Act of Union. It was poverty, lived day by day, experienced on a massive scale. There were of course many parts of Europe in which living conditions were as bad. And there were marked differences between the broadly eastern and western parts of the island as well as between different social classes in the Irish countryside. But there is no denying that the broad tide of poverty edged alarmingly upwards in the decades after 1815. Ultimately, this spilled over into the harrowing

scenes of hunger, disease, and death in the famine years of 1846–49. This was the supreme ordeal of the potato-eating poor. But there were signs of strain in the rural economy long before mid-century. The century opened inauspiciously with failure of the potato crop in the north-east, poor yields from other crops, and inflated food prices.[74] Emergency imports of maize had to be arranged. This indicates, incidentally, that contrary to popular belief, sections of the Irish poor had sampled this grain a half-century before the Great Famine. In the difficult period of adjustment following the end of the Napoleonic wars, there were partial famines in Ulster in 1816 and 1817, and again in 1821.[75] Salaman suggested there were fourteen partial or general failures of the crucially important potato crop in Ireland between 1818 and 1842.[76] The whole issue of the frequency and extent of the failure of major food crops, notably oats and potatoes, still awaits detailed exploration by historians. But the existence of years of distress – pale precursors of the calamity ahead – is not in doubt.

Besides the random shocks from climatic and other natural conditions to which the rural economy was inevitably subject, there was the recurrent problem of seasonal underemployment. Reports compiled by the Poor Law Commission in the mid-1830s are a rich source of evidence on the impoverishing effects of seasonal rhythms in the demand for farm labour, as well as on the problem of poverty generally.[77] In Armaghbreague in County Armagh, out of about fifty labourers, it was claimed that less than ten were in constant employment. Potatoes, sometimes supplemented by milk, were the main food of the labourers and smaller farmers. Their clothing was described as 'very insufficient and mean', and according to the clergyman-witness, 'the fourth part of my parishioners make their apparel their excuse for not attending divine worship.' Farther south, in the parish of Aughnamullen West in County Monaghan, only one in eight labourers was said to be in constant employment: 'When out of employment they subsist on their con acre potatoes, and in many instances are obliged occasionally to beg.' In Castleterra in neigh-bouring Cavan most labourers were underemployed: 'In the summer quarter their wives beg, to support their children and their husbands.'

This picture of limited employment opportunities and under-employment on smallholdings, along with the associated poverty, did not apply uniformly throughout Ulster. In the east higher and more regular incomes were reflected in better clothing and a more varied diet. Thus in the rural parishes of the barony of Belfast Lower, to

26

take a favoured sub-region, there was virtually year-round employ-ment for all. The economic structure was diversified: in addition to farm work, there were employment opportunities in cotton works, lime quarries, road construction, flour mills, bleachgreens, and weaving. Outside of east Ulster in the 1830s, however, there is no doubt that the margin above subsistence for the bulk of the people was uncomfortably narrow, even in an average year. The develop-ing crisis of rural industry, discussed earlier, deepened the problem of subsistence for cottiers and labourers.

The decades preceding the Famine saw a dangerously increased reliance on a single food crop (the potato), reflecting a widespread process of immiseration at the base of rural society. To estimate the degree of dependence on potatoes is difficult. O Tuathaigh suggests that by the mid-1840s 'the potato was the sole food of about one-third of the Irish people.'[78] Very probably, it was the dominant element in the diet of half or more of the population. In Ulster, with its strong tradition of growing oats, there was somewhat greater insurance against food failure. Variations in oat and potato yields might well be out of line with each other; also, of direct relevance to a farming-manufacturing region, there was the likelihood that agricultural and trade fluctuations would not normally coincide. As against these considerations, it must be recalled that Ulster was the most densely populated of all the provinces of Ireland in 1841.

Population pressure, subdivision of holdings, narrowing economic opportunities in agriculture and rural industry, and increasing reliance on the potato were the crucial elements in the build-up to the Famine crisis at mid-century. This was particularly true of south and west Ulster, where a precarious balance between population and economic resources existed. In a very real sense, therefore, the severity of the Great Famine is best understood in terms of the impact of a natural disaster (potato blight and the subsequent destruction of the major food source) on weakened economic structures. But there are other, more dynamic elements in the explanation. The Famine experience was not simply the mechanical outcome of existing economic con-ditions. Once the crisis had arrived, with partial failure of the potato crop in 1845, other forces of both a positive and negative nature intervened to shape the course of the tragedy: decisions by the govern-ment and relief agencies regarding the form and extent of relief measures, decisions by farmers to shift to labour-displacing livestock production, decisions by landlords concerning abatements of rent, evictions, and poor-law rates. Why Ireland was vulnerable to famine is one question. A very different one, involving a socio-political as well as an economic dimension, is why Ireland famished.

The chronology of the crisis, in austere outline, is as follows. There was a partial failure of the potato crop in 1845, Ulster being little affected. Blight struck again in 1846. Virtually the entire crop was destroyed by the mysterious disease. Blight was largely absent in 'black forty-seven', but the acreage of potatoes sown was small. The potato crop failed again in the autumn of 1848. Blight was also present in the two following seasons, though it was clear by 1850 that the disease had spent itself.

The Famine claimed possibly in excess of one million lives, over and above those who would normally have been expected to die in this period.[79] Relatively few actually starved to death. Most were the victims of fever and dysentery, diseases which flourished under conditions of malnutrition, poor hygiene, and inadequate public health measures. One brief illustration of the degree of distress, and of efforts to contain the crisis, must suffice. The description relates to Castledawson in south Derry during the first hungry winter in Ulster (1846–47) and was written by a local gentleman:

> I do not exaggerate when I tell you that from the moment I open my hall door in the morning until dark, I have a crowd of women and children crying out for something to save them from starving ... I have been obliged to turn my kitchen into a Bakery and Soup shop to enable me to feed the miserable children and mothers that cannot be sent away empty. So great is their distress that they actually faint on getting food into their stomachs ... The gentry, the shopkeepers, the clergy are making every effort in their power to relieve the people, by subscriptions, and incessant attention, but what can be done when thousands are daily applying for one meal a day. We are also visited by hordes of wandering poor who come from the mountains ...[80]

Because of its sympathetic middle class, developed retailing system, and income from weaving, Castledawson was better placed than many other districts to withstand the crisis. Elsewhere, these conditions did not apply, and the suffering and mortality were appalling. Excess mortality for the province as a whole has been estimated at about a quarter of a million, a death toll which was very unevenly distributed in terms of both region and social class.[81] Outer Ulster, with its weakened agrarian and proto-industrial structures, suffered dispro-portionately. The southern counties of Cavan and Monaghan were particularly hard hit, with intermediate levels of mortality in Tyrone and Armagh. The north-east, with its stronger and more diversified economic base, its better communications and food-retailing system, was least affected by failure of the staple food crop. It was vulnerable, however, to famine diseases carried by the innumerable emaciated refugees who crowded into towns in search of food, workhouse accommodation, or (if they had some remaining capital) the emigrant ship. As for the class impact of this national tragedy, the great shoals of corpses swept into the Famine abyss were primarily those of cottiers and labourers.

A searing image from this period – one much exploited in later polemical political writing – is that of ships laden with grain leaving a famished land. The peasantry starved that landlord rent might be paid. It is true that Ireland had been a major exporter of grain before the Famine, being part of the granary of urbanising, industrialising Britain. On the eve of the crisis in 1845 just over half a million tons were shipped.[82] In 1846 grain exports were at the lower level of 285,000 tons, sufficient only to feed one to one and a half million people if retained in Ireland. In the following year grain imports dwarfed grain exports by a factor of more than five to one. Yet it can be argued that although grain exports were of minor significance over the Famine period as a whole, a prohibition on these exports in 1846 would have made a strategically important contribution to bridging the 'starvation gap' between failure of the potato crop in August 1846 and the arrival of massive imports of maize a few months later. This is no doubt true, but the apparent implication that there was a shortage of food is not. The emergency slaughter of large numbers of livestock might also have been carried out, to similar effect.[83] But the real problem was not one of the adequacy of overall food supplies at any point during the Famine. The potato eaters starved primarily because they did not have the money or other economic resources necessary to translate their needs into effective demand for food. Only an authoritarian state, committed to the welfare of the poor at all costs, might have effected the redistribution of income and food resources that could have substantially reduced the incidence of hunger.[84] The result, however, would have been major class conflict within Ireland, as the chief beneficiaries of the unrestrained workings of market forces were not landlords, but Irish farmers and merchants. The chief victims were their fellow countrymen from the lower classes. The case with respect to Ulster would have been more complicated, particularly if, as has sometimes been suggested, a Dublin rather than a Westminster government had been handling the crisis. The Protestant people of that province suffered less severely from famine. Ulster Protestants, being separate from the evolving Irish political community whose historic roots lay in Catholic culture and traditions, would have resisted attempts to involve them in financing relief operations elsewhere on the island. Their opposition to a special 'rate in aid' to alleviate distress in other parts of Ireland in 1849 is a revealing case in point.[85] Strongly interventionist action by a Dublin-based government very probably would have induced proto-national conflict at the northern boundaries of Protestant and Catholic Ireland, on top of widespread class conflict embracing the whole island.

The Great Famine was the last major subsistence crisis in Ireland, and indeed in western Europe generally. There were, of course, sharp fluctuations in output and agricultural income at irregular intervals throughout the next half-century owing to bad weather and animal and crop diseases. Improved incomes, better communications, and extensive trading and credit networks softened the impact of further recessions in the rural economy. The Malthusian spectre, like St. Patrick's legendary snakes, had finally been banished. Post-Famine reconstruction, intrinsically bound up with more prudent family strategies (later age of marriage, inheritance by a single heir, greater recourse to migration and emigration), witnessed the conquest of mass poverty.

Two instances of agricultural fluctuations in the second half of the nineteenth century merit attention because they stand out from the usual, if irregular, occurrence of poor farming years. The prolonged depression of 1859–64 was the first major setback to the agricultural economy since mid-century.[86] The primary cause of the crisis lay in the heavens: bad weather in successive seasons, accompanied by potato blight, sheep rot, and foot-and-mouth disease, resulted in greatly diminished agricultural output. The decline in the prices of wheat, oats, and butter in the early 1860s was a further, though less important, factor in depressing agricultural incomes. As during the Great Famine, Ulster fared better than the average experience of the island. Agriculture's link with the linen industry was the major element in dulling the impact of the crisis. The flax acreage more than doubled between 1859 and 1864, reaching a peak at the latter date.[87] The expansion of flax growing, confined mainly to the east and north-east of the province, was most rapid in the early 1860s when boom conditions affected the linen industry because of the wartime disruption of raw-material supplies to the rival cotton industry (see Chapter Two). Ulster farmers could hardly claim credit for the timing of the American Civil War or for the fortuitous fact that agricultural and industrial cycles were out of phase, but their production response to the opportunity offered was rapid, thus helping to offset losses in other farming lines.

The crisis of the late 1870s stemmed from bad weather, resulting in low farm output in three successive years, 1877–79. Unfortunately, these production problems coincided with the first phase of a secular decline in farm prices, which afflicted Irish (and European) agriculture from the mid-1870s to the mid-1890s. The increasing integration of the international food market and the opening up of low-cost sources of supply in the New World exposed Irish agriculture to severe competitive pressure. The impact of outside suppliers on the UK market was perceptible in the cases of grain and butter as early as the 1860s,[88] but it was not until late in the following decade that the full potential of this threat to Irish farmers was revealed. The worst of the three bad years was 1879, characterised by generally low prices and yields as well as a disastrous potato harvest. Where dependence on the potato crop was still marked, as in parts of Donegal, Monaghan, and Cavan, near-famine conditions threatened the smallholder.[89] For stronger farmers the depression of the late 1870s represented a check to rising living standards rather than a traditional subsistence crisis. A recovery in farm incomes in 1880 marked the end of this deep trough. In the long term the significance of the depression lay at the political, not the economic level: the distress and discontent of the late 1870s, translated into political action, was to shake the institution of landlordism to its very foundations.

Landlords, peasant landlords and proletarians
The image of a social pyramid, layered to represent different social classes, conveys some idea of the steep inequalities present in Ulster rural society in the early nineteenth century. At the apex of the pyramid stood the landlord class, numerically insignificant but economically and politically powerful. Its members held estates widely differing in size, ranging from the 100,000 acres of the Marquis of Downshire in 1801 to estates of 1,000 acres or so held by the lesser gentry. In the early nineteenth century one or more strata of middlemen

normally intervened between the landowner and the working tenant farmer. Middlemen leased substantial tracts of land from landowners at a fixed rent over a period of years, in turn renting the land in smaller amounts to lesser middlemen or to tenant farmers. As one descended the tenurial hierarchy, rent per acre naturally rose. Roebuck cites the case of 4,600 acres in county Fermanagh let by the landlord for £315 on a lease for one life to a middleman, Con O'Donnell. O'Donnell in turn sublet the holding to a large number of undertenants, and in 1810 received a gross rental of £1,361, that is, more than four times the amount of the head rent.[90] Ulster was generally characterised by middling and small farms. But there was no homogenous tenant-farmer class (any more than there was a homogeneous landlord one). Commercial farmers, located particularly in the fertile lowlands of the province, employed wage labour and were strongly market-oriented. The smaller farmers, with ten acres or so, were generally self-sufficient in labour (though at particular stages of the family life cycle this might not be the case, and hence the importance of young live-in farm servants). On smallholdings of five to ten acres, it was common to combine farming with domestic weaving, the independent farmer-weaver being especially typical of east Ulster. Farmers frequently sublet land to cottiers and labourers, who represented a semi-proletarianised category in the rural class structure. Even within the bottom stratum of rural society there were intricate variations in economic status. In county Tyrone it was remarked that 'the tenures of the cottiers who derive under the farmers, and are by far the most numerous of the labouring class, are in general very miserable. ...'[91] The bulk of these cottiers, in fact, appears to have been part-time weavers as well as agricultural labourers. Similarly, in the frontier counties of Cavan and Monaghan cottier-weavers were dependent on farmers for a patch of land, a crudely built cabin, and sometimes supplies of yarn as well. In other instances a farmer or farmer-weaver took a cottier as a subtenant, supplying a handloom or two at which the cottier's family worked for the benefit of its dwarf 'landlord'.[92] Most precarious of all was the position of the landless householder who had only a 'dry cot', that is, a cabin without land. 'The dry cottier, or small occupier of land purchases also "corn acres", or "con acres", a name given to land hired for the purpose of raising a single crop of potatoes or oats.' At sowing or harvest time the whole family was mobilised, 'going perhaps two or three miles from their home to cultivate their hired acres'.[93] What these various rental arrangements imply, population pressure and economic inequality notwithstanding, is that there was wide access to land, though under differing conditions, at all levels of rural society in the early decades of the nineteenth century.

In considering the position of smallholders and labourers (some two-thirds of the population in the early nineteenth century), it is important to emphasise that they were not isolated from the market system. There was no subsistence economy in Ulster, though there was widespread production for subsistence needs. The dominant pattern of producing and consuming food within the household unit implied involvement in the land market, either by renting land directly from a landlord or middleman, or by taking land from a tenant farmer. The latter arrangement might be in the form of con-acre; alternatively, it might be on the more permanent basis of subletting.[94] This secondary land market, extending over a minor part of the total farming area but constituting a matter of life or death for many cottiers and labourers, was subject to strong competitive pressures. Agrarian secret societies intervened intermittently to hold down rents; population pressure intensified the struggle to gain access to the means of subsistence.

The main marketable commodity possessed by poorer households was their abundant labour power, not only that of the menfolk but of women and children as well. The latter assisted in such work as sowing potatoes, haymaking, harvesting corn, and tending livestock, though opportunities for many of these activities were confined to short periods in the farming year. A more continuous and more widely available means of supplementing household income, discussed in section one, was the spinning of yarn and other textile pursuits. Indeed, the economic contribution of women (described by one contemporary as working 'more like slaves than labourers')[95] and that of children to the economy of the rural poor can hardly be sufficiently stressed. Surplus adolescents were frequently hired out to other households as farm servants for the half-year or the year.[96] Payment was mainly in the form of food and lodging but at least this relieved pressure on the consumption standards of the servant-supplying family. Employment in agriculture for male adult labourers normally took one of two forms: as an unbound or as a bound labourer. The unbound labourer had to take work on a casual basis and land on the con-acre system. The less insecure bound labourer, engaged by a particular farmer for a season or longer, typically received payment in a variety of ways: food-producing land, provisions, occasionally ground for a flax crop, and the use of a cabin. A money value was attached to each of these payments in kind, and any remaining imbalance in the transaction was settled by a cash payment.[97] Barter of course implies partial monetisation of the economy, but it would be misleading to see this as indicating limited penetration by the market. The two concepts are not conterminous. Bartering arrangements were contained within, and indeed were shaped by, a larger framework of market forces. These forces, bearing on both factor and product markets, emanated from within the regional and the UK economies, though clearly they were somewhat muffled in the early nineteenth century by problems of inadequate knowledge, transport costs, and partial self-sufficiency.[98]

What was the degree of monetisation? We have no adequate measure of this, though in relation to the crucially important labour market we have a large number of observations from the 1830s which provide useful clues. The data summarised in Table 1.4 are based on the evidence of 322 witnesses.[99] Inner Ulster is here defined as Antrim, Down, Armagh, and Londonderry. 'Mixed payments' refer to payments in kind (by provisions, con-acre, etc.), normally with some cash elements as well. It appears that in more than half of the communities for which there are reports, labour was paid largely or exclusively in the form of money. Pure barter was extremely rare. As might be expected, there were discernible differences in levels of monetisation between inner and outer Ulster. It is important to observe that the degree of involvement in cash transactions varied markedly by social class: the farmer or farmer-weaver, buying inputs and selling produce in markets, was involved in a far greater volume of cash transactions than the farm labourer. Lastly, of course, the rural textile industry enveloped Ulster in a web of market relationships, thus helping to make it the most monetised of the Irish provinces.

Table 1.4 *Forms of payment for labour in Ulster, c. 1834*

	Money only (%)	Mainly money (%)	Mixed payments (%)	N
Inner Ulster	17	41	42	182
Outer Ulster	9	44	47	140
All Ulster	13	43	44	322

Source. Poor Law Inquiry: Appendix D.

The foregoing discussion may now briefly be summarised. The large semi-proletariat of cottiers and labourers supplied a factor of production, labour, to the commercial-farming and textile sectors. In addition, labour was expended on household food production – a form of petty farming frequently linked to peasant landlords.[100] Most rural households were involved in either the primary or secondary land market, while towards the base of society labour and rental arrangements commonly intertwined. The existence of barter in these bilateral land and labour exchanges gave rise to market imperfections. Yet, despite limits to the degree of monetisation, and despite a substantial degree of self-sufficiency in food production, the rural economy was strongly subject to market forces in the early decades of the nineteenth century.

The extent of control which head landlords exercised over subletting, subdivision, and other practices on their estates varied considerably over space and time. What complicated matters in the early nineteenth century was the presence of middlemen, a group frequently criticised by contemporary reformers for their laxity in these areas. Loose control seems to have been tied to policies of short-term profit maximisation, with the creation of new tenancies tending initially to swell rent receipts. Even where tenants held directly from landowners, interventionist tendencies were inhibited by the existence of long leases, many of which dated from the eighteenth century. There are also some indications that the owners of small estates, especially if absentee, were less effective managers of their properties.[101] Geographical remoteness was also a relevant factor. In backward and relatively inaccessible parts of the province, such as west Donegal, peasants lived, procreated, and perished with little reference to the prerogatives of landlordism.[102] There is no doubt that by the 1830s landlords were apprehensive about further fragmentation of holdings; their sense of concern was sharpened by proposals for the introduction of a poor-law system financed by a tax on property.[103] The pressures towards partible inheritance and the proliferation of a 'hidden class of occupiers' were not easily resisted. Nonetheless, a reverse process – the consolidation of holdings – was also apparent in this period.[104] Its operation suggests revisions in peasant attitudes as well as more vigorous estate management. It was not, however, until the Famine period that there was a major surge in the elimination of smallholdings.

Two major changes in estate policy, cleary evident in the early nineteenth century, served to enlarge the scope of landlord control. The first was the continuing tendency towards elimination of middlemen, with paid professional land agents taking their place. The second was the granting of shorter leases, or no leases at all (tenancies-at-will), to farmers. In the late eighteenth and early nineteenth centuries agricultural prices had risen steeply, particularly under the stimulus of the wartime conditions of 1793–1813.[105] Ulster landowners, who had tended to give middlemen or direct tenants long leases, extending sometimes over a half-century or more, found themselves unable to benefit from the agricultural prosperity of the period. When leases terminated the opportunity was eagerly seized. The effect of long leases in frustrating the upward movement of rents is well illustrated by the Downshire properties. The average rent per acre over the estates as a whole was only 11*s* in 1815, but it was 20*s* per acre in the case of new lettings in that decade.[106]

Irish agricultural prices slumped in the years after 1813, the price of grain being particularly badly affected.[107] This obviously depressed the net incomes of food producers, though it lowered the cost of living for urban and rural workers who were dependent on purchased food. Arrears of rent mounted. These farming problems were intensified by the potato failures of 1816, 1817, and 1821 noted earlier. Indeed, for smallholders the yield rather than the price of food crops was the major determinant of economic welfare. Grain prices rose in the second half of the 1820s, were depressed in the early 1830s, and recovered again in the late 1830s.[108] The physical output of livestock products and of grains, however, increased over this period, thus moderating the decline in income among commercial farmers.[109] One might also note that, under the conditions of increasing labour supply present in the Ulster rural economy in the decades after 1813, the bargaining power of farmers in relation to suppliers of labour probably improved, thus reducing farm costs. In addition, the terms of trade were moving in favour of agriculture, thereby enhancing the purchasing power of farmers' money incomes.[110] We can thus conclude that although the long deflationary period from 1813 to the early 1840s posed problems for Irish and Ulster agriculture, living standards among the minority of middling and larger farmers improved rather than deteriorated in the two decades before the Famine. This, alas, was not true of the rural poor, whose living standards were very probably declining in the 1830s. These divergent class experiences indicate a deepening of economic inequality in the countryside before the Famine.

How do rents relate to this pattern of change? Information on rent levels and rent movements is rare for the pre-Famine period; only the Downshire estates, most of which lay within Ulster, have been the subject of intensive study.[111] The average rent on these 115,000 acres has been calculated at 12*s* 6*d* per acre in the 1840s, not much above the average for 1815. The course of rents for Kilwarlin, one of the Downshire estates, has also been traced in some detail by Maguire. The data indicate a substantial upward trend from the 1740s until 1815. In the succeeding three decades, however, the rents stipulated in new leases were more or less static, the outcome presumably of two conflicting forces: a tendency to revise rents upwards as leases fell because of under-renting in the past, and downward pressure on rents as a result of low agricultural prices. It is impossible to say if the rent plateau for new lettings observed for Kilwarlin in the pre-Famine decades is broadly representative of what happened elsewhere in Ulster. What can safely be said is that even if the money value of rents was relatively unchanging, the real value of such income would none-theless have increased quite significantly because of the fall in the general price level.

The Great Famine was a crisis period for landlords but not the landlord class. Soaring poor-law rates during the late 1840s bore heavily on proprietors, many of whom were already heavily indebted. The Donegall family, with extensive estates in Antrim (including the town of Belfast) and in the north-west, provides an outstanding example of profligate financial management and consequent vulner-ability to exogenous shocks. Accumulated debts, arrears of rent, and pressure from creditors finally sent parts of this great property tumbling through the Incumbered Estates Court and on to the land market at mid-century.[112] It also appears that the crisis for many other bankrupt or near-bankrupt estates originated long before the 1840s. Over Ireland as a whole, a total of about 5 million acres, or some 25 per cent of the country's land area, was transferred to new owners through the operations of the courts.[113] To a considerable extent, though, these were transactions *within* the landed ascendancy itself. Some commercial wealth also found its way into landed re-spectability in the decades after 1850. It is likely that forced sales of land were proportionately fewer in Ulster than in Ireland generally, though this supposition rests on the indirect evidence of the relative strength of the Ulster economy.

Agrarian violence was less prevalent in Ulster than in any other

Irish province in the pre-Famine period, though in the outer parts of Ulster where the poorer, mainly Catholic peasantry predominated, violent agrarian conspiracies were firmly entrenched.[114] The relatively quiescent state of Ulster rural society may be attributed to the existence of tenant right (see below), opportunities for employment in textile industry, and the safety valve of seasonal and permanent migration. Widespread eviction in the late 1840s and early 1850s strained relationships between landlords and tenant farmers. But given the less severe impact of the Famine in Ulster, and also the fact that the crisis was concentrated among cottiers and labourers (increasingly encumbrances on tenant farmers as well as landlords) the institution of landlordism emerged relatively unscathed. In the longer term, however, particularly in the worst affected and strongly Catholic areas of south and west Ulster, the experience of the late 1840s made available ideological weapons for a later assault on the Protestant landed ascendancy and the union between Britain and Ireland.[115] The short-term response of the better-off tenant farmers was to agitate for the legalisation of Ulster custom, the value of which was being eroded by increased poor rates and low grain prices in the late 1840s. The Ulster Tenant Right Association, promoted by the radical agrarian reformer, Dr James McKnight, and given substantial backing by Presbyterian clergymen, failed to achieve this objective (the recovery in grain prices in the early 1850s delivered the *coup de grâce* to the agitation), but the issue was to recur in more acute form between 1870 and 1881.

What was Ulster custom? In general terms, it was a body of traditional practices regulating landlord-tenant relations, the specific content of which might differ from estate to estate. It has been variously credited with producing a relatively contented tenantry, a progressive agriculture, and a successful textile industry.[116] At its broadest, Ulster custom may be said to have embraced the 'three Fs': fair rent, fixity of tenure, and free sale by the tenant of his interest in the farm. All of these notions are of course ambiguous. A fair rent as defined by whom, using what criteria? Security of tenure, but under what conditions? The right of the tenant to sell his interest in the farm he *rented*, but of what did that interest consist?

The fundamental element in this triad is the level of rent. This had implications for security of tenure and also shaped the value of the tenant's interest in his holding (tenant right). Although the concept of tenant right is somewhat elusive, it merits careful attention because the notion pervades contemporary writing on landlord-tenant relationships and, more important, was deeply rooted in the Ulster popular consciousness.[117] Essentially, an incoming tenant made a lump sum payment to an outgoing tenant (not to the landlord). Payments as high as £8 to £10 per acre were common in east Ulster.[118] To state the matter somewhat differently, the sums involved were frequently in excess of ten times the annual rent of a farm. One obvious explanation for the amount paid by the incoming tenant is that this was compensation for unexhausted improvements carried out by the previous occupant. Yet the very large sums of money involved, relative to rent payments, suggest that this is only a minor part of the explanation. Some of the districts where high tenant-right payments prevailed were anything but exemplars of heavy investment in agricultural improvements.[119] The major component of the tenant-right payment, what might be termed the *pure* tenant right, reflected the extent to which a holding was being let at a rent below the competitive level. The greater this divergence, other things being equal, the greater was the value of tenant right. Competitive and actual rents were not simply a function of agricultural prices, but also of population pressure, closeness to markets, the extent and type of rural industry, and opportunities for earning wages locally or through seasonal migration. The fact that tenant right had a substantial value throughout the nineteenth century indicates that tenant farmers had effective property rights in land (rights not unlike those of landlords), which could be sold to others. That tenant right might indeed be landlord wrong, to paraphrase Lord Palmerston, is clear by reference to the doctrines of nineteenth-century political economy. But popular currents of economic thought and morality – indifferent to abstract theorising, opposed to the unrestrained working of the land market – legitimised tenants' claims to rights in their holdings. Indeed, had there been competitive or 'rack' rents, there would have been no tenant-right payment, other than for unexhausted improvements.

How was the value of this right determined? In some instances the process was an open one: free bidding at a public auction. In other cases the value was limited by restrictions imposed by the landlord or his agent, though these were sometimes difficult to enforce. The payments seem to have been largely independent of the form of tenure, whether leasehold or tenancy-at-will.[120] This is significant, for it suggests that even tenants without formal leases enjoyed *de facto* security of possession, provided that rents were paid. This in turn implies that insecurity of tenure was not a significant barrier to agricultural improvement, contrary to what tenant spokesmen often claimed.

The institution of tenant right had both economic efficiency and distributional implications for the rural economy. It brought the functioning of the land market closer to a regime of competitive rents. Effectively, the tenant paid two rents: an actual rent to the landlord and the equivalent of a rent to the outgoing farmer. (The fact that his second rent was capitalised in a lump sum, rather than being an annual payment, does not alter the logic of the argument). It may seem paradoxical, therefore, that so much popular interest focused on the institution of tenant right. If the end result was to edge closer to competitive rents,[121] was not the custom of little benefit to tenants generally? In fact, it was beneficial. Tenant-right payments represented a transfer of income *within* the tenant-farmer stratum. The tenantry expropriated part of the rental income from land (including any associated locational advantages) at the expense of landlords. From the viewpoint of incoming tenants, of course, the payment of tenant right was an imposition. Landlords in fact feared the rack-renting effect of high payments because the new tenant's ability to pay the landlord's rent might be endangered. But in any given year only a small minority of tenants wished to buy the occupancy rights of other holdings. For the vast majority of tenants the sale value of tenant right was an important index of both the burden of rents and the capital sum being accumulated. Thus, apart from the obvious benefit of tenant-right payments to the small number of outgoing tenants at any single point in time, the custom had a general relevance. It constituted a potentially saleable asset for all existing tenants and also represented a form of insurance, entailing a lump-sum payment in the event of bankruptcy, forced migration, or other unforeseen circumstances. Furthermore, it meant (subject to certain restrictions on some estates) that the vitally important power to select successors resided with tenants rather than landlords. Hence the lively concern with tenant right and the fact that it figured prominently, if episodically, in Ulster political life.

What of claims for wider benefits stemming from the institution of tenant right and, more generally, of Ulster custom? These seem exaggerated. Ulster custom facilitated some capital accumulation, particularly in east Ulster where the practice was most firmly established. This undoubtedly aided capital formation in agriculture, but largely because it left an investible surplus in the hands of tenants rather than through its implications for security of tenure. It is unlikely that insecurity of tenure was a significant economic problem in Irish agriculture generally in the nineteenth century; and after the Famine, agricultural capital was increasingly embodied in farm animals, which were easily movable assets. Furthermore, Ulster custom was neither invariably associated with districts where good farming practices existed, nor confined exclusively to Ulster. A strong connection between Ulster custom and the development of the rural textile industry has sometimes been asserted, though never convincingly demonstrated. It is very likely that some capital was diverted from agriculture into handicraft production, but the contribution cannot have been large, since the industry was labour- rather than capital-intensive. And the extension of the putting-out system in the nineteenth century meant that capital items such as looms and raw materials were financed increasingly by manufacturers rather than rural households. The arrangements for selling tenant right, however, did ease the problem of squeezing inefficient tenants out of agriculture and also of course facilitated the voluntary movement of those transferring to other economic sectors in urban Ulster or abroad.[122] The institution of Ulster custom is therefore incapable of bearing the heavy explanatory load sometimes placed on it in interpreting the distinctive evolution of the northern part of the island.

Relations between landlords and tenants were generally cordial from the early 1850s until 1870. The economic background was favourable: the value of Irish agricultural output rose by over 40 per cent between 1851–55 and 1871–75.[123] This implies an even greater increase in agricultural income per head. Increases of rent lagged well behind, rising by perhaps 20 per cent over the same period.[124] True, Gladstone's land act of 1870, while attempting to give Ulster custom the force of law, had the perverse effect of increasing rather than diminishing uncertainty regarding the rights of tenants.[125] But it was the agricultural depression of the late 1870s, and in particular the disastrous season of 1879 – possibly the worst since the Famine – that brought accumulating frictions to the point of confrontation with Ulster landlords. The mask of deference slipped. Tenant right groups provided the organisational framework through which demands for rent reductions and security of tenure were articulated. These local associations, many of which were based in Presbyterian farming communities, had an especially vigorous existence in east Ulster. It was autumn 1880 before the more militant movement of the southern tenantry, the Land League, had a significant organisational impact on Ulster.[126] The years 1880 and 1881 were in fact good ones for agriculture, but Protestant tenants proved as enthusiastic about farming Westminster as their Catholic counterparts. Bowing to the mass agitation, the Liberal Prime Minister W. E. Gladstone introduced a major set of land reforms in August 1881. The 'three Fs' were conceded. Land courts were set up to fix 'fair' rents; in practice this meant to lower rents. Provisions in the Act for the purchase of land by tenants from their landlords, albeit limited in scope, marked a crucial stage along the legislative road to peasant proprietorship.

Following the 1881 Land Act there was a rush of Ulster tenants into the land courts to have judicial rents fixed. A decline in the intensity of the agitation, especially among Protestant tenants, ensued.[127] Interestingly, the Land League, which from the outset had been a front for conspiratorial nationalism as well as a movement for land reform, succeeded in attracting support from Protestant tenants. Hopes of killing grass-roots unionism with rent reductions were, however, to prove illusory. A further land act in 1882, particularly relevant to the hill tenantry of the province, abolished rent arrears for smallholders. This eliminated a potent source of discontent and a major cause of an upsurge in evictions in Ulster during the years 1879–81. The operations of the land courts commonly resulted in reductions of 15 to 20 per cent, and by 1883 the land war was virtually ended in Ulster.[128] Later agrarian-cum-nationalist agitations, that of the Plan of Campaign, 1886–92, and of the United Irish League, 1898–1903, had little impact on Ulster (with the partial exception of Donegal in the mid-1880s).

A succession of land acts in the quarter-century from the mid 1880s onwards − 'revolution from above' − tightened the screw on landlordism, effecting a relatively peaceful transition to a state of owner occupancy. The provisions of the Wyndham Land Act of 1903, extended in 1909 − the major means whereby tenants became full masters of the soil − succeeded in reconciling tenant right and landlord wrong. The outgoing landlords were favourably compensated with lump sum payments generally ranging in value from fifteen to twenty-five times the annual rent. Tenants were enabled, through state loans, to purchase the landlord interest on the basis of annual repayments which amounted to less than their previous yearly rents. Clearly the rate of return on investment in agitation was a good one. The figures do not add up. But the financial gap between the two sides to this massive transaction was made up by state subsidy, a solution congenial to both. By 1914 the majority of Ulster farmers had become owners of their holdings.[129] Thus was completed the long march of the tenant righters.

The landlord clearances of the early twentieth century had few important economic implications. In view of the low level of evictions in post-Famine Ireland, and the class-specific nature of evictions – those most vulnerable to ejection were smallholders who occupied a minor part of total farm land – strengthening occupancy rights was largely irrelevant to issues of increasing agricultural investment and production. Land reform, the price paid by the state for social stability, did however have a redistributive impact. It transferred wealth to tenant farmers, confirmed the dominant position in the countryside of a rural petty bourgeoisie, and widened the economic gap between farmers and labourers. One might speculate that it also increased inequality within the farming stratum as rent reductions tended to be on a proportional basis.

If the departure of Irish landlords was of relatively little consequence, was their presence during the nineteenth century of similarly slight economic significance? The answer for the second half of the nineteenth century is probably yes, inflated images of self-importance notwithstanding. The position prior to the 1840s presents more problems. The apparatus of the state, particularly at a local government level, was underdeveloped. In addition, alternative means of collecting rents would have been more difficult, though hardly impossible to implement. Rents acted as a spur to the more efficient use of land resources and hence were, in principle, socially desirable. The large rental income from Irish land – some £12 million in the 1840s[130] – might have been diverted into more productive channels than the conspicuous consumption of a landed élite, but this presupposes a very different social order. Arguably the most important function of landlords in pre-Famine Ireland was the economic-demographic one: controlling access to land, hence indirectly controlling household formation, and ultimately influencing population growth. As we have seen, the tightness of estate policy varied in different parts of Ulster and it is virtually impossible to assess the effectiveness and the welfare implications of such policies. Finally, it may be noted that Irish landlords, as compared to their English and Scottish counterparts, were less active in promoting permanent improvements on tenants' farms.[131] Indeed the landlord contribution to fixed capital seems to have been least in Ulster. The comparative inactivity of Irish landlords is probably due to the small size of farms. This would result in higher transaction costs and also a lower rate of return on investment because of the indivisibility of certain items of farm capital. The informal nature of much capital formation on small farms is probably also relevant. Field enclosures, reclamation of marginal land, construction of rough animal shelters, for example, depend primarily on the expenditure of labour rather than money capital. These are most economically undertaken within the framework of the household economy. Looking across the nineteenth century as a whole, it is hardly possible to form a fine judgement of the overall importance of landlords to the Ulster rural economy. One is left with the distinct impression, though, that they were largely peripheral to the central economic processes of that society.

The agricultural labour force, 1851–1911
It is usually contended on both theoretical and empirical grounds that economic development involves a decline in the agricultural sector's share of total employment (and total income). This generalisation has been distilled from the experience of countries which enjoyed population increase *and* economic growth. An industrialising area such as Ulster, which somewhat perversely was also undergoing population decline, usefully tests the scope of this claim.[132] Also, in that Ulster possessed an agricultural, a proto-industrial, and a modern industrial sector, each experiencing different rates of change, a particular outcome is by no means inevitable.

The absolute size of the agricultural labour force, which had been increasing in the years before the Great Famine, went into secular decline thereafter. The number of males classified as securing a livelihood from farming in 1851 was just under 400,000 (out of a total male labour force of 607,000); by 1911 this had shrunk to 250,000. It is also evident from Table 1.5 that the agricultural labour force declined in relative significance during the second half of the nineteenth century. A province-wide focus, however, gives a blurred impression of shifts in occupational structure that accompanied economic change. In the eastern counties where the industrial growth-points of the province were located, the labour force was being substantially restructured. Here the balance between agricultural and non-agricultural employment seems to have been fairly even as early as mid-century. By 1911 only one in every three male workers was

Table 1.5 *The absolute size and proportion of the male labour force in agriculture in the years 1851, 1881 and 1911*

Year	Inner Ulster	Outer Ulster	All Ulster
(a) *Absolute size*			
1851	167,000	226,000	393,000
1881	145,000	178,000	323,000
1911	110,000	140,000	250,000
(b) *Proportion* (%)			
1851	52	80	65
1881	49	82	63
1911	35	79	51

Source. Calculated from occupational data in the Census of Ireland, relevant years.

directly dependent on farming. In south and west Ulster, by contrast, local economies remained firmly rooted in the soil. The numbers of people engaged in agriculture had declined steeply (more so than in the eastern counties), but alternative employment opportunities had not materialised to disturb the overwhelmingly rural character of these sub-regions. Londonderry is an intermediate case with respect to the changing distribution of occupations because of the impact of partial industrialisation west of the Bann.

Not only did the size and relative significance of the agricultural labour force change in the second half of the nineteenth century, but its composition, and hence the rural class structure, also altered. There are formidable difficulties in distinguishing between farmers, various types of family labour, and hired labour.[133] The broad trends, however, are not in doubt. While the number of farmers fell in the period 1850–1914, agricultural labourers declined even faster. By the eve of the Great War the agricultural labourer was a comparatively rare figure. Nearly three-quarters of those working on the land were farm occupiers, their offspring, or other kin. Thus the representative figure in the Ulster farmyard was the family member, contributing to and maintained by the family enterprise.

The resources of the family economy had nonetheless to be supplemented by outside labour. This was particularly true of such counties as Antrim, Down, and Londonderry, where throughout this period farmers accounted for considerably less than half the pool of male farmworkers. Labour needs depended on farm size, on the labour intensity of farm output, and on such demographic features as the size and composition of the household and the life-cycle stage of the family. When there was a labour deficit, the problem was most acute at periods of peak activity in the farm year. A variety of stratagems was used to overcome the problem. Helpers were hired on a daily, seasonal, or yearly basis. In social terms many of these hired workers were not of the labouring class, but rather farmers' sons or co-residing relatives from farm households with a labour surplus. They would not have perceived themselves, or been perceived locally, as merely agricultural labourers. Others whose status was more purely proletarian were almost entirely dependent on the sale of their labour services. Yet it should be remembered that the Famine had greatly weakened this stratum of rural society, and the process of depletion continued through emigration in succeeding decades. Where labourers were obliged to find work beyond their home district, as in south and west Ulster, the hiring fair was an important economic institution linking buyers and sellers of labour power. Paddy Gallagher, born in 1871, who first hired out as a ten-year-old boy, has left us this autobiographical sketch of the system and its economic rationale.

> The year before had been a bad year in Scotland, and my father had not enough money home with him to pay the rent and the shop debts. It was the same with the neighbours. A crowd of us boys were got ready for the hiring fair at Strabane ... When we reached Strabane we all cuddled together, and were scared at first, but the big fellows told us to scatter out so as the farmers would see us. They made us walk up and down to see how we were set up and judge what mettle was in us. Anybody who looked tired or faulty in any way was passed over.[134]

Survivals of this system persisted in Ulster until well into the twentieth century. Yet another means of supplementing the labour resources of the farm household was to pool labour among neighbouring farmers and kinfolk.[135] This practice of mutual aid was especially prevalent at sowing and harvesting times. Finally, of course, the interpenetration of agriculture and rural industry meant that labour could be temporarily drawn away from manufacturing activity, though these transfers diminished in significance during the second half of the nineteenth century.

The 'disappearing' agricultural labourer was responding to poor conditions at home – low and irregular earnings, bad housing, lowly status – and the prospect of improved living standards in urban Ulster or abroad. Data on wage rates in agriculture exist but complications such as the use of non-monetary forms of payment and the frequency of employment make their interpretation difficult. Evidence presented to the Poor Law Commissioners in the 1830s suggests that the average wage paid in the province was 11*d* per day in summer-time.[136] This was without food. In the winter months the rate was somewhat lower, being 10*d* per day. (The first finding is based on 310 usable returns from all over Ulster, the second on 288 such returns.) Given wide variation in wage levels as between different localities, average figures obscure as well as illuminate.

Wages rose after the Famine at a somewhat faster rate than the rise in the cost of living. But the gains achieved were meagre. One set of estimates suggests that the average weekly wages of farm labourers in Ulster in 1860 were about 7*s* to 7*s* 6*d*. This was only marginally more than the earnings of a young factory spinner in the linen industry.[137] County Antrim had the highest level (8*s* 4*d* weekly), while county Fermanagh (6*s* weekly) appears to have been the least rewarding place to pursue a career in labouring. By 1911 differences in wage rates within the province had narrowed, suggesting closer integration of local labour markets. Average weekly earnings had risen to about 11*s*, an improvement certainly, but still roughly the same as the earnings of a Belfast mill girl. A more relevant reference point is that of unskilled male labour in the city, where earnings at around 18*s* per week were some 60 per cent higher. Similarly the comparison with an English agricultural labourer, whose earnings were said to be 17*s* 6*d* per week at this time, is unfavourable.[138] While these various figures are approximations, there is no doubting the existence of large differentials, and hence a powerful motive for leaving the land. Given this rural exodus – the male labour force in Ulster agriculture declined by 37 per cent during the period 1851–1911 – it may seem strange that a more pronounced rise in rural wages did not take place in the later nineteenth century. But changes on the demand side of the rural labour market moderated wage increases; the shift to a less labour-intensive agriculture and, from the 1870s in particular, the adoption of a more capital-intensive form of production involving horse husbandry and farm machinery weakened the demand for labour. As Thomas Kells, a farmer from County Armagh, observed in the 1890s: 'We have machines to mow, reap, thresh, and churn, so we can do with very little men.'[139] Furthermore, the possibilities for effective trade union organisation were slight given the social composition of the labour force, its disperal across tens of thousands of farms, and the face-to-face relationships characteristic of farm employment. The real surprise perhaps was the large numbers still on the land in the Edwardian period, not just rural proletarians, but also farmers and farmers' relatives who made up the bulk of the farm labour force.

Summary and Conclusion

The long run or natural orientation of Ulster agriculture is towards pastoral farming. Between the later eighteenth century and the 1840s, however, there was a pronounced shift towards tillage products, the trinity of oats, potatoes, and flax in particular. From the 1840s, or possibly a little earlier, through to 1914, a reverse long swing occurred. Agricultural resources – land, labour, capital, entrepreneurship – were redeployed in favour of producing animal products. Both swings were in response to changes in relative prices and the cost of farm inputs. In the first half of the century labour was cheap while land was relatively expensive. The major outputs of the rural economy – tillage products and rural textiles – corresponded well to the relative scarcity of these factors of production. Both have a high labour content and are land economising. Labour costs rose after mid century. Rent (the price of land use) showed only a moderate increase; indeed in the late nineteenth century rents were forced downwards (never to recover) under the impact of land legislation. On the demand side, prices moved strongly in favour of pastoral products. Land-extensive husbandry, with diminishing inputs of labour, became increasingly more profitable than labour-intensive crop cultivation. It is probable that technical change, including the revolution in transport in this period, was also biased in favour of livestock farming. The overall outcome in Ulster was intensive mixed farming and significant productivity gains.

While severe fluctuations in incomes and living standards affected the rural economy in the nineteenth century, there was only one major crisis: the Great Famine. The complex nature of the disaster needs teasing out. There was no absolute shortage of food in Ireland; this was an economic and political crisis rather than a problem of food supply as such. Famine cut deeply into the crowded countryside; it did so, not indiscriminately, but along class lines. In these various senses it was a modern famine. But it was also a modified Malthusian crisis. There was a shortage of food relative to human requirements in some districts and among the lowest social groups. True, destruction of the major food crop was due to random elements, perfidious Gods rather than Albions. However, the position of parts of the province, south Ulster especially, was prospectively Malthusian by 1840.[140] Population pressure was leading towards an ecologically precarious form of monoculture among the expanding classes of cottiers and labourers. Harvest failure, superimposed on such conditions, was bound to be calamitous. The peasant propensity to procreate, arguably the major *social* determinant of the Famine in the long term, reaped its own dire harvest. Emphasis on the Malthusian dimension is not, incidentally, meant to imply that disaster was inevitable about mid-century. The broadening stream of migration and emigration in the pre-Famine decades, and a deceleration in population growth rates, offered possible escape routes. In a real and tragic sense Ulster was caught in the last lap; in the absence of repeated harvest failure it might well have slipped past a Malthusian-style confrontation between people and food resources.

Was the Great Famine a watershed in nineteenth-century Ulster and Irish history? If by this is meant the Famine was the pristine source of trends apparent in later periods − a decline in subdivision, increased emphasis on livestock farming, later and less frequent marriage, emigration − then this was clearly not the case. Such a view, while once popular, was never very plausible except under the assumption of a closed economy and society. A less ethnocentric approach to the past would have readily recognised that a small open economy, situated alongside the first industrial nation, and with links to the transplanted European society of North America, would be strongly influenced in its turning points by external forces (international price movements, technology, tastes, employment opportunities). In the case of Ulster, to take a single example, the course of technological change in the linen industry was only partly connected to local conditions. This revised perspective runs the risk, however, of conveying the impression that the Famine was therefore unimportant. It needs stressing that the vast human toll overwhelms all considerations of turning points and origins of change. Mass mortality is the primary historical reality. And of course the Famine did change the *rate* of societal change at the economic, linguistic, religious, and political levels. By compressing historical processes into a short brutal interval it transformed in a qualitative as well as a quantitative sense the course of subsequent development. We may conclude that the Great Hunger still represents a major dividing line in modern Irish history, even if of somewhat blurred relevance in relation to Ulster history.

A two-class model of rural society – landlords frequently predatory, peasants uniformly impoverished – is clearly a distortion of the reality and experience of social relations in the countryside. One aspect of social differentiation on which we lay particular stress is the existence of a category of peasant landlords in the pre-Famine period. Conventional landlords and head rents receive disproportionate attention, being better represented in surviving historical records, but the less visible rental arrangements towards the bottom of society are critically important in terms of the welfare of the rural poor. On the vexed issue of security of tenure and agricultural development, Wakefield's acidic comment of 1812 does service for the century as a whole: 'If encouragement of a longer term could create superior husbandry, Ireland should be a real garden'.[141] Long leases, frequently for the duration of three lives or twenty-one years, were common in the early nineteenth century. The gradual phasing out of such leases does not appear to have diluted the tenant's security nor his co-ownership rights in the soil. It is likely that the real locus of insecurity before mid-century lay among those holding land from peasant landlords. Our discussion of tenant-right claims vindicates the conservative view that these represented an attack on landlord wealth, though there can be little sympathy for a rent-collecting class, 800 of whose members owned half the island in the 1870s. Recent scholarship has established that Irish landlords were generally not rent maximisers, but this, while important, should not be interpreted as constituting a defence or rehabilitation of the landlord system.

The rural textile industry was central to the functioning of the rural economy in the early nineteenth century. More so than farming, it was the subject of major technological and organisational change. It was originally organised on the basis of independent production, with intimate raw material and labour links to agriculture. By the early nineteenth century a new form of capitalistic organisation, the putting-out system, was eroding the position of independent spinners and weavers. Associated with the rise of these large firms of merchant-organisers was a dispersed semi-proletariat. A third distinct form of economic organisation was the factory system which emerged in the Belfast cotton industry in the late eighteenth century, in the spinning of linen yarn in the 1830s, and in linen weaving in the 1850s. This involved full proletarianisation. All three modes of production existed side by side in the first half of the nineteenth century, sometimes in a complementary but ultimately in a competitive relationship. Thus mill spinning gave an initial boost to handloom weaving; further developments in textile technology later undermined handicraft techniques in weaving. The triumph of the factory system implied de-industrialisation in outer Ulster which was essentially a low-cost labour reservation as far as textile production was concerned. For-mation of a local entrepreneurial class, capital accumulation, develop-ment of complementary services, a favourable geographical and transport setting (allowing ready access to energy, raw materials, and markets) − all advantages enjoyed by the Belfast region − were lacking in much of south and west Ulster. Ulster industrialised, but in the Lagan Valley. The Derry area is an exception. If one may regard east Ulster as a peripheral region in terms of industrialising Europe, then the Derry region is a good example of partial industrialisation at the periphery of a periphery.

In 1900 the terms 'rural economy' and 'agricultural economy' were virtually interchangeable; in 1800 this would have been a quite misleading equation. From the second quarter of the nineteenth century a process of agriculturalisation was making progress in south and west Ulster, eventually becoming more general as industry concentrated in urban locations and a scattering of mill villages. This narrowing of the economic base of the rural economy had implications for occupational and class structures. The ranks of those engaged in handicraft production were gradually thinned out. The Great Famine uprooted large numbers of cottiers and labourers. The Famine after-math of migration and emigration was a voluntary continuation of this process. The effect of these class-biased changes was to reduce social divisions in the agricultural community, a development which facilitated mobilisation against landlords in the late nineteenth century. By then there had been a decisive shift in the class balance of rural society in favour of a petty bourgeoisie composed of small propertyholders. Within a few decades the landlord tier was stripped away. Thus, as this century opened, the state of economy and society in rural Ulster was far removed from the complex economic and class structures of a century earlier.

Notes

1. In preparing this chapter I have benefited greatly from the advice and insights of Dr. W. H. Crawford. These were given in a characteristically

generous fashion. David S. Johnson has been a stimulating colleague in our continuing discussions on Irish and Ulster history. I doubt if he can be absolved from all responsibility for interpretations developed here. Professor James S. Donnelly spilled much red ink on the script; his energy and zeal in relation to matters of style and substance are much appreciated. Dr. Christopher McGimpsey strongly impressed on me the importance of the frontier county of Monaghan. Other Irish historians – Peter Solar, Cormac Ó Gráda, W. A. Maguire, Ann McKernan, Debbi Sandel, Brenda Collins, Ken Greer – made helpful comments on various aspects of the work. Judy Kennedy provided assistance for this as for earlier studies. Finally, Dr. Rosalind Marsh, while failing to convince me of the relevance of parallels with Russian peasant agriculture, was a source of encouragement during difficult periods of writing.

2. C. Gill, *The Rise of the Irish Linen Industry*, Oxford, 1925, pp. 341–3; W. H. Crawford, *Domestic Industry in Ireland*, Dublin, 1972, pp. 1–6, 78–80; E. Boyle, *The Economic Development of the Irish Linen Industry, 1825–1913*, unpublished Ph.D. thesis, The Queen's University of Belfast, 1979, p. 279.

3. Gill, *Linen Industry*, p. 342.

4. *Ibid.*, p. 340.

5. The account of the linen industry in this paragraph is based largely on the following: J. Dubourdieu, *Statistical Survey of the County of Down*, Dublin, 1802; Dubourdieu, *Statistical Survey of the County of Antrim*, Dublin, 1812; C. Coote, *Statistical Survey of the County of Armagh*, Dublin, 1804; E. Wakefield, *An Account of Ireland, Statistical and Political*, I and II, London, 1812; Gill, *Linen Industry*; Crawford, *Domestic Industry*; B. Collins, 'Proto-industrialisation and pre-Famine emigration', *Social History*, VII, 1982, pp. 127–46.

6. Coote, *Armagh*, pp. 249–51; Wakefield, *Ireland*, II, p. 740; Crawford, *Domestic Industry*, p. 25.

7. Gill, *Linen Industry*, pp. 271–76; Crawford, *Domestic Industry*, pp. 39–51.

8. E. R. R. Green, *The Lagan Valley*, London, 1949, pp. 97–99.

9. Dubourdieu, *Down*, p. 236.

10. Gill, *Linen Industry*, pp. 265–6.

11. Wakefield, *Ireland*, I, p. 684.

12. *Ibid.*, I, pp. 684–5. Cf. Coote, *Armagh*, p. 255 and Dubourdieu, *Down*, p. 234.

13. Gill, *Linen Industry*, pp. 316–7; Crawford, *Domestic Industry*, p. 43.

14. Green, *Lagan Valley*, pp. 112–5.

15. According to Wakefield (*Ireland*, I, p. 688) sales at the monthly yarn markets of Donegal and Ardara amounted to £1,500 and £2,000 respectively.

16. Collins, 'Proto-industrialisation', pp. 138–9.

17. *Reports from Assistant Handloom Weavers' Commissioners*, BPP, 1840, XXIII, p. 440 (cited hereafter as *Handloom Weavers' Report*).

18. Collins, 'Proto-industrialisation', pp. 140–1.
19. Based on occupational statistics contained in the censuses of Ireland, 1841 and 1851. For a different view see Collins, 'Proto-industrialisation', p. 142.
20. Wakefield, *Ireland*, pp. 706–7; Green, *Lagan Valley*, pp. 99–111.
21. *Handloom Weavers' Report*, pp. 486–9.
22. Crawford, *Domestic Industry*, p. 39.
23. *Handloom Weavers' Report*, pp. 482–3; E.R.R. Green, 'The beginnings of industrial revolution' in T.W. Moody and J.C. Beckett eds., *Ulster since 1800*, London, 1954, p. 33; *Poor Inquiry (Ireland): Appendix D*, BPP, 1936, XXXI, p. 451 (report on Seapatrick).
24. The image is from T.S. Ashton, *An Economic History of England: The Eighteenth Century*, London, 1955, p. 99.
25. Crawford, *Domestic Industry*, pp. 44–6.
26. Green, *Lagan Valley*, pp. 108–9.
27. *Handloom Weavers' Report*, pp. 479–89; Crawford, *Domestic Industry*, pp. 46–51; Gill, *Linen Industry*, p. 274.
28. Gill, *Linen Industry*, p. 273.
29. *Handloom Weavers' Report*, p. 489.
30. Green, *Lagan Valley*, p. 110. The discussion of real earnings draws heavily on data in the following sources: *Handloom Weavers' Report*, pp. 444 *et seq.*; Coote, *Armagh*, pp. 251–6; Dubourdieu, *Down*, pp. 233–6; Wakefield, *Ireland*, I, pp. 685–98; Crawford, *Domestic Industry*, pp. 40–1; Gill, *Linen Industry*, pp. 157–8, 237, 326–8; Boyle, *Irish Linen*, pp. 56–7; B.R. Mitchell and P. Deane, *Abstract of British Historical Statistics*, Cambridge, 1971, pp. 469–71; P. Ollerenshaw, *The Belfast Banks, 1820–1900*, unpublished Ph.D. thesis, University of Sheffield, 1982.
31. The periodic crises which afflicted the industry resulted in acute distress. These fluctuations, which are an integral part of industrialisation, may have been becoming more intense in the first half of the nineteenth century. If true, further adverse implications for welfare are implied, though it should also be remembered that the industry was severely disrupted in the early years of the century due to wartime difficulties.
32. The limited evidence available (discussed in section four) would suggest a rise in the real value of head rents between 1815 and 1840. Cottier rents are more relevant, however. Con-acre rents in Cavan in the 1830s, for instance, generally ranged from £6 to £9 (as compared to head rents of £1 to £2 5s per acre). The pattern in Monaghan was fairly similar. It is unlikely that such high con-acre rents, if measured in real terms, could have existed in the early years of the century in south Ulster. See *Poor Inquiry: Appendix F*.
33. *Report from Assistant Handloom Weavers' Commissioners*, BPP, 1840, XXIV, p. 651. If, however, one is considering household earnings, as distinct from the individual earnings of a cotton handloom weaver, an urban location had definite advantages through opening up opportunities for the employment of wives and children in textile mills.

34. Green, *Lagan Valley*, pp. 100, 103, 105; Gill, *Linen Industry*, pp. 222–4, 324. Boyle, *Irish Linen*, p. 57.
35. Crawford, *Domestic Industry*, p. 57; Gill, *Linen Industry*, p. 279.
36. But see later reservations regarding census data on occupations.
37. Useful accounts of the industry are contained in *The Shirt Industry of North-West Ireland*, prepared and published by the North-West Archaeological and Historical Society, Derry, no date; D. Murphy, *Derry, Donegal and Modern Ulster, 1790–1921*, Derry, 1981. See also L. M. Cullen, *An Economic History of Ireland Since 1660*, London, 1972, pp. 151, 160.
38. *Londonderry Sentinel*, 19 October 1912, as quoted in *Shirt Industry of the North West*, p. 42.
39. See, for example, F. Mendels, 'Proto-industrialisation, the first phase of the industrialisation process', *Journal of Economic History*, XXXII, 1972, pp. 241–61 and E. Almquist, 'Pre-Famine Ireland and the theory of European proto-industrialisation: evidence from the 1841 census', *Journal of Economic History*, XXXIX, 1979, pp. 699–718. For a less than enthusiastic view of this concept see D. C. Coleman, 'Proto-industrialisation: a concept too many'. Economic History Review, XXXVI, 1983, pp. 435–48.
40. Crawford, *Domestic Industry*, p. 26.
41. J. Mokyr, 'Malthusian models and Irish history', *Journal of Economic History*, XL, 1980, p. 165. See also L. Kennedy, 'Studies in Irish econometric history', *Irish Historical Studies*, XXIII, 1983, pp. 203–4.
42. Irregular attendance at the loom and such work-associated patterns of leisure as hunting, bull-baiting, and cockfighting were at variance with the regimentation and time-discipline of modern factory life. On the problems of creating a factory workforce in Ireland see letter from John Marshall of Leeds to Thomas Gataker of Dundalk, 19 November 1801 (Public Record Office, Northern Ireland, Foster-Massereene MSS, D207/28/113). I am indebted to W. H. Crawford for this reference.
43. Boyle, Irish Linen, pp. 29, 40–1; *Report on Standard Time Rates of Wages in the UK*, BPP, 1912–13, XCII, pp. 606, 690.
44. See the annual official publication *Agricultural Statistics of Ireland*, relevant years.
45. T. W. Freeman, *Ireland: A General and Regional Geography*, London, 1972, pp. 56–62.
46. E. E. Evans in the introduction to L. Symons ed., *Land Use in Northern Ireland*, Belfast, 1963, p. 20; Freeman, *Ireland*, pp. 174–200.
47. J. McEvoy, *Tyrone*, pp. 81–2; Wakefield, *Ireland*, I, pp. 323–4; W. S. Mason, *A Statistical Account or Parochial Survey of Ireland*, III, Dublin, 1819, pp. 199, 200; Dubourdieu, *Down*, p. 216.
48. McEvoy, *Tyrone*, p. 29.
49. K. H. Connell, *The Population of Ireland, 1750–1845*, Oxford, 1950, pp. 242–3.
50. On inter-regional trade and specialisation see J. M'Parlan, *A Statistical Survey of the County of Sligo*, Dublin, 1802, p. 14; Wakefield, *Ireland*,

I, pp. 315–6, Dubourdieu, *Down*, pp. 203, 206–7; W. H. Crawford, 'Economy and society in south Ulster in the eighteenth century', *Clogher Record*, VIII, 1975, pp. 241–58; L. Kennedy, 'Regional specialisation, railway development and Irish agriculture', in J. M. Goldstrom and L. A. Clarkson eds., *Population, Economy and Society in Ireland*, Oxford, 1981, pp. 173–93.

51. Cattle aged one year or more numbered 526,000 in 1841, 654,000 in 1847, and 772,000 in 1851. Such a large absolute and proportional increase by 1847 suggests that Ulster agriculture was adopting a stronger livestock orientation before the Famine. See L. Kennedy, 'Ulster agricultural statistics, 1841–1914', unpublished paper, Belfast, 1983.

52. J. Mokyr, *Why Ireland Starved*, London, 1983, p. 19. This major work unfortunately became available after the text of this chapter was essentially completed.

53. J. P. Kennedy, *Digest of Evidence Taken before Her Majesty's Commissioners of Inquiry into the State of the Law and Practice in respect to the Occupation of Land in Ireland* (Devon Digest), I, Dublin, 1847, pp. 372–3.

54. See Lord George Hill, *Facts from Gweedore* (reprint), Belfast, 1971, pp. 40–2, 62–4; J. M'Parlan, *Statistical Survey of the County of Donegal*, Dublin, 1802, p. 64; D. McCourt, 'Infield and outfield in Ireland', *Economic History Review*, VII, 1954–55, pp. 369–76.

55. Pig numbers increased from 247,000 in 1851 to 343,000 in 1912. The rise in the numbers of poultry was more spectacular: from 2·4 million to 9·6 million over the same period.

56. T. Barrington, 'A review of Irish agricultural prices', *Journal of the Statistical and Social Inquiry Society of Ireland*, XV, 1926–7, pp. 251–2.

57. Green, *Lagan Valley*, pp. 130–42.

58. Marginal land in each of the three years has been re-estimated from the agricultural statistics and weighted by a factor of 0·3. Thus the figures for the pastoral area in Table 1.2 are adjusted rather than actual acres. The procedure adopted is explained in Kennedy, 'Ulster statistics' (see n. 51). Note also that labour in this table refers to male labour only.

59. Dubourdieu, *Down*, p. 61; McEvoy, *Tyrone*, p. 106; Wakefield, *Ireland*, I, pp. 468–9.

60. P. Robinson, 'The spread of hedged enclosure in Ulster', *Ulster Folklife*, XXIII, 1977, p. 59. See also R. H. Buchanan, 'Common field and enclosure: an 18th century example from Lecale, Co. Down' in D. McCourt ed. *Studies in Folklife presented to E. E. Evans*, Belfast, 1970.

61. J. MacCloskey, *Statistical Report of the Parishes of Ballinascreen, Kilcronaghan, Desertmartin, Banagher, Dungiven and Boveva in the County of Londonderry*, edited by D. O'Kane, Ballinascreen, 1983, p. 35. See also *Ordnance Survey Memoir for the Parish of Templecorran*, Belfast, no date, p. 25.

62. *Poor Inquiry: Appendix F.*

63. *Handloom Weavers' Report*, p. 479.
64. *Poor Inquiry: Appendix D*. People with some capital resources were over-represented among emigrants from many districts − see, for example, reports on Loughgilly, Creggan, Killevy, Aughabog, and Killevan, and the *Handloom Weavers' Report*, p. 566. This meant that a higher proportion of the *remaining* population was vulnerable to failure of the staple food crop, thus tending to inflate mortality rates during the Great Famine.
65. J. Huttman, 'The impact of land reform on agricultural production in Ireland', *Agricultural History*, XLVI, 1972, p. 358; B. Walker, *Sentry Hill: An Ulster Farm and Family*, Belfast, 1981, p. 105. On manuring see McEvoy, *Tyrone*, pp. 177−8; MacCloskey, *Londonderry*, pp. 36−7; Hill, *Gweedore*, p. 21; Coote, *Armagh*, p. 238.
66. These levels of output per acre compare favourably with average British yields of 17 cwt and 13·5 cwt for wheat and oats respectively in the years 1912−14. See Mitchell and Deane, *Historical Statistics*, p. 90.
67. Dubourdieu, *Down*, p. 49; McEvoy, *Tyrone*, pp. 46−7; Evans in Symons ed., *Land Use*, p. 37.
68. *Ordnance Survey Memoir of Templecorran*, p. 25; Walker, *Sentry Hill*, p. 103.
69. Dubourdieu, *Down*, p. 194.
70. Huttman, 'Land reform', p. 362; J. O'Donovan, *The Economic History of Livestock in Ireland*, Cork, 1940, pp. 180−2, 249. See O'Donovan also on changes in pig breeds (pp. 271−2).
71. L. Kennedy, *Agricultural Co-operation and Irish Rural Society, 1880−1914*, unpublished D.Phil. thesis, University of York, 1978, pp. 22−5.
72. B.A. Kennedy, 'Tenant right before 1870' in T.W. Moody and J.C. Beckett eds., *Ulster since 1800: A Political and Economic Survey*, London, 1974, p. 40.
73. *Report from Handloom Weavers' Commissioners*, p. 674.
74. Green, *Lagan Valley*, p. 127; Gill, *Irish Linen*, p. 341.
75. Murphy, *Modern Ulster*, p. 62; W.A. Maguire, *The Downshire Estates in Ireland, 1801−1845*, Oxford, 1972, p. 31; M. Daly, *Social and Economic History of Ireland since 1800*, Dublin, 1981, p. 20.
76. R.N. Salaman, *The History and Social Influence of the Potato*, Cambridge, 1949, pp. 603−8. J.S. Donnelly (*Landlord and Tenant in Nineteenth-Century Ireland*, Dublin, 1973, p. 14) identifies the following as years of acute distress: 1816−17, 1821−22, 1825−26, 1829−30, 1830−31, and 1839−40.
77. See reports for Armaghleague, Aughnamullan, Castleterra in *Poor Inquiry: Appendix D*.
78. G.Ó Tuathaigh, *Ireland Before the Famine, 1798−1848*, Dublin, 1972, p. 203. For Malthusian-style warnings in 1821 regarding the dangers of rapid population growth and dependence on the potato crop see W. Greig, *General Report on the Gosford Estates in County Armagh 1821* (with an introduction by F.M.L. Thompson and D. Tierney), Belfast, 1976, pp. 154−5.

79. J. Mokyr, 'The deadly fungus', in J. L. Simon ed., *Research in Population Economics*, Greenwich, Conn., 1980, pp. 237–77.
80. Letter from George Dawson to Sir. T. F. Fremantle; reproduced by the Public Record Office, Northern Ireland, in *The Great Famine, 1845–52*, Belfast, no date. For a discussion of famine diseases and public-relief measures see P. MacArthur, 'Medical history of the Famine' in R. D. Edwards and T. D. Williams eds. *The Great Famine*, Dublin, 1962, pp. 263–315.
81. Mokyr, *Why Ireland Starved*, pp. 266–75.
82. Data on the grain trade are from P. M. A. Bourke, 'The Irish Grain Trade, 1839–48', *Irish Historical Studies*, XX, 1976, pp. 156–69.
83. There were 2·6 million cattle of various ages – one-third of them in Ulster – on the island in 1847. In addition there were 2·2 million sheep, 0·6 million pigs, and 5·7 million poultry.
84. The role of the British government, constrained in part by the debilitating principles of a *laissez-faire* ideology, is certainly open to criticism. The vast scale of the relief operations – three million people were being fed by the state in August 1847 – does not compare unfavourably, however, with famine relief measures in other parts of the world even in this century. Given the problems of communication and the under-developed nature of the state apparatus at mid-nineteenth century, this was no mean achievement. Time lags in developing effective policies of food distribution, rather thant he eventual scope of such measures, were the real shortcomings in the response of the state.
85. See, for example, the resolution of the Newry Board of Guardians in February 1849 emphatically denying that 'the industrious population of this province are under any moral obligation to sustain the burden of the poverty of any other province of Ireland', reproduced in *The Great Famine, 1845–52*.
86. The pioneering study of the crisis is J. S. Donnelly, 'The Irish agricultural depression of 1859–64', *Irish Economic and Social History*, III, 1976, pp. 33–54.
87. It is true that in 1861 and 1862 flax yields were below average, but the decline was less than in cereal and potato crops. There were bumper flax harvests in 1863 and 1864.
88. Competition in the case of butter came from continental Europe rather than America. For the already high levels of grain and butter imports into the UK in the early 1860s, see *Annual Statement of the Trade and Navigation of the United Kingdom with Foreign Countries and British Possessions in the year 1865*, BPP, 1866, LXVIII.
89. C. McGimpsey, *To Raise the Banner in the Remotest North: Politics in County Monaghan, 1868–83*, unpublished Ph.D. thesis, University of Edinburgh, 1982. The price of potatoes is a useful index of distress among smallholders and labourers. According to Barrington's price data ('Irish Agricultural Prices', p. 252), this was 83 per cent higher in 1879 than the average for 1874–76. Other years of inflated potato prices later in the century were 1890–91, and 1897–98 (the occasion

C

for inaugurating the socio-political agitation of the United Irish League). The conquest of potato blight about 1900 finally took the potato out of Irish history.

90. P. Roebuck, 'Rent movement, proprietorial incomes and agricultural development, 1730–1830', in Roebuck ed., *Plantation to Partition*, Belfast, 1981, p. 89. See also P. Duffy, 'Irish landholding structures and population in the mid-nineteenth century', *The Maynooth Review*, III, 1977, pp. 12–13, and W. A. Maguire, *The Downshire Estates in Ireland, 1801–45*, Oxford, 1972, p. 249. Preliminary findings by the writer suggest a ratio of 5:1 between con-acre rents and head rents on arable land in Ulster in the 1830s (Kennedy, 'Agricultural statistics'). It should be borne in mind that con-acre rents might include payment for preparation of the ground for a potato or flax crop and possibly also payment for manure.

91. McEvoy, *Tyrone*, p. 99.

92. Crawford, *Domestic Industry*, p. 25. 'It is common for a manufacturing farmer who occupies not more than ten acres of land', according to Wakefield (*Ireland*, I, p. 740), 'to let a part of his "take" to a subtenant at will, who erects thereon a wretched cabin, and employs one or more looms for the benefit of his landlord'.

93. Wakefield, *Ireland*, I, p. 362.

94. Major sources on landholding practices among the rural poor are the *Poor Inquiry (Ireland): Appendix F* and the *Devon Digest* (Kennedy ed.), pp. 519–48.

95. Wakefield, *Ireland*, I, p. 518.

96. See also section five and the discussion there of hiring fairs.

97. J. S. Donnelly, *Landlord and Tenant in Nineteenth-Century Ireland*, Dublin, pp. 11–12.

98. Ulster agriculture was market oriented, responding to local, particularly urban demand, and to the British demand for Irish foodstuffs. The textile industry was increasingly heavily dependent on export markets. Urban, industrialising Ulster offered some incentives for migration within the province, though these were weak in the first half of the nineteenth century. More importantly, conditions of life in Britain and North America influenced the supply of labour in the rural economy through the mechanism of emigration.

99. These results should not be taken literally. Some responses were ambiguous and some respondents were less well informed than others.

100. We define peasant landlords as tenant farmers subletting land to undertenants for a profit rent or renting out land on a short term basis on the con-acre system. To distinguish peasant landlords from middlemen it is necessary to specify some upper limit to farm size. Any dividing line is necessarily arbitrary; but certainly landholders occupying more than one hundred acres are excluded.

101. Duffy, 'Irish landholding', pp. 15, 26; P. McGregor, 'The distribution of landholdings in pre-Famine Ireland', unpublished paper, Belfast, 1984.

102. See, for example, Hill, *Gweedore*, pp. 18–21.
103. Ó Tuathaigh, *Ireland*, pp. 110–13.
104. Donnelly, *Landlord and Tenant*, pp. 22–7; Maguire, *Downshire Estates*, p. 250; *Poor Inquiry (Ireland): Appendix F.*
105. R. D. Crotty, *Irish Agricultural Production*, Cork, 1966, pp. 276–87.
106. Maguire, *Downshire Estates*, pp. 29, 38–9. The new lettings refer to the Kilwarlin estate only.
107. Crotty, *Agricultural Production*, pp. 283–4.
108. Ibid., pp. 283–4; Cullen, *Economic History*, p. 109.
109. Crotty, *Agricultural Production*, pp. 42–9; Bourke, 'Grain trade', pp. 156–69. The relative attractiveness of farming in the 1830s is indicated by the fact that farmers holding ten to twenty acres were abandoning linen manufacture and concentrating on agriculture. See *Handloom Weavers' Report*, p. 480.
110. Recent (unpublished) research by D. S. Johnson on per capita consumption of two semi-luxury items – tea and tobacco – in Ireland in the 1830s and the 1840s is in line with this interpretation.
111. The discussion which follows is based on Maguire, *Downshire Estates*; see especially pp. 29, 38–9, 63.
112. W. A. Maguire, 'Lord Donegall and the sale of Belfast: a case history from the Encumbered Estates Court, *Economic History Review*, XXIX, 1976, pp. 570–84.
113. Donnelly, *Landlord and Tenant*, p. 49.
114. *Papers presented by His Majesty's Command relative to the Disturbed State of Ireland*, BPP, 1822, XIV, pp. 759–79; Donnelly, *Landlord and Tenant*, pp. 35–6.
115. A representative expression of the 'advanced' nationalist view is Arthur Griffith's introduction to J. Mitchell, *Jail Journal*, London, 1983. See also P. Gallagher, *Paddy the Cope: My Story*, Tralee, no date, pp. 103–6.
116. Kennedy, 'Tenant right', pp. 39–49.
117. Penetrating analyses of tenant right are contained in the *Report from the Select Committee on Tenure and Improvement of Land (Ireland) Act*, BPP, XI, 1865, and in B. L. Solow, *The Land Question and the Irish Economy*, London, 1971.
118. Maguire, *Downshire Estates*, pp. 140–4; Kennedy, 'Tenant right', p. 42. For tenant right payments in Ulster in the late nineteenth century see *Report of the Royal Commission on the Land Law (Ireland) Act, 1881, and the Purchase of Land (Ireland) Act, 1885*, BPP, 1887, XXVI.
119. See for example the comments on farming in west Donegal in Hill, *Gweedore*, p. 23.
120. Maguire, *Downshire Estates*, pp. 143–4; Greig, *Gosford Estates*, p. 277.
121. If there had been frequent and extensive sale of tenant right, then effectively a regime of competitive rents would have prevailed. The market in tenant right was not, however, sufficiently active to bring about this result. The fines sometimes paid to landlords on the renewal

of a lease, and which were at variance with the spirit of Ulster custom, also had the effect of raising effective rents.

122. Donnelly, *Landlord and Tenant*, p. 36.

123. Barrington, 'Agricultural prices', pp. 251–2.

124. W. E. Vaughan, 'An assessment of the economic performance of Irish landlords, 1851–81' in F. S. L. Lyons and R. A. J. Hawkins eds., *Ireland under the Union: Varieties of Tension*, Oxford, 1980, pp. 178–9. But see also C. Ó Gráda ('Agricultural head rents, pre-Famine and post-Famine', *Economic and Social Review*, V, 1974, p. 390) who suggests an average increase in rents of about one-third over roughly the same period. Also significant is the wide variation in landlord practices: on the Le Fanu estate in County Cavan, according to Vaughan, rents remained stable, while on the Donegal and Leitrim estates of the third Earl of Leitrim there were exceptionally high increases of 50 per cent or more.

125. B. M. Walker, 'The land question and elections in Ulster, 1868–86' in S. Clark and J. S. Donnelly eds., *Irish Peasants: Violence and Political Unrest, 1780–1914*, Madison, Wisconsin, p. 237. Attempts to give legal expression to traditional rights of an informal nature naturally led to conflicts of interpretation between landlords and tenants.

126. R. W. Kirkpatrick, 'Origins and development of the land war in mid-Ulster, 1879–85' in Lyons and Hawkins eds., *Ireland under the Union*, p. 228.

127. Kirkpatrick, 'Land war', p. 232. Of the 158,000 (self-designated) farmers in 1871, 53 per cent were Roman Catholic, 27 per cent Presbyterian, and 17 per cent Church of Ireland. The last were under-represented among farmers relative to their numbers in the Ulster population. The larger farmers, on the more fertile lowlands, tended on the whole to be Protestant. The proportion of Catholic farmers rose, generally speaking, as one moved outwards towards the south and west of the province.

128. Donnelly, *Landlord and Tenant*, p. 84.

129. In 1913 69 per cent of Ulster farmers owned their holdings, a somewhat higher level of ownership than in any of the other three provinces. See *Agricultural Statistics of Ireland for the year 1913*, BPP, 1914, XCVIII, p. 639.

130. C. Ó Gráda, 'Agricultural head rents, pre-Famine and post-Famine', *Economic and Social Review*, V, 1974, p. 390.

131. C. Ó Gráda, 'The investment behaviour of Irish landlords 1850–75: some preliminary findings', *Agricultural History Review*, XXIII, 1975, pp. 153–4; Donnelly, *Landlord and Tenant*, p. 54.

132. See J. D. Gould, *Economic Growth in History*, London, 1972, pp. 72–4, who calls for such a test.

133. D. Fitzpatrick, 'The disappearance of the Irish agricultural labourer, 1841–1912', *Irish Economic and Social History*, VII, 1980, pp. 66–92.

134. P. Gallagher, *Paddy the Cope: My Story*, Tralee, no date, pp. 8–9.

135. Wakefield, *Ireland*, I, p. 362; Coote, *Armagh*, p. 238; A. O'Dowd,

Meitheal: A Study of Co-operative Labour in Rural Ireland, Dublin, 1981, pp. 30–34.

136. *Poor Inquiry: Appendix D*. The evidential base for the discussion of wages, while large, is also of uneven quality. Actual figures should be treated as approximations. The overall pattern revealed, however, is reassuringly plausible.

137. Fitzpatrick, 'Agricultural labourer', p. 90; Boyle, *Irish Linen*, pp. 98, 163.

138. *Report on Wages in the UK*, pp. 606, 690; *Agricultural Statistics of Ireland for the year 1911*, BPP, 1912–3, pp. 1088–9.

139. Quoted in K. A. Miller, *Emigrants and Exiles*, Oxford, forthcoming.

140. Kennedy, 'Econometric history', pp. 205–6.

141. Wakefield, *Ireland*, I, p. 599.

CHAPTER TWO

INDUSTRY, 1820–1914[1]

Philip Ollerenshaw

It has become increasingly fashionable to emphasise the extent to which industrialisation in nineteenth-century Europe was a regional rather than a national phenomenon, and it has long been recognised that any given industrial region 'may compare, and may co-operate, more closely with an industrial area' in another country 'than it does with its own agricultural hinterland'.[2] Both these observations are highly relevant to Ireland between 1820 and 1914. Industrialisation in Ireland proceeded furthest and fastest in parts of the four north-eastern counties of Antrim, Down, Armagh and Londonderry, and above all in Belfast and its neighbourhood. The nature of industrialisation in north-east Ulster was such that this region did compare and co-operate far more closely with industrial regions in Britain, notably west-central Scotland and north-west England, than it did with other parts of Ireland.

For much of our period industrialisation in the north-east was led by the mechanisation of the linen industry and, after slow beginnings, the related manufacture of textile machinery. Iron and steel shipbuilding and marine engineering became increasingly important in Belfast in the half-century before 1914. The virtual monopoly of Belfast in the field of heavy industry in the province, together with its easy dominance as the leading manufacturing and commercial centre of the linen industry, and its role as key financial centre, combined to ensure that the city towered over the rest of industrial Ulster by 1914 to an extent which would have been inconceivable in 1820. However, neither the rate nor the extent of industrialisation in the north-east should be allowed to obscure the fact that Ulster as a whole remained predominantly rural.

Industrial location in the nineteenth century was bound to be influenced by the absolute and relative cost of water and steampower. In Ulster, waterpower was widely available and was a genuine asset to the pre-1914 economy serving a very large number of different industries either as an exclusive or principal source of power. So long did waterpower (especially in the form of the turbine) remain useful in areas of inland Ulster that it was frequently replaced by electricity in the first half of the twentieth century omitting altogether an intermediate phase of steampower so often experienced elsewhere.[3] General availability of waterpower contrasted strongly with the geographically limited coal deposits. Despite hopes to the contrary, neither the Ballycastle nor east Tyrone collieries ever approached the capacity to meet the demand for coal in the province, and exerted no significant positive influence on the location of industry or the pace of development. For the most part those businesses which did utilise steampower depended on coal imported from Ayrshire, Lancashire and Cumberland. In the 1820s Belfast was by far the most important coal importing town in Ulster: 103,000 tons in 1827 compared to its nearest rivals Newry (34,000 tons) and Derry (8,000), although it still fell below Cork (130,000) and Dublin (266,000).[4]

The degree to which Ulster industry was hampered by the need to import coal is debatable. Overland transport of coal was much more expensive than by sea, particularly before the railway age, and this, together with the availability of waterpower, militated against the rapid diffusion of steampower in the Ulster interior. In coastal areas, however, the price of coal at the quayside could be quite competitive with prices in industrial towns in Britain. During our period the differential between coal prices in Belfast and major British industrial towns was widest in the 1820s but narrowed markedly by mid-century. In the later 1820s, coal averaged between 15s and 17s per ton in Belfast which was well over double prices in Leeds, Manchester and Glasgow. The main complaint in Belfast was that coal imported from Britain was subject to a tax of 1s 9½d per ton. Described by the Belfast Chamber of Commerce in 1827 as 'almost the only and certainly the most obnoxious impediment' to free trade between Britain and Ireland this 'tax on manufactures'[5] was rightly regarded as anomalous and repealed in 1831 after a long and vigorous campaign by the Chamber. Industrial and household consumers of coal in coastal areas of Ulster certainly benefited from their adjacency to British west coast coalfields, and given the narrowing of price differentials it would not be wise to view the lack of local coal and the need to import as significant retardative influences on industrial development in Belfast and other coastal towns.

In the 1820s trade routes between north-east Ulster and Britain were well established and of first importance, although the province did trade with countries in Europe, the West Indies and the Americas. In addition to coal, significant imports into Belfast in the 1820s included timber from the Baltic and Canada; US cotton wool; whisky, cotton yarn, muslins, woollens and hardware from Scotland, and English mill-spun linen yarn.[6] Linen dominated the export trade, which also included printed calicoes and other cotton goods and provisions. Exports of agricultural produce from Belfast supported the town's brewing, distilling and tanning industries.[7] Cross-channel trade, particularly with Liverpool, was, throughout our period, of paramount significance for the north-east and it was greatly strengthened by the inauguration of regular steamship services in the 1820s.[8] Early steamships were so prodigal in their coal consumption that their first conquests were confined to short sea routes such as those between Ulster and north-west Britain and across the English Channel. As early as 1826 steamships carried much of the cross-channel trade and introduced unprecedented regularity, speed and economy to that trade. A result of this dramatic improvement was to highlight the relatively poor state of communications within the province and to trigger demands for investment in inland transport. Calling for such investment in 1828, the *Northern Whig* compared the 'extent, safety and despatch' of cross-channel trade with the 'puny and contemptible' means of internal communications.[9] It was the latter to which the Belfast Chamber of Commerce devoted a great deal of energy from the 1820s, focusing its campaign on demands for private and public investment in road, canal and particularly rail transport throughout the province.

Such was the impact of cross-channel steamship services that in the 1830s the Chamber judged that they had 'effected an entire change in our foreign commerce, which instead of being carried on as formerly by means of vessels sailing direct from Belfast at long and uncertain intervals is now conducted entirely through Liverpool from whence the valuable manufactures of the North of Ireland are transmitted almost daily to their ports of foreign destination'.[10] Exports from Belfast were shipped mainly via the entrepôt of Liverpool, and thus contributed to Liverpool's leading position in the UK export trade. Regular steamship services benefited many Ulster ports, on the north as well as on the east coast, not least by facilitating exports of livestock and provisions.[11] By the same token, of course, they also made easier import penetration from rapidly developing Britain.

In the century before 1914, Ulster's major industries were crucially dependent on cross-channel and overseas demand. A corollary of such dependence was that the province was vulnerable to the effects of commercial crises and industrial depression originating in Britain or indeed outside the UK. For this reason many of the recognised depression years in the British economy — 1826, 1842, 1879, 1886 and 1908 for example — were also depression years in much of industrial Ulster, although local circumstances ensured that the trade cycle in Ulster before 1914 did not always move strictly in tandem with that in Britain.[12]

Industrialisation in the north east rendered the economic base of Ulster far more heterogeneous than other Irish provinces and one effect of this was that industry could help to protect incomes in time of agricultural depression. On at least two occasions, the late 1840s and early 1860s when much of rural Ireland was in serious difficulties, the industrial north east was spared the worst effects of depression because of the relative buoyancy of its linen industry.[13] Although a diversified economic structure sometimes helped in this way, occasionally agricultural and industrial depression coincided, in which case the province was plunged into unusually widespread hardship. The best example of this in our period is 1839–42 when bad harvests and depression in Britain and in Anglo-American trade coincided to make this an exceptionally difficult time for the Ulster economy.[14] Fortunately, however, simultaneous depression in all sectors of this economy was rare betwen 1820 and 1914.

Before looking at the experience of Ulster's leading industries it is useful here to emphasise the fact that most of the businessmen in the province were Protestant, and all the evidence unites to show a massive preponderance of wealth in Protestant hands. One estimate around 1820 put the ratio of Protestant to Roman Catholic capital in Belfast trade and industry at forty to one, and at the end of the nineteenth century it was pointed out that virtually everyone engaged in commerce in Ulster was a Protestant.[15] It was not merely the process of industrialisation but Protestant control of that process that gave the political economy of north-east Ulster its unique character. Easily the largest and most articulate employers' organisation in Ulster was the Belfast Chamber of Commerce. Founded in 1783, the Chamber's size had grown with the importance of the town whose business interests it promoted. Always representative of a cross-section of businesses, membership increased from seventy-six in 1827 to 260 in 1893 at which date only eight members (3 per cent) were Catholics.[16] R. S. Sayers once described the activities of chambers of commerce as 'that middle ground between business and politics'.[17] In the later part of our period that middle ground in Ulster almost disappeared as the fusion of business interests with Unionist politics became explicit and virtually complete. When the Union came under serious threat from the 1880s, the Chamber played an important role in the anti-Home Rule movement which embraced a number of mutually reinforcing cultural, religious and economic arguments. The Chamber attributed the success of industrialisation in the Belfast region to the 'security and protection' afforded by Parliament since the Act of Union, as well as to the 'frugality and enterprise' of its people.[18] As the third Home Rule Bill proceeded successfully through Westminster just before the First World War it had become clear that the business community in the north-east would use its wealth to support a campaign to maintain the Union or, failing that, to defy any attempt to force this region into an independent Ireland.[19] In this sense, industrialisation helped to pave the way for the partition of Ireland and the creation of a Northern Ireland state in 1921.

Textiles: the dominance of linen

The textile history of Ulster from the early eighteenth century is dominated by linen. Irish exports of linen cloth, principally from Ulster, which increased from around two million yards in 1715 to well over forty million yards by the 1790s,[20] are just one index of growth. Until well into the nineteenth century linen was very much an industry of the countryside, but in the Belfast region the cotton industry temporarily eclipsed linen in the forty years or so before 1830. Introduced in the late 1770s, protected until the mid-1820s and exclusively dependent on imported raw material, cotton was significant for the economy of this region in several respects. It pushed Belfast into the factory age, necessitated considerable fixed capital formation, particularly between 1800 and 1825, and successfully developed the system of putting out mill-spun yarn to handloom weavers in Belfast and its hinterland. At the beginning of the nineteenth century Belfast accounted for a quarter of total Irish imports of cotton wool and yarn; by 1820 this proportion had doubled.[21]

The number of mills in operation at any one time is difficult to establish; but it increased rapidly, partly under the stimulus of wartime demand. There were probably ten mills in 1804, several of which had been built since the Union, and about two dozen in 1826 when they were, collectively, the most important industrial consumers of coal in the province.[22] The number of mills declined after 1825; nineteen were in operation in 1832, only four by 1850. There is disagreement on the reasons for this decline. Conventional explanations include a lack of capital, absence of cheap coal, the final abolition of protective barriers in 1824, the effects of the commercial crisis of 1825 and (related to the first three of these) an inability to compete with lower cost producers in Britain. Recently, however, it has been shown that the Belfast cotton industry did not suffer from a capital shortage, nor was a relatively high cost of coal critical since coal accounted for only about two per cent of total input costs and was in any case offset by cheaper labour. Further, 'decline' in the number of cotton spinning mills was mainly a reflection of the fact that mill owners switched to flax spinning after the invention of the wet-spinning process in 1825.[23]

Such modifications to the conventional wisdom have provided a welcome corrective, but our knowledge of the transfer from cotton to powered flax spinning remains incomplete. Certainly the effect of competition from the west of Scotland and Lancashire on Belfast cotton spinning should not be underestimated. Commenting on the virtual disappearance of cotton spinning from Belfast, one of the town's leading bankers in 1848 considered that:

> We were not able to compete with Manchester and Glasgow in the spinning of cotton ... our cotton mills have been converted into linen mills, there are some remaining but they are not doing much; we have a good deal of weaving and bleaching and things of that sort connected with the cotton manufacture but the yarn for that purpose is all imported and a good deal is done on Scotch account.[24]

The evidence suggests that the exit from cotton spinning was to a large extent forced, and that wet spinning of flax was a timely and fortuitous alternative into which cotton spinners might move without massive new investment. Another factor which weakened Belfast cotton spinning, and hastened the move into linen, was the severity of the commercial crisis of 1825 which, although it originated in Britain, began seriously to affect north-east Ulster from the spring of 1826. Unemployment among cotton spinners and weavers reached new heights and the hardship endured in the absence of a poor law (not introduced into Ireland until 1838) was only partially mitigated by local philanthropic activity.[25] Unemployment persisted, and in the cotton weaving trade it was estimated in 1830 that in Belfast alone 700 heads of family together with 3,000 dependents were 'in a state bordering on starvation'.[26]

If the depressive effects of the 1825–26 crisis cannot be doubted, the precise impact of the abolition of protective barriers is much more difficult to assess. The spinning and printing sectors were adversely affected by the removal of protection in 1824, but weaving actually seems to have benefited. Calico printing had grown rapidly from 1800 until the later 1820s from which time there was a sudden decline. By 1834 many printfields were out of work, others barely surviving. The Belfast Chamber of Commerce identified two obvious causes for this: the withdrawal of protective duties and the introduction of steamship services which afforded shopkeepers in the area the opportunity to order from Manchester and Glasgow 'where a greater variety can be had'.[27] Despite this, there were in 1834 three firms printing for the Manchester market, and this trade persisted well beyond mid-century.

Muslin weaving and embroidery were two branches of the Ulster cotton industry which showed significant growth after the mid 1820s, on the basis of imported mill-spun muslin and low paid Irish workers. Both branches were largely controlled by Scottish firms. Exports of muslin from Ireland, predominantly from Ulster, rose very sharply from 560,000 yards in 1823 to eight million in 1830.[28] The sewn muslin trade assumed important dimensions about 1830 and was boosted from 1837 following the introduction of the lithographic press by Cochrane, Brown and Co. of Donaghadee. Lithography was synonymous with quick and cheap printwork and rendered block printing obsolete. In Ulster, muslin was received from the west of Scotland by agents who at first were exclusively Scots but assisted by an increasing number of Ulstermen during the 1840s and 1850s. Either salaried or paid on commission, these agents were responsible both for recruiting women to sew the cloth and for ensuring the quality of the final product. Earnings from this trade, although low and subject to the agent's whim, helped to supplement agricultural earnings throughout Ulster and the ubiquity of outwork is shown by the fact that in the 1850s 'no town in the north of Ireland from Derry to Dublin on the one hand and from Belfast to Sligo on the other was without its sewing agent and in some towns five or six agents were required.'[29] Always subject to market fluctuations, this trade reached its peak just before the commercial crisis of 1857 when employment may have exceeded 100,000. Overproduction and changes in fashion hit trade hard and by 1868 the value of sewn muslins produced in Ireland and Scotland had declined by more than half.

Thus although the spinning and printing sectors of the Ulster cotton industry had contracted by the early 1830s, the weaving and embroidery of muslin grew rapidly and continued on a widespread scale for more than twenty-five years afterwards. In the long term, however, the future of Ulster textiles lay with linen and here the crucial innovation was the wet spinning of flax by power, patented in 1825 by James Kay. In 1820 the Ulster linen industry was predominantly rural and almost all the flax required was home-grown. Of the major processes involved in linen production only bleaching was mechanised; spinning and weaving were not. Since the end of the eighteenth century bleaching, which because of extensive space requirements was and remained a process undertaken outside towns, had been carried on throughout the year and before 1825 was the most capital-intensive process in the linen industry.[30] Indeed bleachers and drapers themselves dominated the industry and their control of linen exports via Belfast rather than Dublin contributed much to Belfast's commercial independence from Dublin which had been increasingly asserted since the late eighteenth century and was virtually complete by 1820.

Dry spinning of flax, possible for coarse yarns since the 1790s, had been widely adopted in Britain by the 1820s. Wet spinning permitted the finest yarns to be machine-spun and was first successfully adopted in Ulster by James and William Murland whose new mill was opened, probably early in 1828, at Annsborough near Castlewellan in County Down. Murlands were wealthy bleachers and manufacturers and their incentive to move into wet spinning derived partly from a difficulty (quite common for early nineteenth-century manufacturers) in obtaining a regular supply of all types of yarn, partly from a rising market for yarns and unusually low flax prices.[31] If linen manufacture was to remain important in Ulster the wet-spinning process was one which manufacturers could ill afford to ignore. Wet spinning, which rapidly and permanently changed yarn production from a domestic to a mechanised factory basis and caused an immediate slump in the earnings of hand spinners,[32] became available at a time when the prospects for cotton spinning in the Belfast area were unpromising, and this helps to explain why several leading cotton spinners moved into flax spinning in the later 1820s and early 1830s.

The first such move was that made by Thomas and Andrew

Mulholland in Belfast in 1829. Mulholland's York Street mill, the first urban steam-driven wet flax-spinning mill in Ireland, was built on the same site, and used the same 100 hp engine as their cotton mill which had been destroyed by fire in 1828. The new mill, which began with 8,000 spindles, laid the foundations of the great York Street Flax Spinning Company which by the end of the nineteenth century was probably the world's largest linen firm, employing more than 5,000 workers.[33] The early and obvious success of the brothers Murland and Mulholland tempted further substantial investment in flax spinning in many parts of Ulster. Capital, labour and enterprise were transferred from cotton as mills, spinners and weavers, and entrepreneurs turned to linen. The availability of these factors of production cut the cost and speeded the rate of transfer, although investment in flax spinning was by no means confined to former cotton spinners.

By 1834 at least a dozen flax mills were in operation, not only in Belfast and Castlewellan but in or near other towns and villages such as Keady, Newry and Ballymena.[34] A similar number was in the course of construction or conversion from cotton spinning and many more additions were made in the next thirty years (see Table 2.1). Although many country mills depended wholly or mainly on waterpower, in Belfast steam was the prime mover and the north and west districts of the town became the principal locations for flax mills from the mid-1830s. From this time flax mills replaced cotton mills not only as Belfast's most important employers of factory labour but also as the town's largest industrial consumers of imported coal. Such was the progress of flax spinning in the north east that, twenty years after the opening of Mulholland's first mill, it was estimated that the steampower requirements of the linen industry necessitated the annual import of 150,000 tons of coal into Belfast which kept 200–300 seamen employed on forty or fifty colliers sailing between Belfast and north-west Britain.[35] Later in the nineteenth century, when total coal imports sometimes exceeded one million tons, most of the steampower in Belfast was employed in the linen industry.[36]

As noted earlier, waterpower continued to be used on an extensive scale before 1914 and several early flax mills were located either on existing or new water sites. The remoteness of such sites frequently required the creation by employers of villages which provided the employer's conception of basic economic, social and spiritual amenities for his workforce. Industrial villages were commonplace in Britain during the early stages of industrialisation and were often associated

Table 2.1 Flaxspinning mills in Ulster, 1839–71

Year	No. of mills	No. of spindles	Driving power				Employees	
			Steam (h.p.)	Water (h.p.)	Average per mill (h.p.)	Proportion from water (%)	Total	Average per mill
1839	35 (a)		823	888	48·9	51·9	7,758	222
1850	61 (a)	345,016	2,051	1,417	56·8	40·8	18,500	303
	1 (b)	11,394	50	–	50·0	–	545	545
1857	77 (a)	397,286	3,570	1,458	65·3	29·0	18,299	237
	8 (b)	108,524	743	280	128·0	27·4	5,965	746
1862	53 (a)	328,037	5,196	1,486	126·1	22·2	15,252	288
	17 (b)	203,392	4,111	383	261·3	8·5	12,045	708
1868	60 (a)	525,311	11,301	2,380	228·0	17·4	25,958	433
	22 (b)	305,848	7,157	556	350·6	7·2	19,757	898
1871	58 (a)	534,968	10,497	1,243	202·4	10·6	23,820	411
	20 (b)	300,536	6,906	521	371·3	7·0	19,580	979

Note. (a) Spinning only. (b) Spinning and weaving.
Source. H. D. Gribbon, *The History of Water Power in Ulster*, Newton Abbot, 1969, p. 97.

with the textile, coal and iron industries. In Ulster most were built around the linen industry and with few exceptions such as Barbour's Plantation near Lisburn, established in 1784, came into existence between 1830 and 1870.[37] As in Britain, both primary and secondary settlements were established in Ulster; the former where no significant village had existed before, the latter where initial village development proceeded very close to an existing town into which it was absorbed at a later date.[38] Primary settlements included Sion Mills in County Tyrone, built by the Herdman family in 1835; Bessbrook in County Armagh by the Quaker Richardsons in the 1840s; and Dunbarton at Gilford, County Down, built in the later 1830s by Dunbar McMaster and Company. Although the narrow economic base of any industrial village was potentially disastrous in the event of failure of the firm around which it was built, it is the case that such firms in our period generally proved to be successful and durable. Industrial villages tended to have high housing standards, and were characterised by a real sense of community. The contrast between life-styles in some industrial villages and Belfast was very great indeed as a description of Bessbrook in 1882 makes clear: 'The village has neither pawn shop, public house nor police office and seems to get on excellently well without any of these customary resources of civilisation.'[39]

Rapid diffusion of power spinning after 1830, especially in the Belfast area, caused major changes in industrial organisation. Previously it had been necessary for weavers, yarn jobbers and manufacturers to attend yarn markets to buy and sort bundles of yarn. Now, however, it became possible to buy from the mill, or to order for delivery, any quantity of evenly spun yarn to nominated fineness. For a short time the finest yarn was still hand-spun but technical improvements quickly took over the complete range. Some owners of spinning mills sought outlet for their yarn by themselves becoming manufacturers, giving out yarn to be woven and arranging for the finishing and marketing of webs. This resulted in some concentration of weavers in close proximity to the mills.[40]

A further important result of power spinning in Ulster was the development of textile engineering. Most of the machinery required for the Ulster cotton industry had been imported from Glasgow and Lancashire and often fitted by technicians from outside the province. Breakdowns could be costly because of the time required to secure spare parts. However, it was not until after 1834 that local engineering firms responded to the great strides made by Ulster linen and began to wean the industry from its overwhelming dependence on British machinery. Indeed, some of Ulster's textile machine makers went one stage further and began to export their products from about 1850 and in this way contributed to the international predominance in textile engineering enjoyed by the United Kingdom before 1914.

Belfast led the way in the manufacture of textile machinery.[41] Samuel Boyd's Belfast Foundry, established in 1811, was a pioneer local maker of flax-spinning machinery from 1834. Other important Belfast firms in the 1840s were founded by Scots, such as James Scrimgeour's Albert Foundry (1843) and James Combe's Falls Foundry (1845). The Albert Foundry was taken over by Scrimgeour's manager James Mackie in 1858, and Mackies went on to become makers of a wide range of flax preparing and spinning machinery as well as a world leader in the manufacture of jute machinery in the twentieth century. The Falls Foundry catered principally for Ulster railway companies during the railway boom of the mid-1840s, but in 1851 branched out into textile engineering and became Ireland's leading maker of machinery for the preparation and spinning of flax, hemp and jute, employing some 1200 workers by 1882. In 1900 the firm became part of Fairbairn, Lawson Combe Barbour Limited, one of the United Kingdom's major engineering groups which continued its Belfast operations until 1955. Only the larger firms could make a wide range of textile machinery, small firms were forced to specialise in machinery for certain processes – frames for hackling, winding, spinning or twisting, for example. Outside Belfast, some textile machinery was made by provincial foundries, the number of which had grown to eighteen by 1914. Some were important general foundries, such as Gardiner's in Armagh, established in 1840, Hugh Kennedy and Co. in Coleraine in 1842, and the Strabane Foundry in 1843, but to the extent that they made textile machinery in addition to their other work, they tended to concentrate on simple devices for flax-breaking and scutching.

Factory-based wet-spinning thus transformed the capacity and organisation of Ulster flax spinning and was responsible for inducing rapid growth in textile engineering especially from the 1840s. The weaving sector of the Ulster linen industry, by contrast, retained its traditional hand technology for more than twenty years after the introduction of wet spinning. Power weaving would be adopted on a wide scale in Ulster only when power looms were capable of weaving medium and fine linens cheaper than handlooms. Early power looms were suited only for coarse linens and so were inappropriate for those areas of the United Kingdom which specialised in the finer cloths: Ulster, Barnsley and Fife.[42] This particular technical problem was not satisfactorily overcome until the 1850s. Furthermore, handloom weavers' wage rates were so low that there was no inducement to invest in power looms in Ulster before mid-century. As far as the manufacturer was concerned, the only disadvantage with dependence on handloom weavers, who combined weaving with agricultural work, was that at harvest time they might be so busy as to have no time left to weave, and hence leave the manufacturer unable to fulfil his orders.[43]

The strongest argument in favour of handloom weaving, its low cost, lost validity quite suddenly in the late 1840s and early 1850s.

North-east Ulster escaped relatively lightly from the Great Famine, but the death or emigration of so many part-time weavers altered dramatically the labour supply. Between 1848 and 1852 weavers' wage rates rose by between 20 and 30 per cent. Decline in the farmer-weaving population presented manufacturers with a major problem, and even the output of the remaining full-time weavers seemed sufficiently inelastic to resolve the difficulty as they took advantage of higher wages, worked fewer hours to maintain a customary income, and increased leisure time.[44] Without power looms there would have been a serious, perhaps chronic, bottleneck in the Ulster linen industry as the weaving sector could not have kept pace with yarn output. Less than sixty power looms in Ulster in 1850 had become more than 4,000 in 1862 and 17,000 by 1875. Power looms were installed either in specialist weaving factories of which there was one in 1850 and fifty-four in 1875; or in weaving sheds attached to spinning mills. The latter, variously known as 'combined', 'double' or 'integrated' mills, were fewer in number and reached their maximum of twenty-two in 1868.[45] After the 1850s combined mills, although small in number, were easily the largest firms in the Ulster linen industry as they were in British cotton.[46] By the 1860s, then, when Ulster had become the largest linen-producing area in the world, both flax spinning and weaving had become generally mechanised and factory production typical. From this period until 1914, improvements in spinning and weaving technology were piecemeal and no single improvement was revolutionary, while finishing techniques remained basically the same throughout the nineteenth century.

Technical change in the linen industry proceeded against a background of widely fluctuating demand conditions, the result of changes in real incomes, fashion, the price and the availability of substitute goods and the height and effectiveness of overseas tariff barriers. Linen lost most of the Irish market to cotton before 1850 but British and overseas markets provided the effective demand to sustain the burgeoning productive capacity of the Ulster linen industry. Of major importance as the market for UK linen was the United States, and this market grew rapidly, if sporadically, to account for over 40 per cent of Ulster's linen exports by the 1850s. Linen exports via Liverpool had made north-east Ulster an integral part of the Atlantic economy after 1815 and the United States played a key role in determining the general level of activity in the Ulster linen industry. Depression in the United States led to a slump in the demand for Ulster

Table 2.2 *Powerloom weaving factories in Ulster, 1850–75*

Year	No. of factories	No. of[a] power looms	Steam (h.p.)	Water (h.p.)	Average per factory (h.p.)	Proportion from water (%)	Total	Average per factory
			Driving power				Employees	
1850	1	34	14	–	14	–	138	138
1857	12	883	250	105	29·6	29·5	1,020	85
1862	13	1,971	460	106	43·5	18·7	2,277	175
1868	38	5,998	1,684	242	50·7	12·6	6,099	160
1871	44	7,734	1,602	302	43·2	15·8	7,585	173
1875	54	9,710	Not recorded	Not recorded	–	–	9,839	182

Note. (a) This table includes only looms in weaving factories. Looms in combined mills were: 1850, 24; 1857, 530; 1862, 2,137; 1868, 6,151; 1871, 6,340; 1875, 7,336.
Source. H. D. Gribbon, *The History of Water Power in Ulster*, Newton Abbot, 1969, p.101.

linen between 1839 and 1842, but exports revived as both the US and British economies recovered and were sustained into the 1850s punctuated only by the commercial crisis of 1847. The most visible effects of this crisis in the Belfast region were that construction of new mills was halted, those partially constructed were left unfinished, and some which had been built were not fitted with machinery.[47] American markets did not collapse during the crisis and recovery in north-east Ulster was led by flax spinning and linen manufacture, a fact reflected in the increase in Irish flax spindlage from 326,000 to 581,000 between 1850 and 1853.

Apart from some disruption to trade routes caused by the Crimean War, which interrupted the supply and drove up the price of Russian flax and so squeezed the profit margins of spinners,[48] the next important downturn in the fortunes of Ulster linen arrived with the commercial crisis of 1857. A financial collapse in the United States in 1857 quickly had transatlantic repercussions. Indeed some regard this as the first worldwide commercial crisis. The demand for Ulster linen fell so sharply that almost all mills in the Belfast region were put on short time from 30 November until early the following year. More generally Belfast trade was brought to a virtual standstill but there were very few failures.[49] Recovery was by no means rapid or sustained, although the conclusion of the Anglo-French commercial treaty of 1860 which substantially reduced tariffs on yarn and cloth imported into the promising French market, gave a timely and much needed psychological boost to an industry which had much spare capacity.[50] No sooner had the treaty come into operation than attention turned to the United States where yet another crisis, the Civil War, seemed to spell disaster for this uniquely precious overseas linen market.

In Belfast the outbreak of the American Civil War in 1861 was greeted with unanimous predictions of adversity which were confirmed by the first few months of hostilities. In the five years ending 31 December 1860 the United States accounted for an average of 41 per cent of total Irish linen exports, but this proportion had declined to just 18 per cent in the eleven months ending 30 November 1861.[51] By late 1862, however, the abject pessimism of the previous year had faded rapidly as it became clear that the same war which eclipsed the United States as a market also seriously disrupted the United Kingdom's main source of raw cotton. The consequent 'cotton famine' led to widespread, but temporary, substitution of linen for cotton and brought a degree of prosperity to the Ulster linen industry unparalleled in the nineteenth century. The linen boom also helped to ensure that the 1866 financial crisis in England did not occur in Ulster. Exports of linen piece goods from the United Kingdom peaked in 1866 at 255 million yards, thread in 1863 at 4·3 million lb and yarn in 1864 at just over forty million lb. These represent increases on the 1861 figures of 119, 78 and 44 per cent respectively and were not surpassed before 1914.[52]

The demand for linen necessitated, and the exports were made possible by, huge increases in spinning and weaving capacity, which are summarised in Table 2.3. Hitherto unemployed spindles were brought into use until capacity output was reached in 1864 after which new spindlage had to be constructed. In power weaving there was little excess capacity at any time until 1868, and without power looms it is inconceivable that Ulster linen manufacturers could have responded to the freak demand conditions. In British cotton manufacturing areas such as Lancashire and the west of Scotland, already weakened by the crisis of 1857, the mid-1860s saw mass unemployment and large numbers of mill closures,[53] but this experience could not have contrasted more starkly with that of Ulster linen. As the *Northern Whig* put it in June 1865, 'New mills and factories are springing up on all sides, while as fast as they can be got started, orders flow in and such a thing as manufacturing for stock is almost unknown.'[54]

Abnormally profitable conditions induced the extension of existing firms as well as the entry of new firms not merely within the traditional linen areas of Antrim, Down and Armagh but also outside it, including Waterford and Cork.[55] At the same time the importance of Belfast as a point of export naturally increased, and as a consequence warehousing became concentrated more than ever in the town. The Chamber of Commerce in 1864 expressed the hope that soon all country firms would have their warehouses in the town so that 'Belfast may become to the linen trade even more than it is what Manchester is to the cotton trade.'[56] A further change in the organisation of the Ulster linen industry was the adoption of limited liability as many firms took advantage of developments in company legislation since 1856 and registered as limited companies. Virtually unknown in this industry before 1865, the majority of firms became limited during the next twenty years.

The strength of the linen boom must have convinced many entrepreneurs that the long term prospects for the industry were bright and

Table 2.3 Spinning mills and powerweaving factories in the Irish linen industry, 1859–68

| | | Spinning mills | | |
| | | | Spindles | |
Year	Mills (a)	Employed	Unemployed	Total
1859	82	560,642	91,230	651,872
1864	74	641,914	8,860	650,774
1866	86	759,452	11,362	770,814
1868	90	841,867	60,439	902,306

| | | Powerweaving factories | | |
| | | | Power looms | |
Year	Factories (a)	Employed	Unemployed	Total
1859	28	3,124	509	3,633
1861	35	4,609	324	4,933
1864	42	7,929	258	8,187
1866	44	10,538	266	10,804
1868	66	11,087	4,130	15,217

Note. (a) Includes combined mills.
Source. F. W. Smith, *The Irish Linen Trade Handbook and Directory*, Belfast, 1876, pp. 108, 112, 129.

for this reason they were prepared to pay hugely inflated prices for plant and equipment.[57] Subscribing to such optimism, the influential *Belfast Linen Trade Circular* noted in January 1864 the substitution of linen for cotton brought about by the Civil War and went on to predict that the durability and strength of linen would cause it 'to take that place permanently which in the first instance had only been vouchsafed to it as a temporary expedient'.[58] This prediction, if true, would have justified in the medium and long terms all the inflated investment costs of the Civil War years. Unfortunately there was no significant long term substitution of linen for cotton, but just as some time had elapsed before Ulster had begun to benefit from the cotton famine, so those benefits did not disappear overnight when the Civil War ended in 1865. Although linen firms in general could not sustain the profit levels of the war years, there is no doubt that the industry fully shared in the international boom of the early 1870s. Within two years of the end of this boom, in 1873, the folly of over-investment in the mid 1860s became fully apparent with a number of large bank-ruptcies the most important of which were Lowry, Valentine and Kirk, flax and tow spinners in 1874, and William Spotten and Company, linen manufacturers and merchants in 1875.[59] These two Belfast firms failed for more than £800,000, and both the size and reper-cussions of these failures were unprecedented in the history of the Ulster linen industry; many other firms were dragged down or weakened as a result and business confidence was so severely shaken that it did not recover completely for more than thirty years.

Certainly in the three decades or so after 1874 the Ulster linen industry was sometimes under great pressure, but it would be inac-curate to view the period as one of unrelieved depression. The trend of flax and linen goods' prices was firmly downwards and competition with European linen and British cotton (and to a small extent wool) intensified as did the trends towards protection of foreign (non-empire) markets. During this period too the geographical base of the industry contracted more or less to its pre-cotton famine dimensions. In the later nineteenth century, however, Ulster linen did gain from the Scottish transfer from linen to jute and the rapid decline of the English linen industry. Exports of fine linens from Ulster to the United States held up remarkably well in the face of generally high tariff barriers and accounted for as much as half of all linen exports from the province before 1914.[60] In the first years of the twentieth century over 65 per cent of all UK linen workers were in Ulster, and the province contributed about 60 per cent of the final value of total product.[61]

The later 1870s and 1885–87 were generally difficult for linen but the interval somewhat easier.[62] In 1885, R.H. Reade, a director of the York Street Flax Spinning Company, judged that foreign com-petition had done much more than protective tariffs to decrease Ulster linen exports and attributed this to the longer hours worked in foreign mills and lower wages paid there. Reade further pointed out that of twelve joint stock flax spinning and linen manufacturing companies with published accounts and regular share quotations in Belfast newspapers four paid no dividend and the dividend of the remainder averaged less than 6 per cent. This had been 'pretty much their state since 1873'. York Street, however, had managed to pay 13·5 per cent for several years before 1885 and was able to do so because its directors had 'had the good sense' to retain most of the abnormal profits made in the mid 1860s.[63] Many companies which had become unprofitable, or had failed, in the period 1874–85 had been floated during the mid 1860s and this underlines the point that they were ill-equipped to weather a significant downturn in linen prices and trading levels given the inflated prices paid for plant and machinery and their necessarily meagre reserves.

Of the different sectors in the linen industry, spinning was undoubtedly under greatest pressure, and Sir William Crawford's view that most flax spinners experienced 'seven lean years to one fat one' in the thirty years or so after the mid 1870s is no exaggeration. During this period some eighteen spinning mills with a total of 200,000 spindles ceased to exist, but this decline was partially offset by a few 'specially fortunate' firms which increased spindlage.[64] Nineteenth century spindlage in Irish linen peaked in 1875 at 925,000 and fell to 828,000 by 1900. This represents capacity; sometimes (as in the mid 1880s) there was a considerable number of unemployed spindles,[65] although it should be noted that with ever finer counts fewer spindles were required to produce the same quantity of yarn. In European terms there was nothing unique about this contraction in spinning capacity. In Scotland, capacity fell by nearly half between 1862 and 1905, while in the last quarter of the century France, Germany and Austria all experienced marked declines.[66] There is no doubt, however, that Ulster spinners increasingly felt the effects of competition from imported yarns from other European countries. One such competitor was heavily protected Russia which, it was reported in 1903, 'now instead of importing from us exports yarns to both Scotland and Ireland to the detriment of spinners in both countries'.[67] More generally, one simple set of statistics is sufficient to show the extent of yarn import penetration. Virtually all imported yarn came into Belfast, and, from less than 100 tons in 1880, the total rose to 6,000 tons in 1895. Imports fluctuated widely but went on to reach a pre-1914 peak of 11,820 tons in 1912.[68]

In the last quarter of the nineteenth century, in addition to the later 1870s and mid 1880s, the later 1890s were also generally difficult for flax spinners. Stockpiling became common and by 1897 'yarn stocks all over the trade had risen to huge proportions'.[69] This was inevitably accompanied by a decline in stock values. Firms in need of capital sometimes, not surprisingly, encountered an outright refusal by shareholders to pay calls on shares. Share values sank to their lowest levels in the 1890s and by 1901 of more than twenty limited companies spinning flax in Belfast in only two, Brookfield and York Street, were there any regular dealings in shares.[70] One of several casualties in the later 1890s was the Belfast Flax Spinning Company. The figures from its balance sheets reproduced in Table 2.4 demonstrate how its financial position had deteriorated between 1886 and 1897. In this period the small amount of uncalled capital had been paid up, reserves had disappeared, debenture indebtedness had almost trebled, while liquid assets had dwindled by more than 40 per cent. When the company went into liquidation it owed the Ulster Bank more than £20,000, and this was merely one of several losses sustained by local banks as a result of serious periodic difficulties in the late nineteenth century Ulster linen industry.

Table 2.4 *The Belfast Flax Spinning Company, 1886–97 (£)*

	Paid-up capital	Reserves	Debentures	Stock and debtors
1886	75,000	12,000	20,000	117,028
1893	80,000	16,000	57,000	87,408
1897	80,000	0	56,000	67,494

Source. Philip Ollerenshaw, *The Belfast Banks 1820–1900* unpublished Ph.D. thesis, University of Sheffield, 1982, p. 273.

Despite, but in a sense because of, the difficulties frequently experienced by flaxspinners, the weaving sector of Ulster linen continued to expand between 1870 and 1914. Yarn prices by the late 1890s were much less than half the levels of the mid 1860s and so the cost of this major input for weaving firms fell correspondingly. The divergent experience of spinning and weaving was conducive to the development of separate weaving factories and the number of looms in such factories in Ireland increased from about 9,000 in 1872 to 27,000 in 1910. By contrast, looms in combined mills declined slightly from a total of some 9,000 in 1872 and accounted for less than a quarter of weaving capacity by 1910.[71] The relentless extension of power-weaving finally sealed the fate of the vast majority of handloom weavers, and in 1898 it was estimated that the number of handlooms in the province did not exceed 2,500.[72] Handweaving in the early twentieth century was confined to the finest products such as damask tablecloths. However, if powerlooms increased productivity and output, manufacturers paid a price for this in recessions as they could no longer depend on handweavers to shoulder the burden. For this reason, continuous production and stockpiling were much more likely in recession under a powerloom regime.

The need to retain skilled powerweavers was another reason why manufacturers were reluctant to cease production at the first sign of recession. One such manufacturer was McCrum, Mercer and Company who produced, *inter alia*, fine cloths at their Milford Mill in Armagh. In the mid 1890s Robert McCrum estimated that two to three months were required to train an efficient powerloom weaver to make fine cloths and the need to pay weekly wages and absorb the cost of defective cloth during that time cost his firm not less than £25. This considerable investment in skill, together with the steady demand for trained powerweavers and a fear of their being poached by his rivals, were the reasons why McCrum felt unable to stop looms whenever immediate market conditions suggested that he should. As he himself stated in 1895:

> If we are to make these goods [i.e. fine cloths and napkins] in quantities great or small, *the looms must go on continuously* with only the needful changes of patterns or of setting, as it is a foolish and disastrous policy to spend large sums in training weavers for our neighbours to reap the benefit of our outlay, they getting nothing but good cloth while we have any quantity that can only be jobbed.[73]

The occasional problems thus encountered by manufacturers should not obscure the massive extension of powerweaving in the late nineteenth and early twentieth century. During this period weaving firms in addition to pure linen cloth also made 'unions' − a mixture of linen and cotton yarns. Unions had long been made in Ulster but at this time there was a rising market for such cloths both printed and dyed, and this goes far to explain why cotton yarn imports into Belfast in most years between 1895 and 1913 exceeded imports of linen yarn. Cotton yarn imports fluctuated much less than those of linen yarn and ranged between 4,100 and 7,200 tons in the period 1895−1913.[74]

Both the elastic supply and relative cheapness of imported yarn, which did so much damage to Ulster flax spinners, are crucial to an explanation of the general buoyancy of firms engaged in weaving and finishing. At the same time there were some growing lines of business such as the hemstitching and embroidery of handkerchiefs and, most importantly, improvements in marketing methods as more firms employed overseas agents to sell Ulster linen goods. In this export-dependent industry overseas agencies assumed strategic significance by the end of the nineteenth century and many firms employed agents all over the world. For all these reasons the weaving and finishing sectors displayed remarkable dynamism before 1914 and even the spinners recovered somewhat from the privations of the 1890s to add over 5 per cent to their capacity between 1900 and 1914. Symptomatic of the increase in activity was a rise in factory employment in Irish linen from 65,000 in 1900 to 75,000 by 1913.[75]

Improvement in the overall condition of the Ulster linen industry in the decade before 1914 is evidenced not only in rising exports and extensions to capacity. The market for linen shares picked up appreciably and firms which had done no more than survive in the 1890s found that their shares regained marketability.[76] Levels of company indebtedness declined and a degree of confidence which had not been experienced since the early 1870s crept back into the industry. This period was one of declining stocks, rising demand, output and profitability although it was marred by one bad year, 1908. The depression of 1908 was caused by a monetary crisis and depression in the United States which began in 1907, and it was a reminder both of the United States' key importance in the international economy and of the ease with which a serious crisis for Ulster linen could materialise quickly out of an apparently blue sky. In Ulster, the Linen Merchants' Association went so far as to declare 1908 the most disastrous in the history of the trade and pointed out with some irritation that the crisis occurred 'at a time when manufacturers and merchants were heavily committed and when every branch was running at high pressure to keep pace with a feverish demand'.[77] Despite the undoubted severity of the 1908 depression, recovery was rapid and the depression must be viewed as an unfortunate but exceptional interruption to an otherwise buoyant decade.

Throughout the considerable fluctuations in the Ulster linen industry between 1870 and 1914 there was little horizontal integration (merger activity) except in linen thread. The development of the Linen Thread Company from 1898 was inspired by similar developments in British cotton thread and it brought together leading firms in the United Kingdom and United States. Barbour's of Lisburn, and Paterson New Jersey and New York were the driving force behind this combine, but other Ulster-based firms involved were the old established F. W. Hayes and Company of Seapatrick County Down and Dunbar McMaster of Gilford, and Greenwich, New York.[78]

More common than merger activity was vertical integration such as spinning and weaving firms which moved into bleaching. In the second half of the nineteenth century the number of bleachgreens in Ulster declined; there were about forty in 1875 and twenty in 1903 and they were heavily concentrated in a few areas such as the Sixmilewater in County Antrim and the Bann Valley. Decline in the number of bleachgreens was accompanied by an increase in average size. Ulster bleachers had an unrivalled international reputation, and large quantities of brown linen were sent from Belgium, France and Germany to be bleached in the province and then returned to the country of origin for sale.[79]

Acquisition of bleaching facilities was a logical step for the large spinning and weaving firms such as York Street which bought William Chaine's Muckamore bleachgreens along the banks of the Sixmilewater for £28,000 in 1883.[80] If York Street was the largest vertically integrated concern in the Ulster linen industry it was by no means the only one. Richardson, Sons and Owden, whose origins lay in bleaching in the eighteenth century had become fully integrated by the 1880s by which time it controlled works in Antrim, Down and Armagh as well as overseas. Another major firm was William Ewart and Sons whose Belfast operations began in flax spinning about 1840. On the eve of the American Civil War Ewarts were already vertically integrated, and in an ideal position to take maximum advantage of the linen boom of the mid 1860s. Profits acquired in this period permitted Ewarts to buy modern, well equipped property at knockdown prices during the depression which followed the massive failures of 1874–75. The size to which the firm had grown by 1883 is indicated by its capitalisation of £500,000 on becoming a limited company in that year. The first directors were Sir William Ewart and his five sons.[81] Although there were several large vertically integrated concerns, it remains the case that before 1914 most firms were involved in a single process with neither the will nor the means to do otherwise.

Between 1820 and 1914 the Irish linen industry was heavily concentrated in north-east Ulster. In the north-west of the province shirtmaking emerged after 1850 as the dominant branch of textiles and indeed this area became the leading centre for this industry in the United Kingdom. From extremely modest beginnings in Derry city in the 1830s the pioneering firm of William Scott laid the basis for the shirtmaking industry which developed very rapidly after 1850. Several leading Derry shirtmakers were Scots and it was the Scottish partnership of William Tillie and John Henderson, formed in 1851, which introduced the sewing machine into the city five years later. Tillie and Henderson opened a new £7,000 factory in Derry in 1857 in which date they already employed 4,000 people, principally outworkers in Counties Londonderry, Tyrone and Donegal. By the mid 1870s the number of factories had risen to twelve, employing 4—5,000 workers in Derry itself and a 'rural and suburban' labour force of about 15,000.[82] Shirtmaking, like muslin embroidery, was largely dependent on low paid women workers who accounted for 80 per cent of the workforce in 1902.

The worst paid process in shirt manufacture was making up and stitching the garment. Until the end of the nineteenth century this process was undertaken overwhelmingly by rural outworkers who collected the necessary parts from factories via 'shirt stations' located within walking distance of their homes, returning the made-up garments, by the dozen, when ready. Laundering and finishing the final product was the best paid stage of manufacture and many Derry factories had laundries attached to them. The total number of factories and laundries in 1902 was thirty-eight, with 113 shirt stations, and the annual wage bill of the 80,000 engaged in this industry exceeded £300,000. Absolute numbers of employees conceal the fact that factory production increased relative to outwork. A ratio of more than four outworkers to one factory worker in 1860 had declined to about two to one by 1908 as assembly line techniques with much improved sewing machines raised productivity. By 1912 such techniques in best practice firms were capable of turning out one shirt every two minutes. Closely related to shirtmaking was the manufacture of collars and cuffs. In addition to Derry, an important centre of this trade was Belfast where one of the first firms was Wilkinson and Turtle, established in 1858. Just over thirty years later exports of collars and cuffs from the two cities amounted to more than 60,000 dozen each week valued at £600,000. In 1907 the Census of Production valued the output of Irish shirt, collar and cuff industry at £1·04 million.[83]

Although this industry provided welcome earnings for women workers both in Derry city and surrounding counties it did emphasise the extent to which Derry lacked those types of employment which before 1914 would have been perceived as appropriate for men. Family dependence on female employment, if not unknown elsewhere, was certainly more obvious in Derry city after 1860 than in other parts of the province, particularly Belfast. The availability of both 'male' and 'female' employment in Belfast was a direct result of increasing industrial and commercial diversification after 1860, and it is the nature of that diversification to which we now turn.

Industrial diversification

Between 1841 and 1911 the population of Belfast rose from 75,000 to 387,000. Such an increase could not have been sustained by the linen industry alone although in percentage terms the greatest decadal increase in this period, 43 per cent between 1861 and 1871, was largely due to the linen boom of the mid 1860s. Between 1870 and 1914 the relative significance of linen in the economy of the Belfast region declined as the growth of other industries, shipbuilding, marine and mechanical engineering, food processing, tobacco manufacture and drink, including whiskey distilling and aerated waters, combined to diversify, strengthen and balance the regional economic base. One recent estimate suggests that about one-third of Irish net industrial output and two-thirds of total industrial exports originated in the Belfast region in 1907.[84]

Outside this region, the industrial experience in the nineteenth century was sometimes an unhappy one, as a reading of the *Select Committee on Irish Industries* of 1885 will show. For example, the number of working breweries in Ulster declined from about forty in 1831 to twenty-five in 1850 and just four remained by 1902: McConnell's and Caffrey's in Belfast, Johnston's in Lurgan and Downes' in Enniskillen. The reasons for this are not altogether clear, but this decline did contrast strongly with the resilience of distilling in the province and particularly with the growth of export oriented distilling between 1870 and 1914. During this period a number of large distilleries was built in Belfast and equipped with complex and expensive patent stills which became more typical of Ulster than other Irish provinces. The largest patent still distilleries in Ulster were in Belfast and there were four in 1902; Dunville's Royal Irish Distillery built in 1869, the Irish Distillery, Higgins' Avoniel Distillery built in 1882 and McConnell's at the end of the nineteenth century. Outside Belfast, seven substantial distilleries survived into the early twentieth century: two in Derry, two in Comber, one in Limavady, one in Coleraine and one (the oldest of them all) in Bushmills.[85]

If the experience of brewing and distilling in Ulster was very different there can be no question about the sharp decline in one of the province's most widespread industries – milling. From the 1870s imports of American flour had a devastating effect on milling in Ulster, and up to two-thirds of the flour mills closed betwen 1873 and 1885. This decline was so rapid, so widespread and apparently so permanent that many Ulster millers called (in vain) for tariff protection.[86] The industry was forced to adopt the same techniques as those used in the United States. Roller milling was introduced in Budapest in 1839, had become widespread in North America after 1870, and was first used in Belfast in the early 1880s.[87] Roller mills were expensive and they tended to be steam driven and located at ports. Such mills were largely responsible for rescuing the Ulster milling industry from annihilation before 1914. Thus although the short term impact of foreign competition was severe, the wide geographical base of the industry destroyed and the number of mills permanently reduced, by the early twentieth century there were signs that the corner had been turned. As E. J. Riordan in his comprehensive survey of Irish trade and industry wrote in 1920, 'No Irish industry has had to face fiercer competition from outside these shores, and has done it more successfully in the long run than the Irish flour milling industry'.[88]

Construction of roller mills added to the industrial base of Belfast. Other industries also contributed including tobacco manufacture where the most important firm was Gallaher's, established in 1879, which rapidly became one of the city's largest employers, about 3,000 by 1907.[89] Aerated water manufacture and export, the provisions trade, paper and printing, were other significant features of industrial Belfast in the late nineteenth and early twentieth centuries. The most obvious growth point in the economy in Belfast in this period, however, was the rise of iron and steel shipbuilding.

On the eve of the first world war, Belfast boasted two of the largest shipyards in the world, but shipbuilding did not become a major industry in Ulster until the 1870s. In the early nineteenth century shipbuilding was widely scattered throughout the United Kingdom in hundreds of yards, the majority of which employed fewer than two dozen men turning out small wooden vessels. By 1900 the industry had been revolutionised in its technology and scale of operations. In terms of employment, several builders were amongst the largest manufacturing enterprises in the United Kingdom, and in 1910 some thirty firms − a quarter of the total − accounted for three-quarters of the industry's output. The principal shipbuilding areas were along the Clyde, the north-east of England between Newcastle and

Middlesborough, Barrow, Birkenhead and Belfast.[90] The rise of Belfast as a shipbuilding centre of international importance was thus part of a process of industrial relocation which began in the mid nineteenth century whereby a small number of centres in the north and west of Britain replaced the south and east of England as the main shipbuilding areas. This relocation was based on the construction and development of iron and later steel steamships.

By the early 1820s Belfast was the single most important centre for shipbuilding in Ulster. In the period 1824–54 it is estimated that some fifty wooden, principally sailing, vessels almost all of which were between 100 and 350 tons were turned out from three yards: Ritchie and McLaine, Charles Connell and Sons and Thompson and Kirwan.[91] Wood had always been the main shipbuilding material, and the doubts surrounding the value of iron as a substitute took more than half a century to overcome after the launch of the first iron barge in 1787. Since the construction of iron ships was technically closest to boilermaking it was natural that a leading firm of engineers and boilermakers, Victor Coates and Company, should build the first iron vessel in Belfast, and continued to build them until the 1860s. This vessel, the *Countess of Caledon*, the first Irish built iron lake steamer, was launched from Coates' Lagan Foundry in December 1838 and put into service on Lough Neagh in the following year.[92] From this date onwards the development of iron shipbuilding in Belfast owed little to previous shipbuilding tradition in the town. Within twenty-five years several factors combined to lay the foundations of the modern shipbuilding industry on the Lagan.

The rapidly growing volume and value of Belfast trade demanded fundamental improvements in port facilities. Tonnage cleared from Belfast rose from 91,000 in 1815 to 291,000 in 1835. Between these dates a long debate between the port authorities, local business interests and several leading engineers including John Rennie and Thomas Telford took place as to what form the improvements should take. In 1837 a decision was taken to straighten and dredge the winding channel approach to Belfast, thereby extending significantly dock and quay space as well as creating three artificial islands. Although this particular phase of improvements, completed in 1849, was by no means the last made to port facilities, it was perhaps the most important undertaken in our period.[93] The long term growth of Belfast trade is indicated by Table 2.5.

Table 2.5 *Registered tonnage and vessels cleared at Belfast, 1840–1900*

Year	Tonnage registered		Vessels cleared	
	Vessels	*Tonnage*	*Vessels*	*Tonnage*
1840	355	45,632	3,323	361,473
1850	463	74,770	4,490	624,113
1860	508	74,049	6,658	885,413
1870	462	62,653	8,303	1,616,908
1880	399	76,386	7,965	1,225,566
1890	293	125,632	8,050	1,840,666
1900	210	147,575	8,318	2,325,936

Source. Thom's Directory.

From 1847 the elected Harbour Commission had overall responsibility for the quality of port facilities, and it quickly established a close working relationship with Belfast shipbuilders which lasted into the twentieth century. Assistance afforded by the commissioners to Belfast shipbuilding was acknowledged by builders themselves and the generous provision of space and dock facilities was a prerequisite for the development of this industry.

One firm which took advantage of space available on one of the artificial islands created by port improvement was that of Robert Hickson which moved into iron shipbuilding on the Queen's Island in 1853. Hickson built ships for both Ulster and Liverpool owners, but the growth of his yard was retarded because several Belfast owners continued to order from yards on the Clyde and Tyne. Eventually in 1858 Edward Harland, Hickson's manager since 1854, took over the yard with the help of money provided by Liverpool merchant and financier G. C. Schwabe, a personal friend. The uncle of Harland's assistant Gustav Wolff, Schwabe provided the critical initial orders for the Queen's Island yard through his connection with the Bibby Line of Liverpool and Bibbys continued to order from Harland and Wolff until after 1914. Launched between 1859 and 1860 *Venetian, Sicilian*, and *Syrian* were numbered one, two and three respectively on Harland and Wolff's order book. All three were around 1500 gross tons iron hulled, barque rigged, single screw steamers. Since Harland's did not yet build engines these three vessels were towed to the Clyde where the machinery was installed by McNab of Greenock. An unusually high ratio of length (270 feet) to breadth (thirty-four feet) was introduced

89

D

on these ships and subsequently became common in Harland's vessels. Later in the nineteenth century the ratio was stretched further, to more than eleven to one. In addition, Harland incorporated an iron deck, flat bottom and wide bilge to increase strength and stability.[94] Such designs became popular, although by no means universal, on larger liners and cargo ships, and contributed much to Harland's prestige after 1860. In essence Harland and Wolff were innovative but usually practical and did much to redefine the art of the possible in large scale iron shipbuilding from 1860 onwards.

If Harland's contribution to ship design should not be forgotten, it was never a sufficient condition for the growth of Belfast shipbuilding and there has been a tendency to overlook or underestimate other factors which all played contributory roles. Apart from the highly positive part played by the Harbour Commission, and the strategic intermediation and finance of Schwabe, as well as the ready availability of skilled British labour which Harland brought over in the 1850s and 1860s to do much of the actual construction work, another favourable influence on Belfast shipbuilding was the growth of world trade. Indeed this last was the single most favourable omnipresent influence on shipbuilding in the United Kingdom before 1914. The current price value of UK trade (exports, imports and re-exports) totalled £375 million in 1860, £1403 million in 1913. In the same period merchant shipping tonnage rose from 4·7 million to 11·6 million, and the nation's share of world tonnage remained the same at about one-third.[95] Such was the price competitiveness and quality of United Kingdom shipbuilders that it was exceptionally rare for British shipping companies to buy ships built elsewhere, and for this reason the trade and tonnage figures obviously reflect a massive growth in UK shipbuilding between 1860 and 1914. British preeminence in iron, steel and engineering between 1860 and 1880 permitted British shipbuilders to capture the vast home market and retain it down to 1914.[96] Belfast, given the ease with which it could draw raw materials and engineering expertise from the Clyde and elsewhere, and given the other favourable influences already discussed, was in an ideal position to share fully in this market. Harland and Wolff could hardly have become partners at a more fortunate time.

The emergence by mid-century of many Liverpool shipping magnates provided a stream of orders for Harland and Wolff from 1860. Ulster shipping companies, by contrast, provided a relatively modest demand, the most important in the early years of Harland and Wolff was J. P. Corry and Company, bulk timber and jute traders for whom ten vessels were built between 1860 and 1874. Moreover Belfast never dominated the construction of cross channel steamships or of vessels employed on lakes and waterways within Ulster itself. Most of these were ordered from yards on the Clyde or on the north-east coast of England. Harland and Wolff did secure their first Admiralty contract in 1867,[97] but by far the greatest proportion of their output before 1914 was non-naval.

Before 1870 the development of Belfast shipbuilding was promising and employment at Harland's had grown from 500 in 1861 to 2,200 ten years later, but this was insignificant compared to growth thereafter. If Bibby Line orders were crucial in enabling Harland and Wolff to build a business and a reputation, the White Star Line connection, which was established just before 1870, was the single most important source of orders for this shipyard before 1914. Once again Schwabe's influence and connections seem to have played a key role since it was allegedly at his home in 1869, playing billiards with a Liverpool shipowner T. H. Ismay, that Schwabe persuaded the latter to place orders for his newly registered company with the Belfast yard.[98] From 1870 Ismay, Imrie and Company, in which both Harland and Wolff were shareholders, and their White Star Line developed a relationship with their shipbuilders which was exceptionally close even by late nineteenth and early twentieth century standards in this industry.

The first tangible result of this relationship was the remarkable *Oceanic* launched in 1871 at a cost of £120,000, one of an initial batch of four ships ordered by White Star. This ship marked the complete separation of the species of passenger vessels from the genus of long distance steamers and, as one historian has written, 'seldom has a single vessel contained so many innovations'.[99] These innovations, the result of collaboration between Harland and Ismay, included the revolutionary decision to move the first class accommodation from the conventional position at the rear of the vessel to a more comfortable midships location. With the *Oceanic*, 420 feet by forty-one feet, 3,800 gross tons, engined by Maudsley in London and capable of fourteen knots, White Star set new standards on the North Atlantic which fashion-conscious rivals such as Cunard ignored at their peril.

Harland and Wolff did build several sailing ships for White Star, the last in 1890, but a brief account of White Star steamship orders, which numbered more than sixty between 1870 and 1914, will illustrate the kind of technical advance and increase in size which put this shipyard in the vanguard of large liner construction. Iron was used throughout the 1870s to be replaced by steel beginning with the 4,400 gross tons *Arabic* and *Coptic* in 1881. Single screws were used until 1889 when the 10,000 gross tons *Teutonic* and *Majestic*, the first merchant cruisers, were fitted with twin screws. From 1909 triple screws were installed, above all on the *Olympic, Titanic* and *Britannic*, each of which was around 850 feet by ninety-two feet and 45,000 gross tons. When completed between 1910 and 1914 these were amongst the world's largest liners, and they were fitted with a combination of triple expansion and turbine propulsion, first employed on the North Atlantic in 1905.[100] By 1914 Harland and Wolff had built some 750,000 gross tonnage for White Star, about a third of their total output between 1870 and 1914.

The rise of Harland and Wolff led not only to increasing demands for male labour (some 14,000 were employed in 1914), it also required an unprecedented degree of skill supplied by workers in dozens of different trades, and resulted in a number of important spin offs including rope making and marine engineering. Neither of these was new in Belfast in the 1870s, but both developed to an unprecedented extent from this period onwards. The Belfast Ropeworks, managed by W. H. Smiles, son of Samuel Smiles, opened in 1876 on a four acre site on the banks of the Connswater River in Ballymacarrett, and was easily the largest ropeworks ever seen in Ireland. A 420 yard enclosed ropewalk was built with machinery driven by two pairs of marine type compound engines adapted for this particular use by John Rowan and Sons of Belfast. Initially American machinery was installed, but by 1882 this had been 'largely added to and improved upon' by the introduction of machinery made by the Falls Foundry in Belfast.[101] By this date 300 people were employed, twenty years later there were 3,000. The demand for heavy rope came to a significant extent from the shipbuilding and shipping industries but before 1914 there was an increasing demand for all types of sash and blind cord as well as binder twine for wheat growing countries, and fishing lines and trawler twines for North Sea and other fisheries. The Belfast Ropeworks made all types of rope and twine and had become the largest single works of its kind in the early twentieth century.[102]

Another industry which owed its rapid development to shipbuilding was marine engineering. Prior to 1880, at which time Harland and Wolff began to make marine engines, their ships were either engined on the Clyde or the Thames, or engines were brought to Belfast on a custom built steamship for installation. Virtually every major UK shipyard acquired its own marine engineering facilities in the later nineteenth century and Harland and Wolff were no exception.[103] The engine works not only contributed much to the firm's independence but also quickly became a major employer of labour; of 7,000 employees at Harland's in 1892 some 2,500 were employed in the engine works.[104] The search for independence was taken further by Belfast shipbuilders than by most other yards because of the geographical remoteness of Belfast from the largest shipbuilding areas, the Clyde and north-east England, where subcontracting was common. This search was successful and necessitated the development of a yard which was at once larger and more integrated than most contemporary yards. Harland and Wolff's four acres in 1859 had become ninety-five acres by 1916. On the culmination of pre-1914 merchant ship-building, the launch of the *Olympic* and *Titanic* in Belfast, the *Shipbuilder* magazine of 1911 remarked:

> Unlike many shipbuilding firms, Messrs. Harland and Wolff may be termed builders in the most complete sense of the word. As in the case of all vessels built by them, not only have they constructed the hulls of the *Olympic* and *Titanic*, but also their propelling machinery, while much of the outfit usually supplied by sub-contractors for ships built in other yards has been manufactured in their own works.[105]

Edward Harland and, to a much smaller extent, Gustav Wolff directed the yard until 1874 when two employees W. H. Wilson and W. J. Pirrie were taken into partnership. From then until Harland's death in 1895 these four men worked closely together although Pirrie emerged as the dominant force by the end of the nineteenth century. In 1885 the firm had taken private limited liability with a capital of £600,000 divided into 600 shares of £1,000 each. Pirrie, raised to the peerage in 1906, stamped his personality on the firm and reorganised its divisional management structure. In an industry where connections with 'builders' friends' counted for so much, few were better placed than he. A peerage, together with many directorships in financial, industrial, shipping and shipbuilding companies made Pirrie an extraordinarily powerful figure in shipbuilding until his death in 1924, and he was largely responsible for ensuring that Harland and Wolff were key builders for one of the largest pre-war shipping combinations, the International Mercantile Marine (which included White Star) from

1902. Under Pirrie the firm also became actively involved in the Armaments Ring from 1907 and oil tanker construction from 1907–08, in addition to the acquisition after 1909 of yards for building on the Clyde and for repair at other locations including Southampton. Harland's also developed a keen interest in diesel engines from 1912 through a holding in the Burmeister and Wain Oil Engine Company at their Finnieston works in Glasgow.[106]

If Harland and Wolff dominated Ulster shipbuilding after 1860, another Belfast firm, Workman Clark and Company, made a much greater contribution than they are usually given credit for. Frank Workman and William Campbell, both former employees at Harland and Wolff, set up a four acre yard on the north bank of the Lagan in 1879. The first keel was laid in spring 1880 when the yard employed 150 men, and in that same year George Clark, a Scot of considerable financial means, became a partner. As had been the case with Harland and Wolff, it was a family connection that provided Workman Clark with their crucial opportunity. Workman's family connection with the Smith family and its City Line of Glasgow bore first fruit with the construction of the 2,600 gross tons passenger and cargo ship the *City of Cambridge* in 1882.[107] This particular connection survived the takeover of Smith by Ellerman Lines in 1901 and continued until after 1914 by which time eighteen vessels had been built. The Smith-Ellerman orders, although important, were never so significant in the long term for Workman Clark as the White Star orders were for Harland and Wolff. The development of Workman Clark was impressive by any standards: 7,000 were employed on a fifty acre site by 1902, the first of two years before 1914 in which this shipyard turned out more gross tonnage (75,800) than any other yard in the United Kingdom

Like Harland and Wolff, Workman Clark did not for many years possess an engine works and it was only in 1892 that they turned out their first vessel engined by themselves. Prior to this date engines for Workman Clark steamers had come from the Clyde. Since the Clyde had long been at the forefront of marine engine technology, it was entirely appropriate that the engineering department should first be directed by Charles Allan whose family owned the Allan Line of Glasgow and whose apprenticeship had been served at J. and G. Thomson of Clydebank.[108] In 1893 Workman Clark took over the shipbuilding, engineering and boilermaking business of MacIlwaine and MacColl. The latter had a long history, but had been building ships since the 1860s, and in 1886 had taken a new yard laid out by the Belfast Harbour Commissioners.[109] From then until 1893 almost sixty vessels were constructed and fitted with their own engines. Extensions to capacity in the early 1890s were responsible for Workman Clark's rapid growth in the next twenty years (see Table 2.6).

Between 1880 and 1914 Workman Clark turned out about 310 vessels, only thirty-two of which were sailing ships built, between 1884 and 1896, at the end of the sail era. Their ships tended to be much smaller than those of Harland and Wolff, the largest before 1914 were a pair of passenger liners, *Nestor* and *Ulysses*, each of 14,500 gross tons built for Alfred Holt in 1912–13. Workman Clark built for a bewildering variety of owners and never specialised in liner construction to the same extent as Harland and Wolff, although one of their ships, the 10,600 ton *Victorian* built for the Allan Line was the first turbine liner on the North Atlantic in March 1905. In the early twentieth century Workman Clark developed strong interests in the construction of frozen meat carriers, particularly for the Shaw, Savill and Albion Company, and fruit and passenger ships. Some of the latter were built for Elder and Fyffes but a majority was for the United Fruit Company of Boston for whom nineteen, with a total gross tonnage of 98,000, were built between 1903 and 1914.

Both Workman Clark and Harland and Wolff had a scale and diversity of output which helped to insulate them from the most violent fluctuations with which this industry is often associated. The size of these yards and the relative stability of output combined to ensure that shipbuilding not only played an increasingly important

Table 2.6 *Approximate output of two Belfast shipbuilders, 1885–1912 ('000 tons gross, four year totals)*[111]

Year	Harland and Wolff	Workman Clark
1885–88	100	29
1889–92	239	78
1893–96	270	129
1897–1900	309	182
1901–04	313	218
1905–08	350	235
1909–12	342	290

Sources. S. Pollard, *An Economic History of British Shipbuilding 1870–1914*, Ph.D. thesis, University of London, 1951, Table A.7; Workman Clark (1928) Ltd., *Shipbuilding at Belfast 1880–1933*, Belfast, 1934, p. 58.

but also a stabilising role in the economy of the Belfast region before 1914. At the beginning of the twentieth century the shipyards' weekly wage bill amounted to between £15,000 and £18,000; by 1915 it was running at £35,000.[110] On the outbreak of war in August 1914, the future of no Ulster industry seemed so secure as that of shipbuilding.

Banking

The need to import raw materials such as coal as well as intermediate goods such as iron, steel and cotton yarn, together with a dependence on British and overseas markets for final products all made a contribution to the leading position of Belfast in industrial Ulster before 1914. Between 1820 and 1914 Belfast was also the premier financial centre in the province. The mechanics of business finance in this period are little understood, and this section is confined to some general observations. The sources of finance were several, the needs of borrowers varied from a few hundred pounds to tens of thousands and some required credit for a few weeks while others needed extended loans. Again, many loans were made available through some kind of intermediary such as an attorney or bank, while in other cases no financial intermediation was required.

Reinvestment of profits was a perfectly normal method of industrial finance and expansion in Ulster as in the rest of the United Kingdom in this period, but the importance of external finance should not be played down. The most important sources of external finance in Ulster before 1914 were commercial banks, but in the early nineteenth century in particular attorneys performed pivotal functions as financial intermediaries. Attorneys in north-east Ulster, as in other industrialising areas such as Lancashire and West Yorkshire, were able to use their high professional status and financial connections to act as intermediaries between lenders and borrowers who were neither related nor even known to each other.[112] In the 1820s since several attorneys had offices in Belfast as well as in provincial towns they were in a unique position to find rural lenders for urban borrowers or *vice versa*, and thereby reduce the problems posed by the need to supply funds to a rapidly growing industrial town like Belfast from a large number of dispersed sources. Some idea of the attorney's role as financial intermediary can be gathered from newspaper advertisements. In the 1820s, for example, sums offered through attorneys ranged from £30 to over £30,000 although usually the larger sums were divisible into smaller individual lots, and many loans were offered on an explicitly long term basis. It is also worth noting that English-based attorneys advertised funds in Belfast from the mid-1820s. On the demand side the largest individual sums required by attorneys for clients were smaller than those offered, but occasionally exceeded £10,000 with a diverse range of security tendered, such as unencumbered land and turnpike tolls. The frequency with which advertisements appear in newspapers is a strong indication that the capital market in early nineteenth century Belfast was an active one and that the attorney was a key figure in that market.[113]

Of growing importance in the Ulster economy from 1820 were the commercial banks. In the early 1820s the commercial banking system in Ulster was limited to offices of three banks based in Belfast: Batt, Houston and Batt, known as Batt's or the Belfast Bank; Orr, McCance, Montgomery and McNeile, known as Montgomery's or the Northern Bank; and Tennent, Callwell, Luke and Thomson, known as Tennent's or the Commercial Bank. The first of these opened in 1808, the last two in 1809, and each operated agencies in towns and villages in north-east Ulster. Agents pushed notes into circulation through discounting bills, and they combined work for the bank with other business interests such as linen bleaching or the legal profession. Agents were located in areas most likely to maximise banknote circulation because note issue made a crucial contribution to bank profits before mid-century. All these banks were private concerns with unlimited liability and restricted to a maximum of six partners. Legal changes between 1821 and 1824 permitted the formation of banks with an unrestricted number of partners. Such 'joint-stock' banks were permitted to issue notes so long as they had no office within a fifty Irish mile radius from Dublin, although this prohibition ceased after 1845. The three banks in Belfast quickly availed themselves of legal changes and converted to joint-stock status. Montgomery's became the Northern Banking Company in 1824; Batt's and Tennent's merged in 1827 to become the Belfast Banking Company, after which no private banks remained in Ulster. A third joint stock concern, the Ulster Banking Company, was established in 1836 and was the last bank to be established with its head office in the province. The Belfast banks had very similar structures of management and organisation and offered an identical range of services. In many ways they modelled themselves explicitly on Scottish banks which had an unrivalled reputation within the United Kingdom for stability and for their contribution to economic growth. From 1825 branches of banks based outside Ulster began to appear in the province and the process of branch expansion was rapid. By 1852, some seventy bank offices had been established in Ulster, fifty of them operated by the Belfast banks, fifteen by the Provincial Bank of Ireland (a bank with an administrative head office in London set up in 1824), four by the Bank of Ireland (a Dublin-based chartered bank established in 1783) and one by the National Bank of Ireland (set up in London in 1835).[114] One other bank operated in Ulster before 1850, the Agricultural and Commercial, which opened in 1834 and failed in 1841 for a variety of reasons including a too-rapid rate of branch expansion, dishonest and incompetent directors, lack of managerial experience at branch level, a poor inspectorate and shoddy bookkeeping.[115]

Throughout our period the relationships between commercial banks and Ulster agriculture, industry and trade were close. Indeed the role of banks in financing industrial development in the province was important from the 1820s, and Mokyr's recently expressed view that it is 'unlikely ... that the banks were instrumental in producing major increments to the productive resources of the country'[116] can be firmly rejected for north-east Ulster. The three Belfast based banks were owned principally by shareholders in Ulster. Each of these banks had an advisory committee which comprised local businessmen, who also had to be substantial shareholders, with a sound knowledge of the regional economy, the credit needs of customers and the creditworthiness of firms. They met regularly to advise bank directors on the overall operations of the bank. Local ownership and control, together with recruitment of staff overwhelmingly from within the province, were features of the Belfast banks, which rendered them integral parts of the Ulster economy before 1914. Commercial banks, both in towns and country areas, catered for the credit needs and saving habits of the 'middle class' and upwards. Two types of savings bank, Trustee from 1816 and Post Office from 1861, served those members of the working class who wished and could afford to save with a bank. Before 1914, the extent to which the working class held accounts with commercial banks anywhere in Ulster was very limited indeed.

Banks assisted the Ulster economy in a number of ways between 1820 and 1914. The power of note issue was especially important in the first half of the nineteenth century: it promoted the use of an economical and portable currency in a region which was short of coin, it lowered discount rates and raised bank profits. Moreover the power of issue enabled banks to operate country agencies which were crucial to the efficient operation of Ulster fairs and markets; such agencies laid the basis for modern branch networks. Cheques became more common from the 1830s and the rapid diffusion of branches from this time did much to increase the availability of credit facilities (bill discounts, overdrafts and fixed period loans) and decrease the amount of hoarded cash by offering interest-bearing deposit accounts.

Throughout our period much banking business was seasonal, reflecting the seasonal nature of economic activity in rural Ulster. One of the best indicators of this is the annual cycle of banknote circulation which began to rise sharply after the harvest and reached its peak around January and declined thereafter until the next harvest. Many bank customers such as provision traders and flax spinners often required short term credit every year and these two groups were important recipients of short term bank finance in nineteenth-century Ulster. The banks were generally averse to granting explicitly long-term loans, and preferred to reserve the option of calling in loans at a few months' notice. In practice, credit could be extended for many years provided the account had a satisfactory turnover. Sometimes security was required for advances, on other occasions personal reputation of the customer concerned was quite adequate.

Branch systems appeared much earlier in Ireland than in England and Wales, and in the last two countries the localised nature of banking was a contributory factor in weakening banks themselves and so was conducive to economic instability until well into the second half of the nineteenth century. In Ulster, branch systems acted as a stabilising force on the banking structure, and such systems also facilitated the transfer of funds within the province. As a representative of the Belfast banks told a parliamentary enquiry in 1875, deposits were gathered 'chiefly' in agricultural districts and 'our loans are made in the towns'.[117] A snapshot picture of deposits and current accounts in the Northern Bank in January 1860, as given in Table 2.7, helps to indicate the importance of Belfast in overdraft business *vis-à-vis* all other branches. Indeed, these figures are a useful indicator of the overwhelming importance of Belfast in the Ulster banking system, and in our example Belfast accounts for 43 per cent of deposits, 78 per cent of overdrafts and 80 per cent of credit balances.

The evidence suggests that all banks which operated in Ulster were

Table 2.7 *Northern Bank deposits and current accounts, 28 January 1860 (£ '000)*

Branch	Deposits	Current accounts	
		D r	*Cr*
Armagh	31·8	30·7	6·0
Ballymena	79·0	11·3	2·4
Ballynahinch Agency	5·6	–	–
Carrickfergus	61·8	3·3	1·9
Castlewellan	30·0	0·8	2·0
Clones	60·8	21·4	6·8
Coleraine	61·6	15·2	4·4
Derry	111·9	79·6	36·2
Downpatrick	138·0	78·7	21·7
Limavady	59·1	5·5	4·8
Lisburn	92·5	4·7	6·9
Lurgan	46·0	3·7	2·9
Magherafelt	38·2	6·0	4·6
Branch total	816·3	260·9	100·6
Head Office (Belfast)	614·6	935·3	409·3
Total	1,430·9	1,196·2	509·9

Source. Northern Bank Abstract of Branch Balances, PRONI D3145.

heavily involved in lending to industry. This is true not merely of the Belfast banks but of the Bank of Ireland, the National, the Provincial and the Hibernian. Predictably, at certain times there was a noticeable restriction of credit. For example in the early 1860s and late 1870s, the discount of farmers' and shopkeepers' bills was discouraged because of the difficulties experienced in Ulster agriculture. Similarly, there were several periods in the late nineteenth century when banks refused to extend further credit to many linen firms. Banks sometimes lost heavily as a result of failures in the linen industry. Examples here included the Provincial Bank which lost some £75,000 following the bankruptcy of Lowry, Valentine and Kirk in 1874, and the Northern Bank which had to write off a debt of £60,000 owed by William Spotten and Company which failed in 1875.[118]

In general, banks in Ulster before 1914 avoided large bad debts, and probably the largest single bad debt (£135,000) was incurred in 1873, not in the ordinary course of bank lending but as a result of fraud on the part of two officers of the Belfast Banking Company. Fortunately, both for the bank itself and the stability of the banking system as a whole, the reserve fund was more than adequate to meet this potentially catastrophic loss. Given that the banks lent on a large scale, particularly in the north-east, the consequences of a failure of one or more of them would have been very grave indeed, but the fact that the banks were stable meant that there were no financial crises induced by bank failure and apart from the special case of the Agricultural and Commercial Bank, the province was free from bank failure from the early 1820s through to 1914.

Conclusion
It was noted earlier in this chapter that north-east Ulster had more in common, and maintained much closer contact, with industrial regions of Britain than it did with other parts of Ireland. This characteristic was already apparent in the 1820s and became increasingly obvious towards 1914. In several important respects north-east Ulster and especially Belfast benefited from a proximity to Britain, and from excellent cross-channel communications. If Britain was an unbeatable competitor in some markets, it was itself a lucrative market for other goods such as linen and Belfast-built ships. Moreover, Liverpool was an extremely convenient entrepot for shipment of Ulster goods worldwide. The ease with which Belfast in particular could import coal, iron and other items, together with the low cost of cross-channel transport suggests that we should beware of overstressing the handicaps under which the north-east is sometimes alleged to have laboured. Some accounts assume that the lack of local coal and iron were major handicaps and that high calibre entrepreneurship came to the rescue. It remains the case, however, that very little is known about the quality of entrepreneurship in Ulster before 1914, and it is manifestly inadequate to list a number of successful businessmen as 'proof' of a higher order of entrepreneurial talent. Certainly there were some shrewd and capable businessmen in nineteenth and early twentieth century Ulster, several of them 'immigrants' from Britain, but they cannot be given exclusive credit for industrialisation in the north east. Savings appear to have been ample and were channelled into productive uses particularly by the banking system which maintained strong local links throughout our period. Labour costs were often lower than in Britain and this also helped in the struggle for competitiveness.

Before 1914 the Belfast region was proud of its industrial achievement and many northern commentators were fond of pointing to the contrast between Belfast and Dublin. On the eve of the First World War the prospects for linen, engineering and shipbuilding seemed bright. Appearances were deceptive, however, since 1913 was one of the last peacetime years in the twentieth century that it was reasonble to feel confident about the industrial future of this region. The interwar depression which devastated so many major export-dependent industries in the United Kingdom had serious effects in Northern Ireland.[119] 'From the vantage point of later years', writes Professor Pollard, 'it is not difficult to point to weaknesses in the British industrial structure before 1914, but they would not have been easy to prove to contemporaries'.[120] The same comment applies equally to the cornerstones of industrial Ulster.

Notes

1. Sincere thanks are due to Dr. W. H. Crawford, Dr. H. D. Gribbon, D. S. Johnson and Dr. C. W. Munn for helpful criticism of an earlier draft of this chapter, and to Dr. D. E. Bland and Professor S. Pollard for supervising the research on which it is based.
2. Clive Trebilcock, *The Industrialisation of the Continental Powers 1780–1914*, London, 1981, p. 3; Sidney Pollard, *Peaceful Conquest*, Oxford, 1981, esp. pp. 111–23.
3. H. D. Gribbon, 'The industrial archaeology of Northern Ireland', *Irish Economic and Social History*, VIII, 1981, p. 99; *The History of Water Power in Ulster*, Newton Abbot, 1969, passim.
4. See in particular W. A. McCutcheon, *The Industrial Archaeology of Northern Ireland*, Belfast, 1980, ch. 6; *Belfast Newsletter*, 18 April 1828.
5. Petition of Belfast merchants and traders to the House of Commons, 9 February 1827; *Belfast Chamber of Commerce* (hereafter BCC) *Out-letter Book 1821–44*, PRONI D1857/2/1. This is one of many similar petitions sent before 1831.
6. For useful accounts of imports and exports respectively see *Northern Whig*, 26 January, 2 February 1826.
7. E. R. R. Green, 'Early industrial Belfast' in J. C. Beckett and R. E. Glasscock eds., *Belfast: The Origin and Growth of an Industrial City*, London, 1967, p. 84.
8. For a comprehensive survey, see D. B. McNeill, *Irish Passenger Steamship Services*, I, Newton Abbot, 1969.
9. *Northern Whig*, 27 March 1828.
10. BCC to Viscount Morpeth, February 1839, *BCC Out-letter Book*.
11. Peter Solar, 'The agricultural trade statistics in the Irish railway commissioners' report', *Irish Economic and Social History*, VI, 1979; W. H. Crawford, 'The evolution of Ulster towns 1750–1850', in Peter Roebuck ed., *Plantation to Partition*, Belfast, 1981, p. 150.

12. The existence of a trade cycle began to be appreciated in Ireland from about 1840. See in particular Mountiford Longfield, 'Banking and currency', *Dublin University Magazine*, XV, 1840, esp. p. 223.
13. For the early recovery of Ulster linen after the temporary setback of 1848 see Provincial Bank of Ireland Annual Report 16 May 1850, *Bankers' Magazine*, X, 1850, p. 392; on the early 1860s see James S. Donnelly Jr., 'The Irish agricultural depression of 1859–64', *Irish Economic and Social History*, III, 1976, pp. 33–54.
14. *Belfast Mercantile Register*, 3 January 1843.
15. T. M. Devine and David Dickson, 'A review of the symposium' in Tom Devine and David Dickson eds., *Ireland and Scotland 1600–1850*, Edinburgh, 1983, p. 271; *Mr. Gladstone and the Belfast Chamber of Commerce*, Belfast, 1893, p. 3.
16. *BCC Annual Report* 1827, PRONI D1857/1; *Mr. Gladstone and the Belfast Chamber of Commerce*, p. 3.
17. R. S. Sayers, *Lloyds in the History of English Banking*, Oxford, 1957, p. 33.
18. *Mr. Gladstone and the Belfast Chamber of Commerce*, p. 5.
19. See Ian Budge and Cornelius O'Leary, *Belfast: Approach to Crisis*, London, 1973, ch. 4; A. T. Q. Stewart, *The Ulster Crisis*, London, 1967.
20. Conrad Gill, *The Rise of the Irish Linen Industry*, Oxford, 1925, pp. 341–2.
21. David Dickson, 'Aspects of the rise and fall of the Irish cotton industry' in L. M. Cullen and T. C. Smout eds., *Comparative Aspects of Scottish and Irish Economic and Social History 1600–1900*, Edinburgh, 1977, p. 108. In absolute terms, the imports increased more than this. Dickson calculates three-year averages of cotton wool and yarn imports into Belfast at 3,741 and 1,095 cwt respectively in the period 1799–1801; by 1820–22 these totals had become 19,962 cwt and 6,272 cwt.
22. For information on the coal consumption of individual cotton mills and other enterprises, see 'Return of consumption of coals, March 1829', *BCC Out-letter Book*.
23. F. Geary, 'The rise and fall of the Belfast cotton industry: some problems', *Irish Economic and Social History*, VIII, 1981, pp. 30–49.
24. *Secret Committee of the House of Lords on Commercial Distress*, BPP 1848, VIII, QQ. 7308–9.
25. Such activity included a charity ball and theatre performances. *Belfast Newsletter*, 19 May 1826. See also *Northern Whig*, 11 May 1826.
26. *Belfast Newsletter*, 8 October 1830.
27. BCC to G. R. Porter, 17 April 1834; *BCC Out-letter Book, loc. cit.*
28. E. R. R. Green, *The Lagan Valley 1800–50*, London, 1949, p. 105.
29. David Bremner, *The Industries of Scotland*, Edinburgh, 1869, pp. 306ff.
30. Emily Boyle, *The Economic Development of the Irish Linen Industry 1820–1913*, unpublished Ph.D. thesis, Queen's University of Belfast, 1979, p. 25.
31. Hugh McCall, *Ireland And Her Staple Manufactures*, Belfast, 1870 edition, pp. 390–1.

32. BCC to Thomas Lack, Privy Council for Trade, Whitehall, 5 December 1832, *BCC Out-letter Book*.
33. Alec Wilson, 'Belfast: its trade and commerce', in *Guide to Belfast*, Belfast, 1902, p. 42.
34. BCC to G. R. Porter, 17 April 1834; *BCC Out-letter Book*.
35. *Henderson's Belfast Directory and Northern Repository*, Belfast, 1849, p. 13.
36. It is impossible to be precise about total steampower in Belfast. For a review of some evidence see John W. Kanefsky, 'Motive power and the accuracy of the 1870 factory return', *Economic History Review*, XXXII, 1979, esp. pp. 364–5.
37. An illuminating account of village development is D. S. Macneice, 'Industrial villages of Ulster 1800–1900' in Peter Roebuck ed., *Plantation to Partition*, pp. 172–90.
38. This terminology is taken from J. D. Marshall, 'Colonisation as a factor in the planting of towns in north-west England', in H. J. Dyos ed., *The Study of Urban History*, London, 1968, pp. 215–30.
39. G. Clark ed., *The Industries of Ulster: Present and Prospective*, Belfast, 1882, p. 9.
40. Conrad Gill, *Rise of Irish Linen Industry*, p. 325; E. R. R. Green, *The Lagan Valley*, pp. 112–23.
41. The indispensable reference here is W. E. Coe, *The Engineering Industry of the North of Ireland*, Newton Abbot, 1969, pp. 22–8, 46–76. See also W. A. McCutcheon, *Industrial Archaeology of Northern Ireland*, pp. 299, 301–2.
42. O. N. Greeves, *The Effects of the American Civil War on the Linen and Wool Textile Industries of the UK*, unpublished Ph.D. thesis, University of Bristol, 1968–9, p. 26.
43. This had also been a problem for Ulster cotton manufacturers. For an example see James Boomer to John Todd, 11 September 1827, and James Boomer to William Henry, 8 October 1827, *Out-letter Book of James Boomer and Co.*, PRONI D2450/2/1.
44. *Belfast Linen Trade Circular*, 25, 6 August 1852; *Belfast Commercial Chronicle*, 22 January 1853.
45. See Boyle, *Economic Development*, p. 96.
46. On the size of integrated mills in the British cotton industry after 1850 see C. H. Lee, 'The cotton textile industry' in Roy Church ed., *The Dynamics of Victorian Business*, London, 1980, p. 173.
47. *Secret Committee of the House of Lords on Commercial Distress 1848*, Q.7298.
48. *Belfast Linen Trade Circular*, 205, 18 January 1856.
49. F. W. Smith, *The Irish Linen Trade Handbook and Directory*, Belfast, 1876, pp. 98–9.
50. *Belfast Linen Trade Circular*, 453, 7 January 1861.
51. *Belfast Linen Trade Circular*, 505, 6 January 1862.
52. B. R. Mitchell and Phyllis Deane, *Abstract of British Historical Statistics*, Cambridge, 1971, pp. 202–3.

53. See in particular W.O. Henderson, *The Lancashire Cotton Famine 1861–5*, Manchester, 1934; Anthony Slaven, *The Development of the West of Scotland 1750–1960*, London, 1975, pp.108–9.

54. *Northern Whig*, 2 June 1865, quoted in N.W. Todd, *A Social and Economic Study of Part of South County Antrim in the Second Half of the Nineteenth Century*, unpublished M.A. thesis, Queen's University Belfast, 1975, p.133. This excellent study contains a massive amount of useful information on this interesting and industrially diverse area.

55. Boyle, *Economic Development*, pp.97ff.

56. *BCC Annual Report*, 15 January 1864.

57. Greeves, *Impact of American Civil War*, pp.431–2.

58. *Belfast Linen Trade Circular*, 610, 11 January 1864.

59. The boom of the early 1870s and subsequent downturn are described in *Belfast Linen Trade Circular*, 976, 16 January 1871; 1,029, 22 January 1872; 1,081, 20 January 1873; 1,185, 18 January 1875.

60. Exports of United Kingdom fine linens to the United States held up well between 1870 and 1914. See S.B. Saul, *Studies in British Overseas Trade 1870–1914*, Liverpool, 1960, pp.157–9.

61. Estimated from figures in Phyllis Deane and W.A. Cole, *British Economic Growth 1688–1959*, 2nd edn., Cambridge, 1967, p.205.

62. *Linen Merchants' Association Annual Report*, 30 January 1883, p.13; 29 January 1884, p.20; PRONI D2088/17.

63. *Select Committee on Industries (Ireland)*, BPP 1884–5, IX, QQ.11731–47. In 1885 York Street's reserves amounted to £300,000.

64. Sir William Crawford, *Irish Linen and Some Features of its Production*, Belfast, 1910, p.9.

65. See Wilson, *Belfast: its trade and commerce*, p.39.

66. Alastair J. Durie, *The Scottish Linen Industry in the Eighteenth Century*, Edinburgh, 1979, p.168; R. Lloyd Patterson, 'The British flax and linen industry' in William Ashley ed., *British Industries*, London, 1903, pp.128–9.

67. Lloyd Patterson, 'Flax and linen', p.129.

68. Todd, *South County Antrim*, p.138; *Linen Merchants' Association Annual Reports*, 2 February 1906, p.8, 28 January 1914, p.10, PRONI D2088/17.

69. H.C. Lawlor, 'The Genesis of the linen thread industry – 3', *Fibres, Flax and Cordage*, March 1945, p.99, PRONI D1286, Box 1.

70. William Boyd to Messrs. Storey, Cowland and Hill, London, 3 September 1901, *Blackstaff Flax Spinning and Weaving Company, Secretary's Letter Book*, PRONI D2120/1/1.

71. Crawford, *Irish Linen*, p.9.

72. *Linen Merchants' Association Annual Report*, 26 January 1898, p.17, PRONI D2088/17.

73. Robert McCrum to James Girdwood, New York, 1 October 1895; *McCrum, Mercer and Watson Out-letter Book*, PRONI D2518/1.

74. For a complete set of statistics of cotton and linen yarn imports into Belfast between 1895 and 1913 *see Linen Merchants' Association Annual Reports*, cited above, n.68.

75. D. L. Armstrong, 'Social and economic conditions in the Belfast linen industry 1850–1900', *Irish Historical Studies*, VII, 1951, p. 240, contains figures for employment in linen mills and factories between 1850 and 1904; see also Boyle, *Economic Development*, p. 125.

76. Useful sources which contain much relevant detail on the difficulties of the late nineteenth century and recovery after 1905 are the *Letter Books of the Blackstaff Flax Spinning and Weaving Company*, PRONI D2120/1/1 and 2.

77. *Linen Merchants' Association Annual Report*, 5 February 1909, PRONI D2088/17.

78. H. C. Lawlor, 'The Barbours of Hilden', *Fibres and Flax Journal*, October 1942, PRONI D1286 Box 1. See also E. R. R. Green, 'Thomas Barbour and the American linen thread industry' in J. M. Goldstrom and L. A. Clarkson eds., *Irish Population, Economy and Society*, Oxford, 1981, p. 215.

79. Lloyd Patterson, 'Flax and linen', p. 143.

80. N. W. Todd, *South County Antrim*, p. 151.

81. H. C. Lawlor, 'The Ewarts of Belfast', *Fibres and Flax Journal*, April 1943, pp. 178–9, PRONI D1286, Box 1.

82. Duncan Bythell, *The Sweated Trades*, London, 1978, p. 73.

83. This account of shirtmaking relies on Bythell, *Sweated Trades*; 'The Derry shirtmaking industry' in W. P. Coyne ed., *Ireland Industrial and Agricultural*, Dublin, 1902, pp. 417–9; North-West Teachers Centre, *Shirtmaking in Derry*, Derry, nd; E. J. Riordan, *Modern Irish Trade and Industry*, London, 1920, pp. 122–3.

84. L. M. Cullen, *An Economic History of Ireland Since 1660*, London, 1972, p. 162.

85. See the articles on brewing and distilling in W. P. Coyne ed., *Ireland*, pp. 451–512. Descriptions of Ulster distilleries can be found in A. Barnard, *The Whisky Distilleries of the United Kingdom*, London, 1887, pp. 426ff.

86. *Select Committee on Irish Industries 1885*, Appendices 17 and 18, reprint letters from Ulster millers and grain merchants. See also Felicity Walton, 'Ulster milling through the ages', in W. M. Scott ed., *A Hundred Years A-Milling*, Dundalk, 1951, p. 136.

87. A useful local survey of these developments is E. R. R. Green, 'History of the Belfast grain trade', *Proceedings of the Belfast Natural History and Philosophical Society*, 2nd series, VIII (1971), pp. 38–47.

88. Riordan, *Trade and Industry*, p. 88.

89. Christine Shaw, 'The large manufacturing employers of 1907', *Business History*, XXV, 1983, p. 53.

90. Sidney Pollard and Paul Robertson, *The British Shipbuilding Industry 1870–1914*, Cambridge, Mass. 1979, pp. 49–52; Anthony Slaven, 'The shipbuilding industry' in Church, *Dynamics of Victorian Business*, pp. 107–25.

91. C. H. Oldham, 'The history of Belfast shipbuilding', *Journal of the Statistical and Social Inquiry Society of Ireland*, XII, 1911, p. 418.

92. *Belfast Evening Telegraph*, 15 June 1950.
93. Anthony Marmion, *The Ancient and Modern History of the Maritime Ports of Ireland*, 4th edn., London, 1860, pp. 341–8. See also James Bird, *The Major Seaports of the United Kingdom*, London, 1963, ch. 4.
94. S. Pollard, *An Economic History of British Shipbuilding 1870–1914*, unpublished Ph.D. thesis, University of London, 1951, p. 133.
95. H. J. Dyos and D. H. Aldcroft, *British Transport*, London, 1974 edn., p. 248.
96. S. Pollard, 'British and world shipbuilding 1890–1914: a study in comparative costs', *Journal of Economic History*, XVII, 1957, p. 432.
97. Dennis Rebbeck, *The History of Iron Shipbuilding on the Queen's Island up to July 1874*, unpublished Ph.D. thesis, Queen's University of Belfast, 1950, p. 199.
98. Roy Anderson, *White Star*, Prescot, 1964, p. 42.
99. Pollard, *British Shipbuilding*, p. 365.
100. Laurence Dunn, *Famous Liners of the Past Belfast Built*, London, 1964, p. 26.
101. Clark, *Industries of Ulster*, pp. 26–7.
102. *Belfast Evening Telegraph*, 12 February 1944.
103. Pollard, *British Shipbuilding*, p. 67.
104. Shaw, 'The large manufacturing employers of 1907', p. 55, n. 22.
105. *The Shipbuilder*, VI, 1911, p. 7.
106. Dunn, *Famous Liners*, p. 13.
107. Workman Clark (1928) Ltd., *Shipbuilding at Belfast*, Belfast, 1934, p. 59.
108. *Shipbuilding at Belfast*, p. 8.
109. *The Industries of Ireland. Part I: Belfast and the Towns of the North*, London, 1891, p. 71.
110. Wilson, 'Belfast', p. 46; *idem*, 'The shipbuilding industry in Belfast', *Proceedings of the Belfast Natural History and Philosophical Society*, 1915–16, p. 28. Large liner companies had the resources to order in time of recession and so helped to steady the output of yards which built for them; Pollard and Robertson, *Shipbuilding Industry*, p. 85. The White Star Line maintained its earnings per gross ton in the often difficult trading conditions of the nineteenth century and was thus able to sustain its orders with Harland and Wolff. On White Star see Dyos and Aldcroft, *British Transport*, pp. 258, 279, 287.
111. Harland and Wolff's output was abnormally low in 1904 because of the changeover to electricity as well as other modernisation schemes, and in 1909 when three berths were cleared to form two massive berths to commence work on Olympic and Titanic. Pollard, *British Shipbuilding*, p. 78, n. 1.
112. See in particular the seminal work of B. L. Anderson, 'The attorney and the early capital market in Lancashire' in J. R. Harris ed., *Liverpool and Merseyside: Essays in the Economic and Social History of the Port and its Hinterland*, London, 1969; M. Miles, 'The money market in the early industrial revolution: the evidence from West Riding attorneys c. 1750–1800', *Business History*, XXIII, 1981.

113. For further examples of the attorney's role see Philip Ollerenshaw, *The Belfast Banks 1820–1900*, unpublished Ph.D. thesis, University of Sheffield, 1982, pp. 5–7.

114. J. W. Gilbart, 'On the laws of currency in Ireland', *Journal of the Statistical Society*, XVI, 1852, p. 319.

115. 'The Agricultural Bank of Ireland', *Bankers' Magazine*, III, 1845, pp. 200–6; IV, 1845, pp. 280–5.

116. Joel Mokyr, *Why Ireland Starved*, London, 1983, p. 186.

117. *Select Committee on Banks of Issue*, BPP 1875, IX, QQ. 3459–60. On the instability of banks in England and Wales see P. L. Cottrell, *Industrial Finance 1830–1914*, London, 1980, p. 16.

118. For more discussion of late nineteenth-century bank lending see Ollerenshaw, *Belfast Banks*, pp. 170–93, 262–91, 314–35, 347–51.

119. A convenient brief survey is F. S. L. Lyons, *Ireland Since the Famine*, London, 1971, pp. 706–14.

120. Sidney Pollard, *The Development of the British Economy 1914–67*, London, 1969, p. 3.

CHAPTER THREE

TRANSPORT, 1820–1914

W. A. McCutcheon

Between 1820 and 1914 Ulster experienced a revolution in internal transport which was more fundamental and far-reaching than anything experienced either before or since. By 1914 Ulster had become the most intensively industrialised part of Ireland. Thus while there were large areas such as the Antrim moorlands, the Sperrin uplands and the mountains of south Down and south Armagh which remained sparsely populated and little changed, the effects of large scale industrialisation in the lower Lagan valley and to a lesser extent in the Derry catchment and in and around many of the old-established market towns were reflected in a remarkable expansion of population and services. One of the most vital of these services was improved communications which can be seen as both a result of a series of fundamental changes in social and economic activity which had occurred since 1830 and also as a potent force moulding and, to an extent, controlling the development of industry and the distribution of population as these had emerged during the second half of the nineteenth century.

This chapter considers how facilities for the internal movement of both freight and passenger traffic changed during the period under review, comments briefly on the complementary development of harbour facilities and shipping services to and from a number of Ulster ports, and analyses the relationship between developing transport services and the economic infrastructure of that part of Ireland which in the nineteenth century had assumed a character very different from that encountered elsewhere on the island – a character more akin in many ways to that of corresponding areas of northern England and central Scotland.

Roads

In Ulster, as elsewhere, the oldest and most basic form of overland movement was by foot or on horseback along forest paths and trackways. There was to some slight extent a rudimentary road system from early times but the greater part of the country was quite devoid of such highways. Until the subjugation and 'planting' of Ulster in the sixteenth and early seventeenth centuries internal commercial intercourse was very slight and 'passenger traffic' consisted almost entirely of warring parties of one sort or another or, to a lesser extent, the movement of clerics, monks and scribes making their way perilously from one monastic retreat to another.[1]

As a result of various external influences in the early seventeenth century, including the establishment of an Irish parliament in Dublin, the importance of improving internal communications throughout the island was recognised. As early as 1613 an act was passed in Dublin which made Ireland independent of Britain in the matter of road making and repair.[2] This paved the way for the remarkable and sustained development of roads throughout the country. In 1780 that seasoned traveller, Arthur Young, remarked with some surprise that '... for a country so very far behind us as Ireland to have got suddenly so much the start on us in the article of roads is a spectacle that cannot fail to strike the English traveller exceedingly... .'[3]

During the period 1613 to 1765 the construction and maintenance of Irish roads was basically the responsibility of the parish, operating a system of direct statutory labour, but by about 1750 this *modus operandi* had already shown its inadequacy in coping with the demands of a developing economy.[4] This was particularly the case in Ulster where the system of statutory labour imposed by the parish vestry could be extremely disruptive in a prosperous economy based on the twin pillars of agriculture and linen.[5] An act[6] of 1765 formally established the County Grand Juries as the principal road-building agencies in the country. These replaced the parochial involvement in major schemes of road and bridge construction and maintenance which had been in operation since 1613 with a system which permitted a wider degree of planning co-operation and skilled supervision through professional and semi-professional overseers. This 'present-ment' system, as it was called[7] from the statutory function of the Grand Jury to 'present' or levy '... such sum or sums of money, as they shall think fit, upon any barony or baronies in such county for the repairing old roads or making new roads through such barony or baronies ...' was by no means flawless. Between 1765 and 1898, however, when the Local Government (Ireland) Act ended the Grand Juries' responsibilities in all matters connected with road and bridge construction, it was the foundation on which the excellent reputation of Ireland's road network was largely based. In Ulster, it was in no small measure due to the relative efficiency of the presentment system (formally introduced in 1765 but foreshadowed as early as 1710) that the local road network advanced so rapidly in little over a century.[8]

The actual method of operation has been described elsewhere,[9] but pertinent in the present context is the calculation that between 1770 and 1890 over 70 per cent of the Ulster road network was made or modified under presentment, with contracts growing larger and more ambitious as the nineteenth century progressed and the demands of an increasing volume of vehicular traffic, as yet of course entirely horse-drawn, intensified in both the commercial (freight) and passenger sectors.

Side by side with the presentment system there existed in Ulster a few important turnpike roads. These were constructed by 'trusts' or private companies statutorily established to build and maintain important roads by means of funds which the trusts were empowered to collect in the form of tolls or dues at the various gates or 'turnpikes' along the line of the road. In Ulster the first turnpike roads appeared in the 1730s and the system lasted through until the 1850s when it was finally stifled by the spread of the railways, many lines being built in direct and deliberate competition for the lucrative traffic hitherto moving slowly and laboriously along the parallel turnpikes close by.[10] The quickening pace of industry, too, was intolerant of this leisurely system of organised road transportation and there were frequent and bitter complaints in the Belfast area of both the exorbitant demands of the turnpike trusts in their collection of tolls and of the slowness and interruption of traffic resulting from the system of collection itself. The condition of the turnpike roads in Ulster was very variable and a great deal depended on the local landowner, who was usually the chairman of Trustees, and his engineer. The first northern turnpike, from Dundalk to Newry, Banbridge, Dromore, Hillsborough, Lisburn and Belfast, was established in 1733; in 1858 the last turnpike, from Antrim to Ballymena, Ballymoney and Coleraine, closed down. In both instances control of the important roads in question passed directly to the County Grand Juries who were in a position to maintain and improve such arterial roads under the presentment system already described, frequently with substantial financial assistance from the Irish Board of Public Works, founded in 1831.[11]

This governmental body was yet another road and bridge-building agency active in Ireland during the period under review.[12] It was to the Board of Works that Grand Juries now applied in the first instance for financial assistance in major schemes of road construction or extension, and the Government at Westminster usually accepted or rejected such proposals on the recommendations of the Board. There were few trunk roads in Ulster which were not improved or extended by the Board of Public Works in the nineteenth century, whilst new lines constructed under its direction or with substantial financial assistance included the great 'coast road' in County Antrim, from Larne to Ballycastle;[13] the roads from Ballycastle to Coleraine; Ballymoney to Cushendun; Fivemiletown to Clones; Strabane to Derry and Downpatrick to Strangford.[14]

From these various systems emerged a tightly-knit and effective network of trunk, main, secondary and tertiary roads serving northeast Ireland. A mesh of minor or tertiary distributive roads constitutes the initial matrix and reflects the prolonged role of the Irish parish during the seventeenth and early eighteenth centuries as the main agent of road construction and husbandry. On to this have been superimposed the main roads of the province which in many instances can be traced back to the period 1770–1850 when construction under the presentment system was at its peak. The demands of an expanding economy were reflected in numerous major schemes of road and bridge construction (often road realignment and bridge reconstruction) made necessary by the quickening pace of commercial intercourse and the increased movement of raw materials and manufactured goods from one part of the province to another. As the dominance of Belfast increased in relation to all other Ulster seaports – particularly after the major improvements carried out in the lower reaches of river Lagan in the 1840s, which afforded safe passage and adequate berthage to much larger vessels at all stages of the tide – so the role of the Lagan valley as a corridor of communication intensified. The turnpike roads, which provided the main arteries, were serviced by a network of secondary and distributive roads feeding into the main lines and linking many peripheral towns and villages with the more important market and linen manufacturing towns lying close to the river.[15]

This was a pattern repeated throughout the province, the more demanding requirements of horse-drawn traffic (as opposed to trains of pack horses) in regard to road alignment and gradient having a marked effect on the developing Ulster road network. Many of the older, higher roads constructed along or above the tree line in the eighteenth century were abandoned in favour of new alignments at lower levels which in their construction necessitated the use of Victorian steam technology and hundreds of men and horses to provide the earth-moving facility which the previous century had not possessed. Bridges were often rebuilt to handle increased loads and provide wider and safer carriageways, while the relative importance of wayside inns declined with the coming of the railway age and the greater speed of the last coaching services operating int he 1830s and 1840s.[16] The Ulster landscape was opened up as never before to a new breed, the itinerant tourist. Major schemes such as the construction of the remarkable coast road in County Antrim, running along a reinforced raised beach platform from Larne northwards to Cushendall and thence up over the moors by Loughaveema to Ballycastle, or the noteworthy and distinctive reconstruction of the main street in Banbridge in response to the demands of an increasing traffic in both goods and passengers between Dublin and Belfast, were commented on at length by English visitors and tourists.[17]

For a time road and rail transport services existed in many areas side by side, but from about 1860 the role of the expanding railway network became of major importance in the internal movement of both goods and passengers. The condition and relative importance of the province's roads deteriorated steadily until the 1920s and 1930s when the introduction of regular and motorised road services highlighted the neglect which had attended the road system from the later nineteenth century.

Inland waterways

The system of inland waterways used for commercial navigation focused on Lough Neagh, the largest freshwater lake in the British Isles. Lough Neagh was linked to the open sea by lowland corridors in which natural waterways and relatively level terrain prompted canal construction from an early date. In fact, the first canal to be built in the province, from Newry up to Whitecoat Point on the Upper Bann just south of Portadown, was the earliest true summit level navigation of the canal era, antedating both the Sankey Cut at St. Helens and the Bridgewater Canal at Manchester by nearly twenty years. It was completed and opened in 1742.

The Newry Canal was soon followed by the Lagan Navigation

which was begun in 1756, reached Lisburn in 1763, but was not completed through to Lough Neagh until 1794. The Tyrone Navigation, including the tub-boat canal extension usually referred to as Ducart's Canal, was built over a protracted period (1733–87) specifically to ease the outward movement of coal from the developing coalfield around Coalisland in east Tyrone to Lough Neagh, Newry and (ultimately by coastwise shipment) to Dublin. Later the Ulster Canal was built (1825–42) as a major link in a great composite waterway across Ireland, from Belfast to Limerick. It connected Lough Neagh and the river Blackwater with Upper Lough Erne. Finally, the course of the Lower Bann was made navigable from Lough Neagh to the sea beyond Coleraine in the mid-nineteenth century (1847–58) under the Irish Board of Public Works. The only other artificial navigation of any commercial importance in Ulster was the short Strabane Canal built in the 1790s as part of the Foyle navigation system. This linked the quays at Derry with the important market town of Strabane and the adjoining county town of Lifford, across the river in Donegal.[18]

By 1860 the commercial importance of these canals had already been thrown into considerable doubt, for a variety of reasons. With the failure of the Tyrone coalfield to develop, the Newry and Tyrone navigation systems were robbed of their fundamental *raison d'être*. Traffic being carried was by then but a pale shadow of what had been expected when the waterways were built. Even with the construction of a new and much larger ship canal below the town, opened in 1850, Newry was rapidly falling behind Belfast, which was already siphoning off much of the traffic formerly using the inland canal southwards from Portadown. The Lagan Canal, especially the lower (older) section from Belfast up to Lisburn and Sprucefield, maintained a position of modest commercial importance but the unexpected success of the Ulster Railway in carrying a wide range of goods traffic and coal up and down the valley was already robbing the waterway of a great deal of the type of cargo for which water transport is usually considered ideal. The fact was that in the Lagan valley, and even in the Lough Neagh basin as a whole, the distances involved were too short in economic terms to enable barge traffic to maximise its basic advantages, that is, the slow uninterrupted movement of large quantities of heavy, bulky raw materials and fuel over considerable distances. On the Lagan Canal this applied particularly to the upstream movement of coal, grain, and a wide range of imported raw materials. Furthermore, the absence of a steady and substantial coal export from beyond Lough Neagh meant that to an increasing extent the downstream cargoes consisted of agricultural produce, building sand and gravel, native timber and to a lesser degree bricks, tiles and fireclay goods moving across the southern waters of Lough Neagh from Maghery to Ellis's Gut, near Aghalee. The canal linking Belfast with the hinterland of the Lagan valley and the Lough Neagh basin beyond became increasingly a relatively unimportant appendage to the city's growing commercial infrastructure – a picturesque relic of a more leisurely age, though it still continued to carry modest tonnages until 1914. Increasing rail and (later) road competition over the short hauls of the Lagan valley, a general slowness of transit, and a sustained hostility from the powerful industrialists along the river who regarded the canal company as something of a threat in its competing demands for limited water resources (particularly in the Lisburn-Belfast section) all contributed to its continuing difficulties.[19]

The Ulster Canal was nothing short of a commercial disaster. It was completed in 1842 as an extended (forty-six mile) link in the great line of inland navigation across Ireland from Belfast to the Shannon and Limerick. Seen at the time as a northern rival to the Grand and Royal Canals to the south, the Ulster Canal was constructed to Thomas Telford's general design in the fashion of many of his later canals. These tended to be more direct and less influenced by the vagaries of terrain than the earlier waterways of the canal era, epitomised in the work of James Brindley. This was largely due to the need to avoid costly and time-wasting deviations from a direct line whenever a canal was being built close to parallel and competing lines of road and rail transport, as many of these later canals were bound to be. The Ulster Canal was certainly direct, but the cardinal error made in its construction, and from which it never recovered, was that many of its locks were much too narrow to take the lighters from the chief 'feeder' navigations to the east, the Newry and Lagan, thereby necessitating a laborious transhipment of cargoes at Charlemont or Maghery. Rail competition from the extended Ulster Railway (Armagh-Monaghan-Clones), a frequent severe shortage of water on the higher levels, and the total failure of the Ballinamore and Ballyconnell Canal (beyond Upper Lough Erne) to provide an effective link through to the headwaters of the river Shannon – all these factors led to its rapid commercial eclipse and relatively early closure.[20]

While the improvements effected by the Board of Public Works on

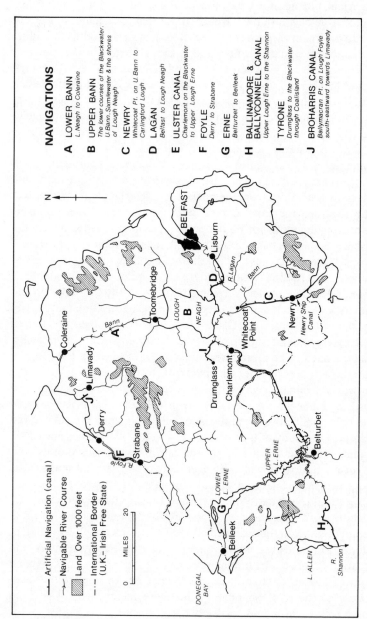

NAVIGATIONS

A LOWER BANN
L.Neagh to Coleraine

B UPPER BANN
The lower courses of the Blackwater.
U.Bann, Sixmilewater & the shores
of Lough Neagh

C NEWRY
Whitecoat Pt. on U.Bann to
Carlingford Lough

D LAGAN
Belfast to Lough Neagh

E ULSTER CANAL
Charlemont on the Blackwater
to Upper Lough Erne

F FOYLE
Derry to Strabane

G ERNE
Belturbet to Belleek

H BALLINAMORE &
BALLYCONNELL CANAL
Upper Lough Erne to the Shannon

I TYRONE
Drumglass to the Blackwater
through Coalisland

J BROHARRIS CANAL
Ballymacran Pt. on Lough Foyle
south-eastward towards Limavady

Map 2   Canals and navigable waterways of Ulster

— + — Artificial Navigation (canal)

∿ Navigable River Course

▨ Land Over 1000 feet

– – – International Border
(U.K.– Irish Free State)

0 ___ 20
MILES

116

the Blackwater, Upper and Lower Bann, and Lough Neagh in the mid-nineteenth century did for a time stimulate local traffic, they came much too late to fulfil the glowing expectations which had existed at the outset. Lough Neagh had for long been of great importance in linking east Tyrone, south Derry and north Armagh with the Lagan valley, providing opportunities for the movement of population and economic contact,[21] but the rapid growth of lines of rail communication throughout the Lough Neagh basin between 1850 and 1870 soon resulted in the orientation of the entire area towards the expanding port and manufacturing centre of Belfast.

Finally, let us consider the Erne Navigation and the Foyle Navigation. The former, implemented piecemeal between 1842 and 1891, provided a continuous, elongated navigation channel through the lakes from Belleek by Enniskillen to Belturbet; the latter consisted of ten miles of navigable river channel upstream from the Derry quays and a short four-mile cut thence up to an extensive basin in the prosperous market town of Strabane on the Abercorn estates. Both were of limited commercial importance. The Strabane Canal was of direct utility to the town it served and contributed substantially to its commercial and industrial vigour throughout the nineteenth century, albeit under increasing competition from both broad (5 ft 3 in.) and narrow (3 ft) gauge railways. The Erne Navigation, however, was merely an elongated navigational facility of some fifty-two miles, with a number of isolated rural landing slips and quays along the shores of the upper and lower lakes. It was never of any great economic significance.[22]

Railways

Construction of the Ulster canal system began in 1733 and finished in 1858. Chronologically the canals were succeeded by the railways as the principal arteries of commerce and internal population movement. In both absolute and relative terms, however, the railways were of far greater significance and dominated the local transport scene from 1850 until 1925. Their construction may be considered in three phases. First there was the initial surge between 1837 and 1860 when the main trunk lines were built (often piecemeal and by several distinct companies which subsequently amalgamated), linking principal centres of population and following natural routeways in the physical landscape. Secondly, from 1860 to 1880, there was the infill of this basic grid with numerous branch lines. Quite a number of these were of less sound economic justification, being frequently constructed to satisfy the social aspirations or business ambitions of local landlords. Many landlords held positions of influence on the boards of parent companies and sought to extend their spheres of influence into virgin territory or to thwart the efforts of rival interests by gaining access to potentially lucrative rail-heads, port catchments of growing importance, or expanding watering places. Finally, and this was a distinctly Irish phenomenon, there developed a widespread and significant railway system constructed on the narrow-gauge principle of 3 ft gauge track (as opposed to the standard Irish gauge of 5 ft 3 in., itself in fact a broad gauge compared with the normal British gauge of 4 ft 8½ in.). Narrow-gauge lines in many instances formed adjuncts to the three major rail systems which had already emerged in Ulster by the time the first narrow-gauge lines were built. The narrow-gauge lines were constructed between 1872 and 1909 and were in many ways closely comparable with the tub-boat canals of the previous century, seeking out rich but relatively inaccessible mineral deposits in the uplands of County Antrim, advancing into sparsely populated but scenically spectacular areas of County Donegal at a time when such places were becoming of increasing importance to visiting tourists, and serving isolated but productive agricultural areas like the farmlands of the Clogher valley and the Leitrim valleys and foothills which were enabled thereby to provide increasing quantities of agricultural produce and greater numbers of livestock for the growing populations of the province's towns and cities.[23]

This third phase included a few lines which in an Irish context are usually referred to as 'light' railways, though they were in fact built by government on the broad gauge into the remotest and most picturesque corners of the country in an attempt to bring some economic improvement to those 'congested districts' where there were few natural resources worthy of commercial exploitation.[24]

The remarkable development of the railway network in north-east Ireland between 1839 and 1922 can be seen in Map 3. It is difficult to grasp the impact and dominance of the railways in the internal transport network of late nineteenth century Ulster. The railway era began in 1839 with the opening of the seven and a half mile Belfast-Lisburn line. This was the first section of the Ulster Railway (Belfast-Lisburn-Portadown-Armagh completed in 1848). By the end of the century the railway network (both broad and narrow gauge) totalled approximately a thousand miles, much of it double track, and had

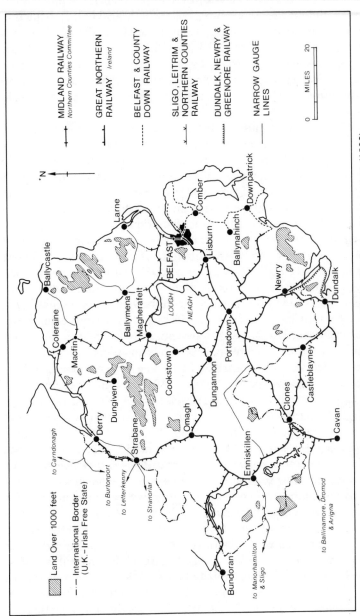

Map 3   Railway network of Northern Ireland at its greatest extent (1922)

Land Over 1000 feet

— — International Border
(U.K.–Irish Free State)

MIDLAND RAILWAY
Northern Counties Committee

GREAT NORTHERN
RAILWAY *Ireland*

BELFAST & COUNTY
DOWN RAILWAY

SLIGO, LEITRIM &
NORTHERN COUNTIES
RAILWAY

DUNDALK, NEWRY &
GREENORE RAILWAY

NARROW GAUGE
LINES

0   MILES   20

N

Ballycastle

Larne

Coleraine

Macfin

Ballymena

Magherafelt

BELFAST

Comber

Lisburn

Ballynahinch

Downpatrick

LOUGH NEAGH

Cookstown

Portadown

Newry

Dundalk

Dungiven

Derry

Strabane

Omagh

Dungannon

Clones

Castleblayney

Cavan

Enniskillen

Bundoran

to Carndonagh

to Burtonport

to Letterkenny

to Stranorlar

to Manorhamilton
& Sligo

to Ballinamore, Dromod
& Arigna

reached to within five miles of over 90 per cent of the population. In the mid-nineteenth century, rail services quickly stifled the pre-existing horse-drawn road passenger services, though Bianconi continued to operate in west Ulster (Sligo to Letterkenny, Strabane and Enniskillen) well into the 1860s, at least. For the internal movement of passenger and goods traffic the railways had no effective competitor until the years immediately preceding the Second World War.[25]

Much of the capital for the early growth of the Ulster railway network was forthcoming in a remarkable flurry in the years of 'railway mania' (1844–45) when it has been estimated that some 80 per cent of all the capital authorised for Irish railways betwen 1825 and 1850 was invested in a deluge of unbridled enthusiasm.[26] As early as 1835 railway speculation increased sharply in Ireland – the only line then in operation was that from Dublin to Kingstown, opened the previous year – but of the twenty-six schemes sanctioned in that year only two, from Dublin to Drogheda and from Belfast to Armagh (the Ulster Railway) succeeded in raising capital from their lists of subscribers in the years immediately following. In the case of the Ulster Railway, the original directors were almost entirely local businessmen and included John McNeile of the Northern Bank and James Goddard of the Bank of Ireland, with the significant addition soon afterwards of a director specifically appointed to represent the shareholders of Merseyside and Manchester. When the company was floated in 1836 the shares, 12,000 of £50 each, were taken up rapidly in Liverpool and Manchester as well as in Belfast and Dublin.

The Ulster Railway was something of an exception in these difficult years of railway financing and apart from its extension beyond Lisburn to Lurgan and Portadown, reached in 1842, it was not until after the intense speculation of the mid-1840s that sufficient capital was forthcoming to ensure its completion to Armagh and also the construction of the nucleii of the other two railway systems which later came to dominate the north of Ireland – the lines from Belfast to Ballymena and from Belfast to Holywood. There was no real economic reason why construction of these lines should have been delayed well into the 1840s, during the difficult famine years, and one can but point to the intensity of the panic affecting the British stock market at this time to account for the rapidity with which Irish railway investment burgeoned during and immediately after the mania of 1844–45. By 1850 it has been estimated that on the Ulster Railway of £537,000 capital invested from private sources £510,000 was from Irish investors; on the Belfast and Ballymena Railway of £363,000 invested £190,000 was from Irish sources; and on the Belfast and County Down Railway of a capital of £156,000 some £90,000 represented Irish investment.[27]

Before the coming of the railways all goods which could not be carried on the person had to be transported by pack-horse train, by road wagon, by canal or navigable waterway, or in privately-owned cars or carts. The first of these was by its nature extremely limited in scale, unreliable in the face of adverse weather, and subject to the depredations of the countless roving vagabonds and footpads with whom the roads and tracks were infested in the seventeenth and eighteenth centuries.[28] The road wagon was a considerable advance in terms of the bulk and volume of goods which could be transported. However, while a few regular services were established (between Dublin and Belfast for example) it was a slow and laborious method of conveying goods and raw materials about the country and never attained any great significance in Ireland.[29] In this context the coming of the canals was a major step forward and the north of Ireland lent itself to their construction, with commercial arteries radiating from Lough Neagh towards Belfast, Newry, the Erne lowlands and the Shannon, the Coalisland area of east Tyrone, and the Lower Bann valley, Coleraine and the North Atlantic. However, the role of these canals was strictly limited in terms of the volume of goods they were capable of transporting. The industrial development which did occur in the late eighteenth and early nineteenth centuries, particularly in linen, was assisted by, but was by no means dependent on, the facilities which existed within the province for the conveyance by water of manufactured goods, raw materials and fuel. Thus, in 1777 it was estimated that land carriage was accounting for the greater proportion of goods moving about the country, the bulk of it in small lots of less than a ton being conveyed in two-wheeled cars.[30] Soon the Scotch or Scottish dray became important in Ulster, where linen was brought to the new markets in Belfast from numerous outlying bleachgreens, and carts returned with bleaching materials, woollen cloth and imported foodstuffs. The absence of any great areas of heavy manufacturing industry in the interior meant that during the early nineteenth century the canal barge, the two-wheeled car and an increasing number of larger Scotch carts between them accommodated the requirements of agriculture and at the same time catered for those

E

few dispersed centres of manufacturing industry which already existed in the province. As the Railway Commissioners noted in 1837, 'It (the inland traffic) is carried on for the most part by the common cars of the country at a very low rate — the charge not exceeding, on an average, 5*d* per ton per statute mile; and the average distance of carriage is not less than forty miles ...'[31] Within a few years the coming of the railways reduced all horse-drawn freight traffic on Irish roads to a subsidiary role, feeding to or distributing from railway stations.

The rapid spread of a railway network throughout the province in the mid-nineteenth century coincided with a remarkable surge forward in the general level of industrial production; from ports such as Derry, Coleraine, Larne, Belfast, Newry, and Dundalk imported coal was rapidly conveyed to the mills and factories of the interior, with a wide variety of manufactured goods and agricultural produce channelled back through these ports for export. The ports themselves developed a new industrial vitality though, as we shall see, the relative commercial importance of some which were located at the head of tidal river estuaries declined as the average size of vessels increased.

In the earlier phases of railway development the actual construction of the lines provided employment for thousands of itinerant labourers and tenant farmers, labouring on the railways being for many an alternative to idleness and poverty and for others to the seasonal demands of the domestic linen manufacture.[32] Once a line was built there was an immediate effect on the countryside through which it passed and the towns and villages which it served. Railway work had a certain prestige value (rather similar to the current regard for airline employemnt, in whatever capacity) and in the second half of the nineteenth cetury there was great competition even for unskilled railway jobs, which it was quickly recognised had the one great advantage of relative security of tenure. There were also sickness benefits, widows' pensions, company houses and, not least, the possibilities of promotion.

Travel times were suddenly reduced to a fraction of what they had been in the pre-railway era and manufacturers were enabled to import supplies of fuel and raw materials more quickly and with greater regularity (though not necessarily more cheaply) than hitherto, with a complementary expansion of distributing and marketing horizons.[33] Farmers could buy bulky feedstuffs, fertilisers and heavy machinery more easily and sell their produce in markets hitherto lying beyond the range of perishable products of the land. The countryside was opened up to visitors and tourists to a degree unknown in the days of travel by pack horse, post chaise, stagecoach or canal fly boat.[34] Taking the waters at coastal resorts became fashionable in Ulster, as elsewhere, and the scenic gradeur of the Antrim coast in particular soon encouraged the railway company serving the area (from 1870 the Belfast and Northern Counties Railway Company, with headquarters at York Road) to develop special services and excursions to cater for the curious visitor and local tourist alike. The rapid growth of a variety of industry in many Ulster towns and villages was both a reflection of the improved transport facilities provided by the railway and a further stimulus to seasonal passenger traffic to resorts and excursion places like Bundoran, Portrush, Bangor and Newcastle.

In social terms the sudden, dramatic increase in speed of communications was quickly accepted and the railways soon came to play an important role in determining subsequent movements of population within the province. As the lower Lagan valley and Belfast emerged rapidly as the industrial and commercial nucleus of Ulster so the three railway companies operating from the city − the Great Northern Railway Company (Ireland), the Belfast and Northern Counties Railway Company and the Belfast and County Down Railway Company − contributed to an increasing extent to the internal migration of population into that relatively small area, a movement which had begun in the pre-railway era and had gathered momentum throughout the first half of the nineteenth century. In this general eastward drift of population the railways provided the means by which wage earners, and subsequently whole families, could be drawn permanently from rural areas to the new industrial growth and its associated urban spread of high-density terrace housing so typical of Ballymacarrett, Sandy Row and the Falls, Shankill, Crumlin and Oldpark areas of Belfast. It is a recognised fact in Ulster society that in countless Belfast households of the middle and artisan class there is very often but one, at most two generations separating the heads of household from their roots in the Ulster countryside. In many cases it was the railways which provided the initial contact between rural and urban lifestyles and subsequently led to the permanent migration of population on a major scale.

In other ways, too, the railway was a great liberator, enabling more people to live in country areas or in market towns within easy travelling distance of places of employment in the city. The commuter emerged as a direct result of the alteration in space/time relationships made possible by the introduction of specific railway services. Outside the lower Lagan valley it is simplistic to assume a straightforward link between the coming of the railways and a demographic shift from country to town. Some towns benefited markedly from the arrival of this new and revolutionary means of travel and conveyance, others did not − or at least not to anything like the same extent. In other words, the railways enhanced and improved population mobility and migration throughout Ulster in general, but apart from the Lagan valley and Belfast did not necessarily determine the direction of that movement.

In some areas of the province the railways performed quite specific functions. During the last quarter of the nineteenth century, for example, narrow-gauge lines were built solely to facilitate the extraction of valuable minerals (iron ore and bauxite) from the inter-basaltic horizons of the Antrim plateau or to convey intrepid tourists to the Antrim glens and coast, where the remarkable hydro-electric tramway or road railway from Portrush to the Giant's Causeway, opened in 1883, became an international tourist attraction in its own right. In County Donegal, the Donegal Railway Company and the Londonderry and Lough Swilly Railway Company penetrated the mountain fastnesses of Ireland's rugged north-western corner. Here the little red and yellow trains were dwarfed by the magnificence of the Barnesmore Gap, and the rugged grandeur and operational difficulties of the Burtonport extension underlined the fact that in such terrain steam railways were being worked at the very limit of their capacity. At the other end of the province the great flax-spinning mills at Bessbrook erected by the Richardson family earlier in the century were linked to the port of Newry in 1885 by a short hydro-electric railway powered by water turbines in a former flour mill along the three-mile route. As with many Ulster mills and factories − Dickson of Dungannon, Herdman of Sion Mills, Andrews of Comber, for example − a railway siding ran right into the works and rail transport played a vital role over many years in providing direct transport links to and from the nearest port.

Each of the three main railway companies operating from Belfast made determined efforts to develop tourist facilities in the areas which it served, with Bundoran and Warrenpoint (GNR), Portrush (BNCR) and Bangor and Newcastle (BCDR) emerging as the principal watering places. At Bundoran, Warrenpoint, Portrush and Newcastle the railway company concerned either built or acquired and greatly extended a large hotel and used this as a focal point for a whole range of special tourist services and excursion fares. Bangor was somewhat different in that proximity to Belfast soon resulted in the emergence of a dual role, as both tourist resort and dormitory town, though even in its tourist function it catered more extensively for the Belfast day trippers who for some years at the beginning of the twentieth century could make at least part of their journey by paddle steamer. All five towns developed in similar fashion, with tall grey or painted stucco late Victorian terraces lining the seafront within walking distance of the railway terminus to cater for the seasonal influx of visitors. A central commercial core developed in each case, consisting of a tasteless and bizarre sprawl of souvenir shops, tea rooms, amusement arcades and public houses.

It should not be forgotten that even after the lines were built and opened, subsequent amalgamations combined with growing commercial success to release funds which were frequently used in part to replace inadequate public accommodation. This programme of replacement and extension continued throughout the period 1870 to 1914 and brought a great deal of employment to the Ulster construction industry.[35] Line features such as viaducts, bridges, embankments, cuttings, culverts and tunnels were quite often replaced as trains became heavier, and prosperous lines were provided with double track, the work involved often benefiting the local engineering industry in Belfast, Newry, Dundalk and Derry.

The prosperity of the railways was reflected in sustained dividends which were well above the Irish average. On the Ulster Railway profits rose rapidly and by the early 1870s dividends of 5 and 6 per cent, declared twice yearly, were possible from total annual receipts of over £200,000. In the years immediately preceding the amalgamation of 1875–76 when the Great Northern Railway Company (Ireland) was formed by the merger of four smaller companies of which the 'Ulster' was one, the financial prosperity of the latter was such that it was the last to surrender its independence and then only on an assurance that its Ordinary stock would be valued at a premium of 24·5 per cent compared with that of the recently formed Northern Railway Company. While dividends on the GNR(I) fell somewhat in the years immediately following 1876 due to massive capital expenditure on processes of standardisation, improvement and modernisation, by 1890 and through until 1910 an uninterrupted twice yearly dividend of 6½ per cent on all ordinary shares was maintained and the company was regarded as one of the most prosperous in Ireland.

The Belfast and Ballymena Railway Company became the Belfast and Northern Counties Railway Company in 1862, a title more in keeping with its ultimate extent, and a high level of prosperity was maintained right through the remainder of the nineteenth century until its absorption into the Midland Railway Company of England in 1903. Dividends payable half yearly on ordinary shares during the period 1850–1900 were as follows:

1850	2½ per cent	1880	4⅛ per cent
1855	4½ per cent	1885	2¾ per cent
1860	4½ per cent	1890	5¼ per cent
1865	4¼ per cent	1895	5¾ per cent
1870	5 per cent	1900	5¼ per cent
1875	7¼ per cent		

The terms by which the powerful Midland Railway Company acquired the BNCR in 1903 reflect the latter's prosperity at the time, and immediately increased the value of the Belfast company's debentures by £36,000, of its 4 per cent preference shares by £34,000, of its 3 per cent preference shares by £3,000 and of its ordinary shares by some £150,000.

On the County Down system, a much smaller network of some eighty miles which enjoyed the twin advantages of serving some of the most productive agricultural land in Ireland and also an expanding population in the immediate environs of Belfast, the level of prosperity was also well above the Irish average. After a slow start when annual dividends were either passed or of the order of 1½–2 per cent, by the early 1880s the position was improving rapidly under a newly constituted board of directors. A steady dividend of between 5 and 6½ per cent was paid twice yearly from 1882 until the eve of the Great War some twenty years later. In the first decade of the twentieth century annual receipts per track mile had risen to the highest figure ($>£2,000$) for any Irish railway company while average fares per passenger mile ($1 \cdot 72d$, $1 \cdot 21d$ and $0 \cdot 80d$ single journey) were amongst the lowest. Over three-quarters of the total receipts of this company were now coming from passenger traffic.[36]

In Belfast the Central Railway, opened in 1875, linked the three main termini and in the years which followed thousands of cattle, sheep and pigs were brought to the acres of lairages at Maysfields alongside the railway to supply the extensive municipal abattoir which had been constructed close by. From the coal quays on the Down side of the river sidings led to the Lagan viaduct and thousands of tons of coal were distributed annually by rail throughout Ulster. From the grain silos flanking the harbour wheat and maize in particular were transported directly by rail to many inland locations (Coalisland, Lisburn, Ballymena, Portadown, Armagh, Cookstown) as the essential raw material for many large flour and provender mills which supplied the provincial bakeries and thousands of livestock farmers. In both these traffics − coal and grain − the railway to a large extent took over the role of the Lagan Navigation, though from both Belfast and Newry upstream barge traffic in coal and grain continued until the inter-war years.

Derry was unique in that it was served by four separate railway stations − the termini of four different railway systems, two broad-gauge and two narrow-gauge. The Waterside and Foyle Road stations were linked across the Foyle by the Carlisle Bridge, opened in 1863, and later both the Londonderry and Lough Swilly Railway to Buncrana, Cardonagh, Letterkenny and Burtonport and the Strabane-Derry line of the Donegal Railway Company were connected along the quays and across the river in a complex mixed-gauge system of conventional railway track and tramlines sunk into the quayside setts to avoid interruption to horse-drawn traffic.

At Strabane the broad-gauge track of the Great Northern Railway came into immediate contact with the narrow-gauge system of the Donegal Railway Company (from 1906 'The County Donegal Railways Joint Committee') with the lines from Letterkenny through Convoy and Lifford and from Stranorlar through Killygordon and Castlefinn converging in a large narrow-gauge complex alongside the Great Northern station. Strabane was at one time in direct contact by narrow-gauge railway with Derry, Letterkenny, Stranorlar, Donegal, Killybegs and Ballyshannon and the extensive railway complex on the western edge of the town was for many years a bustling centre of activity.

Portadown was another railway junction of prime importance in the Ulster railway network, with the main line from Belfast to Dublin passing through Macneill's impressive station at Watson Street before swinging away southwards over the flat lands of the Cusher-Bann confluence, crossing and recrossing the Newry Canal as both canal and railway sought and followed the easy gradients of the Poyntzpass glacial overflow channel. Through Portadown also passed the original Ulster Railway from Belfast to Armagh; in addition it was the point of divergence of the line to Dungannon and Omagh across the Sperrin uplands by Pomeroy and Sixmilecross. With additional significance as a river port linked with Lough Neagh by the Upper Bann Navigation and with Newry and Carlingford Lough down the inland canal by Scarva and Poyntzpass, it was a major centre of manufacture, marketing and trade throughout the period under consideration and a hub in the transport network of mid-Ulster.

Newry was a seaport of international importance in the eighteenth century and one of the chief trading towns in Ireland. In the nineteenth century its commercial links with the Lough Neagh basin and beyond, originally established with the construction of the inland canal in the 1730s, were greatly changed. Though the inland canal remained in use throughout the period under review its relative importance declined with the coming of the railways in the mid-nineteenth century. The first railway serving the town was the short six-mile line between Newry and Warrenpoint, which was completed in 1849. Newry lay some distance from the Portadown-Dundalk section of the main line from Belfast to Dublin, completed in 1852, but it was linked to this important artery soon afterwards with the construction of a line from Armagh, which intersected the main line at Goraghwood. In 1876 the town was connected with Greenore, Carlingford and Dundalk, while from 1885 it was linked with the important mill village of Bessbrook by a notable hydro-electric roadside railway. Railways passed through the town and along the canal quays to the Albert Basin and the new ship canal, opened in 1850, contributing to the commercial prosperity of a busy port with a substantial import traffic in coal and timber, grain, salt and chemicals.

Thus, the railways had brought increased commercial prosperity to a number of Ulster towns and ports and had made a sustained contribution to the great advance in industrial production and technological sophistication which occurred throughout the province during the period 1850–1910. Increased mobility of population and the coming of the electric telegraph led to a quicker and more efficient dissemination of information, while the internal distribution of fuel and raw materials from point of import was speeded up, marketing horizons were greatly widened, and new social patterns of work, residence and leisure were created in a relatively short space of time. The heyday of Ulster railways was undoubtedly around 1910 for although individual services were much improved in the inter-war years and amalgamations increased efficiency in a contracting network, never again did the railways make such a broad impact on economy and society.

Within a relatively brief period of little over half a century the developing technology of steam-powered locomotion had revolutionised Ulster's internal transport system and had boosted certain elements in its industrial economy — notably the linen industry and associated textile engineering, a variety of food processing based on native agriculture, the milling of imported grain, general engineering depending on imported raw materials and the export of finished products, and not least the overall pattern of agricultural production itself — to a position of great apparent stability and strength. It is inconceivable to think of this development without the sound transport base provided by the steam railways which reduced both horse-drawn transport and inland water transport to supporting roles.

However, within the north of Ireland as elsewhere the railway age was relatively short lived. The railways blossomed throughout the second half of the nineteenth century, reaching a peak in the Edwardian years, but the inability of the province to provide abundant and reliable traffic in minerals or in industrial and agricultural produce of a bulky, heavy nature, unsuited to road transport, and also the uneven demand for long-distance passenger traffic, were fundamental weaknesses which were concealed only by the absence of effective competition. Apart from the Belfast area there were no great industrial conurbations, no coalfields of importance, no great centres of population requiring frequent and reliable intercommunication, no great ports into whose hinterlands fast and efficient rail links were essential. Thus, when road transport emerged during the inter-war years its greater flexibility of service throughout an area of dispersed rural population and its ability to handle what goods and mineral traffic existed over the greater part of the province led to the rapid undermining of a substantial proportion of the railway network.

However in 1920 no such developments were foreseen and the extensive railway network in Ulster was confidently preparing to resume normal peace-time working, aided by substantial compensation payments made by government for the enforced disruption and operational difficulties resulting from the recent international conflict.[37]

Port improvement

A brief consideration of the role played by the principal ports – Derry, Coleraine, Larne, Belfast and Newry – is an integral part of the history of transport in Ulster. During the nineteenth century Belfast came to dominate this aspect of the province's economy to such an extent that only Derry and, to a lesser extent, Newry were able to compete for commercial traffic. Newry suffered from its 'inland' position as the average size of vessels increased, even after the completion in 1850 of the new ship canal connecting the Albert Basin in the centre of the town with the large Victoria Lock at Upper Fathom, at the head of commercial navigation in the estuary of the Newry (Clanrye) River. Below the lock the estuary widened towards Warrenpoint and Carlingford Lough but access to the ship canal for incoming steamers was limited to a relatively short time on either side of high water – and even then only for vessels of limited draught and tonnage. The same was true in reverse for steamships and coasters moving down the ship canal from Newry. As the nineteenth century progressed this tidal regime proved a considerable commercial handicap in terms of the expected re-emergence of Newry as a port of international importance. As early as the 1850s the average tonnage of vessels entering the port annually was around 120,000 compared with 150,000 for Derry and 575,000 for Belfast.[38] The failure of the Tyrone coalfield to provide a steady and substantial coal export down the inland canal from Lough Neagh, for coastwise shipment to Dublin, was a major disappointment, though this traffic was to an increasing extent replaced by a substantial coal import from Wales, Merseyside and Cumbria which moved inland by canal and more particularly by rail to the mills, factories and bleachgreens of south-central Ulster. However, with the rapid growth of Belfast after the major river improvements of the late 1840s and the remarkable commercial success of the Ulster Railway, from Belfast south-westwards by Lurgan and Portadown to Armagh, much of the traffic which hitherto might have moved southwards from Portadown, Armagh and Dungannon was siphoned off along the Lagan Navigation or the Ulster Railway to the head of Belfast Lough. Thus, for various reasons, while the commercial prosperity of Newry continued throughout the period, it was on a strictly limited scale and the port never again recovered the position of national importance which it had enjoyed in the pre-railway era.

The development of Larne was linked with attempts to establish a regular and reliable short sea route between Great Britain and Ireland to handle the Royal Mail in modern steam packets. At Portpatrick in Wigtownshire and at Donaghadee in County Down harbour works were carried out by the government of the day in the years following 1820, and a steam packet service introduced in March 1825 carrying mails, passengers and livestock.[39] The service proved unsuccessful and after a great deal of dissatisfaction and loss of public money it was eventually withdrawn in 1849. The railway from Newtownards to Donaghadee was completed between 1859 and 1861 and a further attempt was made, in 1865, to establish a regular steam packet service across the treacherous North Channel, with thousands of tons of rock cleared from the bed of Donaghadee harbour in an attempt to provide sufficient depth of water for the cross-channel steamers. However, the new service was short-lived and the entire scheme proved disastrous, since the Scottish railway company serving Portpatrick refused to carry the mails at the rate proposed by the Post Office, and heavy seas badly damaged the harbour at Portpatrick. As early as 1867 the more sheltered Larne-Stranraer route took the place of the ill-fated southerly crossing and henceforth the harbour at Larne was improved to handle an increasing size of passenger steamer, with both broad and narrow-gauge railways running right up to the quayside. Much was made of the shortest sea crossing between Ireland and Great Britain in the torrent of tourist literature and advertising poured out by the progressive Belfast and Northern Counties Railway Company in the years after 1870. In contrast, the 'grand harbour' at Donaghadee – built of Anglesea limestone between 1821 and 1837 to designs by the elder Rennie under the direction of his son – lapsed into a prolonged and continuing somnolence. There was for a time a short coal siding on the pier, running out from the terminus of the branch railway from Newtownards, and this was serviced by a steam crane, but for the greater part of its existence Rennie's masterpiece has provided anchorage for a few fishing boats, a renowned lifeboat, and a seasonal flotilla of assorted pleasure craft.

The development of Coleraine and of Portrush were closely related. Coleraine was an important and historic bridging town on the Lower Bann but in terms of modern commerce it was handicapped by the winding and hazardous river navigation below the town, and more particularly by the natural phenomenon of the sand bar across the mouth of the river caused by the interaction of tide and current where the outflow of fresh water comes up against the turbulent waters of the North Atlantic. In 1814 George Sampson recognised that:

'... several projects for improving the harbour at Coleraine had been suggested. A canal to pass from the dam behind the town to the road of Portrush. A railway to the same place to accompany the new line of road. A canal from the river near the Laughin-island to the above mentioned basin or dam. All of these have been spoken of but none of them has hitherto been much pressed upon the public attention not because the practical ability is doubtful but because the advantages are uncertain and the risk of course would be serious. ...'[40]

This proposal canal was felt to be needed because of the dangerous navigational approaches to the port of Coleraine by the 'bar mouth' and the lower estuary of the Bann, but when a major harbour was built at Portrush under John Rennie's direction between 1827 and 1836 – initially planned as an outport for Coleraine but soon enabling Portrush to become a major port in its own right – the need for such an inland navigation disappeared. With the coming of the railways in the late 1840s and early 1850s the proposal was never revived. The sand bar and lower reaches of the river Bann were much improved later in the century, between 1879 and 1884, with greater ease of access to and from the Coleraine quays situated immediately below the handsome new bridge completed in 1844. There was still, however, need for a river pilot based at the fishery harbour of Portstewart, across the bay.

The history and development of the province's two main ports – Derry and Belfast – is a theme the full development of which lies somewhat beyond the scope of this chapter. Both are river ports at the head of major sea loughs; both depended very substantially on the improvement of natural facilities for their importance as major centres for commercial shipping; both have long and distinguished histories in the fields of maritime commerce; and both have made major contributions to the industrial and commercial life of the cities of which they form an integral part. Belfast had the great advantage of being closer to and looking directly towards the pacemaker of Britain's industrial revolution – northern England and central Scotland – and took full advantage of a steady and prolonged interchange of men and ideas across what might be described as a technological continuum formed by the northern part of the Irish Sea, which continues to this day. Derry, on the other hand, was more remote and tended to export men, livestock and agricultural produce to Scotland, and further afield, importing coal, foreign timber, grain, chemicals and luxury goods. Derry's natural hinterland included a large part of County Donegal and though of great natural beauty it was a good deal poorer than that of Belfast in terms of both agriculture and indigenous industrial development. This fact was reflected in the industrial life of the city itself which did not attain the same level of development or diversity. Both cities were well served by railways and both had splendid natural waterways leading upstream to artificial navigations which penetrated deeply into their economic catchments. Both grew around important bridging points and both had comparable developments 'without the walls', as it were, on the opposite (east) bank of the river from the original, fortified nucleus.

At Belfast the development of the port and harbour is a story which effectively begins with the spectacular straightening of the course of the lower Lagan by William Dargan in the 1840s. This splendid feat of Victorian engineering not only increased overnight the commercial potential of the port but provided the essential elements in the physical environment which were subsequently utilised to such effect by the technical and entrepreneurial skills of Gustav Wolff, Edward Harland, William Pirrie and Charles Allan.[41] In Victorian Belfast the port *was* the town. By 1910 when the city reached the end of its period of maximum growth and in many respects the zenith of its commercial prosperity,[42] the role of the port and harbour was of vital importance: providing industry with a phenomenal range of raw materials, exporting the products of the city's rich and varied industrial establishment to all parts of the world, importing from Great Britain the essential supplies of coal which by now supported a wide range of steam-powered industrial activity in a province which was to a very large extent dependent on such imports, and providing a harbour estate in which one of the country's industrial giants, Harland and Wolff, was at the peak of its powers as shipbuilders to the world, then engaged on the construction of that remarkable trio of huge passenger liners *Olympic, Titanic* and *Britannic*. The Great War which broke out a few years later marked the end of an era, not only in shipbuilding and other industry, but in the general development of the Ulster economy.

Notes

1. J. H. Andrews, 'Road planning in Ireland before the railway age', *Irish Geography*, V, 1964, pp. 17–41; W. A. McCutcheon, 'Roads and bridges', *Ulster Folklife*, X, 1964, pp. 73–81.
2. 11–13 Jas I cap 7.
3. Arthur Young, *A Tour in Ireland in 1777 and 1778*, 2 vols., 1780: II, p. 39.
4. W. A. McCutcheon, *The Industrial Archaeology of Northern Ireland*, Belfast, 1980, pp. 1–2; J. T. Fulton, *The Roads of County Down 1600–1900*, unpublished Ph.D. thesis, Queen's University of Belfast, 1972, pp. 36–40.
5. W. H. Crawford, 'Economy and society in south Ulster in the eighteenth century, *The Clogher Record*, 1975, pp. 241–58; see also L. M. Cullen, *The Emergence of Modern Ireland, 1600–1900*, 1981.
6. 5 Geo III cap 14, s. 33.
7. McCutcheon, *Industrial Archaeology*, pp. 2–4.
8. A wide range of presentment records is available in the Public Record Office of Northern Ireland and, while these are somewhat uneven, a clear picture of the important role of the presentment system in moulding the development of Ulster's road pattern over a considerable period (1711–1898) can be gained from a close perusal of these documents and ledgers; I. J. Herring, 'Ulster roads on the eve of the railway age', *Irish Historical Studies*, II, 1940, pp. 160–88; see also K. B. Nowlan, 'Communications' in T. W. Moody and J. C. Beckett eds., *Ulster Since 1800*, London, 1957, pp. 138–47.
9. McCutcheon, *Industrial Archaeology*, pp. 2–6.
10. As, for example, on the Lisburn-Moira section of the main Lagan valley turnpike from Belfast to Portadown and Armagh. See *Report from the Select Committee on Turnpike Roads in Ireland*, BPP, 1831–2, XVII, E. R. R. Green, *The Lagan Valley*, London, 1949, p. 39; and the original Ordnance Survey memoir for the Parish of Magheramisk, County Antrim.
11. 1 & 2 Wm IV cap 33: see also *Report of the Committee appointed to inquire into the Board of Public Works, Ireland*, BPP, 1878, XXIII, and *An Epitome of the Acts of Parliament relating to the powers and duties of the Commissioners of Public Works in Ireland*, 5th edn., Dublin, 1903.
12. The Irish Post Office, which was amalgamated with the Post Office of Great Britain in 1831, had played a lesser role in surveying many Irish roads in the first quarter of the nineteenth century and in recommending certain improvements to be carried out in the interests of improving the efficiency of the carriage of His Majesty's Mail. Not many of these were implemented but in Ulster the following roads were constructed or modified as a result of the Post Office interest, viz. Monaghan-Aughnacloy-Omagh-Strabane, and Belfast-Newtownards by Bradshaw's Brae.
13. Margaret C. Storrie 'William Bald, FRSE, *c.* 1789–1857, Cartographer

and Civil Engineer Surveyor', *Trans. and Papers of the Institute of British Geographers*, 47, 1969, pp.205–31; see also McCutcheon, *Industrial Archaeology*, pp.32–3, and the first few annual reports of the Commissioners of Public Works in Ireland, beginning in 1831–2.

14. For the student of engineering history and public works in nineteenth-century Ireland there is a great deal of documentary material relating to Ulster in the library of the Office of Public Works in St. Stephen's Green, Dublin. This ranges from various plans and sections (1826–28) by John Rennie of a new bridge to be built over the river Lagan at Belfast to a plan (1827) for a new fishery harbour at Portstewart by James Donnell, and includes a very large number of plans and sections of roads and bridges being built or improved throughout the province. The newly reconstituted library of the Institution of Engineers of Ireland at Clyde Road, Dublin, is also an extremely valuable repository of historical material and by arrangement this can be made available for consultation, though as yet on a limited basis.

15. Green, *Lagan Valley*, pp.33–56.

16. McCutcheon, *Industrial Archaeology*, pp.16–23; see also Herring, 'Ulster roads'.

17. Individual accounts of Irish (Ulster) roads and road travel appear in the following travellers' writings – Carr (1806), Hoare (1807), Newenham (1809), Atkinson (1823), Scott (1825), Barrow (1836), Thackeray (1843), Hall (1841–43) and Kohl (1844).

18. W.A. McCutcheon, *The Canals of the North of Ireland*, Dawlish, 1965.

19. W.A. McCutcheon, 'Inland navigations of the north of Ireland', *Technology and Culture*, VI, 1965, pp.596–620.

20. McCutcheon, *Industrial Archaeology*, pp.76ff.

21. H.L. Glasgow, *The Upper Bann Navigation Rate*, Cookstown, 1916.

22. *Final Report of the Royal Commission appointed to inquire into the Canals and Inland Navigations of the United Kingdom:* XI (Ireland), BPP, 1911, XIII, paras. 125–6. See also D.B. McNeill, *Coastal Passenger Steamers and Inland Navigations in the North of Ireland*, Belfast, 1960.

23. A great deal has been written on the Irish narrow gauge. The following is a selection of the more interesting and reliable work: P.J. Flanagan, *The Cavan and Leitrim Railway*, Newton Abbot, 1966; and four books by E.M. Patterson: *The County Donegal Railways*, Dawlish, 1962; *The Lough Swilly Railway*, Dawlish, 1964; *The Ballymena Lines*, Newton Abbot, 1968, and *The Clogher Valley Railway*, Newton Abbot, 1972. See also McCutcheon, *Industrial Archaeology*, pp.187ff. for further extensive notes and bibliographical references.

24. McCutcheon, *Industrial Archaeology*, pp.220, n.272.

25. For an exhaustive commentary on the position of Irish railways at the peak of their prosperity see the *Reports of the Vice-Regal Commission on Irish Railways*, published between 1905 and 1910, especially Cmnd. 4481 of 1909 and Cmnd. 5248 of 1910.

26. Joseph Lee, 'The provision of capital of early Irish railways 1830–53', *Irish Historical Studies*, XVI, 1968, pp. 33–63.
27. Joseph Lee, 'The construction costs of Irish railways 1830–53', *Business History*, IX, 1967, pp. 95–109.
28. McCutcheon, *Industrial Archaeology*, pp. 17–19.
29. Constantia Maxwell, *Country and Town in Ireland under the Georges*, London, 1940, pp. 217–8.
30. Young, *Tour in Ireland*, II, p. 156.
31. *Railway Commissioner's Report 1837–38*, I, p. 14.
32. W. H. Crawford, *Domestic Industry in Ireland*. See also half-yearly engineers' reports for the Ulster Railway, the Belfast and Ballymena Railway and the Belfast and County Down Railway, at the Public Record Office of Northern Ireland.
33. For a detailed example: coal from Belfast to Lisburn, Lurgan, Portadown, Lough Neagh and Coalisland in 1882, see McCutcheon, *Industrial Archaeology*, p. 94.
34. K. B. Nowlan ed., *Travel and Transport in Ireland*, Dublin, 1973.
35. McCutcheon, *Industrial Archaeology*, pp. 158ff.
36. *Ibid.*, pp. 95ff.
37. Report of a Commission established by the Rt. Hon. J. M. Andrews, Minister of Labour in the first Government of Northern Ireland on 25 May 1922, Cmd. 10, 1922, '... to inquire and advise the Government of Northern Ireland as to what changes, if any, are desirable in the administration of the railway undertakings in Northern Ireland. ...' This report contains valuable summaries and tabulated statistics as well as a coloured map of the Ulster railway network at its greatest extent.
38. A. Marmion, *The Ancient and Modern History of the Maritime Ports of Ireland*, London, 1855, pp. 311, 353, 413. See also *Tidal Harbours Commission, Second Report*, Appendix A, BPP, 1846, XVIII, Pt. II and *Return from the Authorities of the Harbours, etc. of the United Kingdom giving a description of works executed within the last twenty years*, BPP, 1903, LXIII. Two theses are of direct relevance: S. Ward, *Geographical Factors in the Growth and Decline of the Ports of North East Ireland*, unpublished M.A., Queen's University of Belfast, 1950; B. A. McNeill, *The Growth and Decline of Several North Down Sea Ports*, unpublished M.A., Queen's University of Belfast, 1958.
39. McCutcheon, *Industrial Archaeology*, p. 217, n. 209–17; E. R. R. Green, *Industrial Archaeology of County Down*, Belfast, 1963, pp. 25–7.
40. G. V. Sampson, *Memoir ... of the County of Londonderry*, Dublin, 1814, p. 238.
41. Emrys Jones, *A Social Geography of Belfast*, London, 1960, pp. 43–50; Denis Rebbeck, 'The Belfast Shipyards 1791–1947', *Presidential Address of the Belfast Association of Engineers*, 1947.
42. Between 1914 and 1918 there was, of course, an artificial stimulus which boosted rail traffic, linen production, agricultural output and shipbuilding. As D. S. Johnson shows in Chapter Six this level of production and prosperity continued until 1920, when there was a dramatic collapse.

CHAPTER FOUR

POPULATION CHANGE AND URBANISATION

1821–1911

L.A. Clarkson

Between the first and last censuses taken in an unpartitioned Ireland there were three main demographic trends in Ulster. First, the population of the province, after rising from 2 million to 2·4 million between 1821 and 1841, fell to 1·6 million in 1911. Second, Ulster's share of the population of Ireland increased from 29 to 36 per cent. Third, the proportion of the population in the province living in towns grew from less than 10 per cent to almost 40 per cent. There was a further development, not strictly demographic, but related nevertheless, and worthy of note in view of the way that it has coloured Ulster's history. The proportion of Roman Catholics in the province declined slowly from around 50 per cent in 1861 (the earliest year for which figures are available) to 44 per cent in 1911. The purpose of this chapter is to elaborate these trends and to explain them, principally by focusing on the demographic dynamics – i.e. changes in marriage, fertility, mortality and migration – and more briefly by setting out the underlying economic and social influences.

I

Table 4.1 summarises the changes occurring in the population of Ulster and of Ireland as a whole between 1821 and 1911. Before the Famine population trends in Ulster were broadly similar to those in other provinces but thereafter their experiences diverged considerably. During the critical Famine decade Ireland lost almost 20 per cent of its population whereas Ulster lost less than 16 per cent; and over the whole period 1841–1911 Ireland's population declined by 46 per cent and Ulster's by 34 per cent. Table 4.2 elaborates the information in Table 4.1 by showing the population of Ulster, county by county, (treating Belfast as a separate unit) between 1821 and 1911. It also

137

Table 4.1 *Population change in Ireland and in Ulster, 1821–1911*

| | Ireland | | Ulster | | |
Year	Population ('000)	Percentage change over decade	Population ('000)	Percentage change over decade	Ulster as a proportion of Ireland (%)
1821	6802		1998		29·4
1831	7767	+ 14·2	2287	+ 14·4	29·4
1841	8175	+ 5·3	2386	+ 4·4	29·4
1851	6552	− 19·9	2012	− 15·7	30·7
1861	5799	− 11·5	1914	− 4·9	33·0
1871	5412	− 6·7	1833	− 4·2	33·9
1881	5175	− 4·4	1743	− 4·9	33·7
1891	4705	− 9·1	1620	− 7·1	34·4
1901	4459	− 5·2	1583	− 2·3	35·5
1911	4390	− 1·5	1582	− 0·1	36·0

Source. W. E. Vaughan and A. J. Fitzpatrick eds., *Irish Historical Statistics. Population 1821–1971.* Dublin, Royal Irish Academy, 1978, pp. 3, 16.

presents the county populations in the form of index numbers, treating the county populations in 1841 as equivalent to one hundred. From this it can be seen that the greatest losses of population occurred in the Famine decade, 1841–51, with declines ranging from 10 per cent in county Antrim to almost 30 per cent in counties Cavan and Monaghan. During the 1850s and '60s the losses were less severe but they increased during the 1870s and '80s, only to slacken again at the end of the century and to diminish further in the early part of the twentieth century. Throughout the whole period 1841–1911 the greatest declines in population were experienced by the three south-western counties of Cavan, Fermanagh and Monaghan where they exceeded 60 per cent. The smallest (43 per cent or less) occurred in counties Antrim, Donegal, Down and Londonderry. In Antrim and Down some of the decline is explained, not by emigration or mortality, but simply by the encroachment of the boundaries of Belfast, the area of which was enlarged eightfold during the period. In contrast to all the counties, Belfast grew in population from 37,000 in 1821, to 75,000 in 1841 and to 387,000 in 1911, a remarkable expansion by the standards, not merely of Ireland, but of the United Kingdom as well. In 1821 barely 2 per cent of Ulster's population had lived in Belfast; in 1911 the proportion was almost one-quarter.

The growth of Belfast was the most obvious example of urban

Population change and urbanisation

Table 4.2 *The population of Ulster by counties (including Belfast)*

Year	Antrim (exc. B'fast)	Armagh	Belfast	Cavan	Donegal	Down (exc. B'fast)	F'nagh	L'derry	M'han	Tyrone
			(a) *Numbers ('000)*							
1821	234	197	37	195	248	325	131	194	175	262
1831	272	220	53	228	289	352	150	222	196	304
1841	286	232	75	243	296	361	156	222	200	313
1851	260	196	98	174	255	321	116	192	142	256
1861	257	190	119	154	237	299	106	184	126	239
1871	246	179	174	141	218	277	93	174	115	216
1881	238	163	208	129	206	248	85	165	103	198
1891	215	143	256	112	186	224	74	152	86	171
1901	196	125	349	98	174	206	65	144	75	151
1911	194	120	387	91	169	204	62	141	71	143
			(b) *Indices* 1841 = 100							
1821	82	85	49	80	84	90	84	87	88	84
1831	95	95	71	94	98	96	96	100	98	97
1841	100	100	100	100	100	100	100	100	100	100
1851	90	85	131	72	86	89	74	86	71	82
1861	90	82	159	63	80	83	68	83	63	76
1871	86	77	232	58	74	78	60	78	58	69
1881	83	70	277	53	70	69	55	74	52	63
1891	76	62	341	46	63	62	47	68	43	55
1901	69	54	465	40	59	57	42	65	38	48
1911	68	52	516	37	57	57	40	64	36	46

Source. Vaughan and Fitzpatrick, *Irish Historical Statistics*, pp. 10–13.

development in nineteenth century Ulster. Before the Famine less than 10 per cent of the population lived in communities of more than 2,000 people (the census definition of a town) compared with 16 per cent in Munster and 22 per cent in Leinster; only Connacht had a smaller urban fraction. By 1911, however, Ulster was substantially more urbanised than either Munster or Connacht, although less so than Leinster which contained the city of Dublin. Nevertheless, between 1841 and 1911 the rate of urban growth was faster in Ulster than elsewhere in Ireland.

Urbanisation was not just a matter of towns becoming larger but of some losing population more slowly than the surrounding countryside. This point is illustrated by Table 4.3 and Map 4. Table 4.3 shows that counties Antrim, Armagh, Down and Londonderry were much

Table 4.2 *The urban population of Ulster, 1821–1911 (The population of towns with 2,000 or more people at some time during the period as a percentage of the total population of Ulster, and of the individual counties)*

Year	Ulster	Antrim (a)	Armagh	Cavan	Donegal	Down	F'nagh	L'derry	M'han	Tyrone
1821	7·6	9·7	5·8	3·3	2·5	9·5	1·8	8·4	4·4	4·0
1831	9·0	10·0	6·3	3·2	2·1	11·2	4·0	12·5	5·6	4·4
1841	9·5	10·2	7·5	3·4	2·0	12·3	3·6	11·1	5·7	4·6
1851	12·6	10·4	8·1	4·1	2·4	14·9	5·0	15·0	7·2	5·5
1861	14·5	11·6	11·7	4·5	2·6	16·1	5·4	15·7	8·0	6·3
1871	19·3	13·3	15·9	5·0	2·7	18·6	6·3	19·6	8·4	7·1
1881	22·9	16·9	19·1	5·2	2·8	20·1	6·7	23·0	9·1	8·2
1891	27·6	18·9	21·5	5·7	3·0	21·5	7·5	28·2	9·8	9·8
1901	34·8	21·4	26·0	6·0	3·2	24·1	8·3	34·4	11·3	11·3
1911	38·4	24·2	28·2	6·5	3·8	25·9	7·8	36·3	14·7	12·2

Note. (a) Excluding Belfast.
Source. Vaughan and Fitzpatrick, *Irish Historical Statistics*, pp. 36–9.

more urbanised than the rest; it also shows that after the Famine the proportion of town dwellers increased in all nine Ulster counties, even in Cavan, Donegal, Fermanagh, Monaghan and Tyrone although these counties between them possessed only two towns that actually increased in size. Between 1841 and 1911 there were forty-two towns in Ulster that at one time or another had a population of at least 2,000.[1] Twenty-three of these experienced population growth of 10 per cent or more between 1841 and 1911; in five the population stagnated; and in fourteen it fell by at least 10 per cent. Only five growing towns were west of the Bann; the remainder were all contained in a north-eastern wedge bounded by the Upper and Lower Bann and Lagan valleys. By contrast, only two decaying communities – Antrim town and Donaghadee – were located in this region. The remaining twelve, except for Limavady in county Londonderry, were strung along a southern arc stretching from Ballyshannon in the west to Downpatrick and Portaferry in the east. The stagnating communities were all located west of the Upper and Lower Bann. The nineteenth century urban pattern in Ulster was thus largely a new one. Derry and Belfast provided a certain continuity with the past, but in general the province possessed a different urban profile after 1800 from that of the eighteenth century.

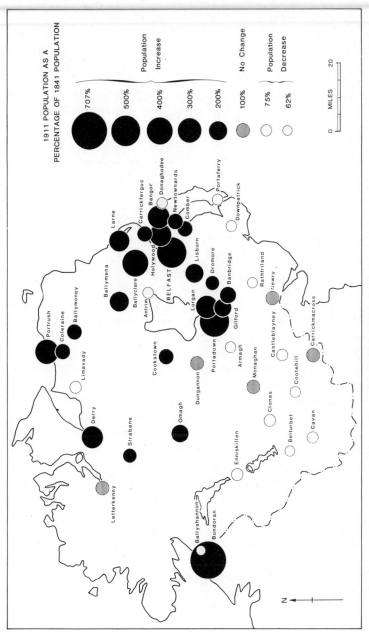

Map 4 Urban population change in Ulster, 1845–1911

II

The broad features of demographic change in nineteenth century Ireland are familiar. The increase in population before 1841 was the final phase on a long expansion stretching back to the mid-eighteenth century; but by the 1820s the rate of increase had slackened and the Famine devastated a society already moving into a new demographic era. Between 1841 and 1851 there were more than one million deaths in Ireland over and above what might have occurred had there been no famine, and a further 1·2 million people emigrated. Thereafter population decline persisted in a manner unparalleled in any other European nation. Part of this continuing loss was the outcome of declining fertility brought about by a rise in the age at first marriage and by a reduction in nuptiality;[2] and part was the result of an unceasing stream of emigration that eventually resulted in more Irishmen living in Great Britain, America and Australasia than in Ireland itself.

The general pattern holds for Ulster as elsewhere, but it requires elaboration to take account of the fact that post-Famine adjustment in the province was less extreme than elsewhere, and also to accommodate the varying experiences of the Ulster counties. Even during the years 1821–41, when population growth in Ulster seems at first sight to have been similar to the rest of Ireland, appearances are deceptive, for the underlying patterns were different. The estimated birth rate in Ulster (thirty-nine per 1,000) was almost identical with the national average, but the death rate (twenty-one per 1,000) was substantially lower. A greater natural increase thus occurred in Ulster but was offset by a higher level of emigration occasioned principally by the contraction of the rural linen industry. According to Mokyr the annual rate of emigration from Ulster betwen 1821 and 1841 was between 8·4 and 9·4 per 1,000 compared with a level of 7 per 1,000 for the island as a whole.[3]

Although the birth rate in pre-Famine Ulster was at the national average, there were marked intra-provincial differences with the eastern counties displaying lower fertility than the western counties because of lower nuptiality. Taking the proportion of women aged 46–55 who were married as a measure of nuptiality, the highest proportions in 1841 were in Cavan (90 per cent) and Monaghan (89 per cent); and in lowest proportions in Antrim (85 per cent) and Down and Londonderry (both 82 per cent). It is highly likely that these regional differences had begun to emerge in the 1820s and that they had been accompanied by a rise in the mean age at first marriage.[4]

On the eve of the Famine, therefore, Ulster was a society of high but declining fertility, high emigration, and low mortality. When the potato failed in 1845−49 the east and north-east of the province weathered the crisis more successfully than elsewhere. Famine mortality in Ulster as a whole was lower than in either Munster or Connacht − and about the same as in Leinster. Cousens has suggested that Ulster landlords had a more benevolent attitude towards their tenants than landlords in other parts of Ireland and so cushioned them from the worst ravages of the Famine; more likely, Ulster, or rather the eastern part, was less ravaged by poverty to begin with. The labouring population in the east of the province enjoyed a somewhat more varied diet than labourers elsewhere; even so, the nutritional support derived from the potato throughout Ulster was crucial and its loss had the most serious consequences.[5]

Emigration from Ulster during the Famine was very uneven. Between 1846 and 1851 Cavan and Monaghan lost 16 to 20 per cent of their 1841 populations as a result of emigration. In these counties the failure of the potato intensified existing distress arising from the decline of the linen industry during the 1830s and '40s. By contrast, barely 10 per cent of the population of the northern and eastern counties of Ulster emigrated. In counties Donegal and Londonderry there had been heavy emigration in the 1820s and '30s (the result of an earlier decay of linen) and so a good deal of demographic adjustment had already taken place by the time of the Famine. In counties Antrim and Down, proximity to Belfast helped to curtail net emigration. Similarly, in County Armagh the rate of emigration was relatively low because Lurgan as a linen manufacturing town and Portadown as a linen and transport centre, held population in the county. Between the extremes were the predominantly rural counties in Fermanagh and Tyrone where emigration was less severe than in Cavan and Monaghan but a good deal heavier than in the east.[6]

The population of Ulster fell by 374,000 between 1841 and 1851. In principle, it should be possible to apportion this decline to deaths caused by the Famine, to emigration following the Famine, and to reduced fertility during the Famine. But we must also remember that births during the decade 1841−51 partly offset the losses caused by death and departure. Thus:

population 1851 = population 1841 − deaths, 1841−51
− emigration, 1841−51
+ births, 1841−51

For a proper measure of the impact of the Famine it is necessary to distinguish between 'normal mortality' 1841–51 and 'Famine mortality' 1846–51; and also between 'pre-Famine emigration' 1841–45 and 'Famine emigration' 1846–51. Less obviously, perhaps, we need to divide births before and after 1845. This is because a famine can be expected to lower fertility in three ways. Most directly death brings some marriages to an end before the wife has reached the end of her child-bearing years. Less directly, a famine will cause some projected marriages to be abandoned, either because one or both of the partners die before the ceremony takes place, or because of hardship. And finally, hunger and disease depress sexual activity and induce amenorrhea among women. Thus we should expect the birth rate in Ireland between 1846 and 1851 to be lower than in the years 1841–45.

Mortality, emigration and birth rates for the years 1841–51 all have to be deduced from information contained in the censuses. The estimates are discussed in the appendix to this chapter, and they contain a good deal of approximation. Nevertheless, they are robust enough to support two conclusions. First, emigration and mortality arising directly from the Famine played roughly equal parts in reducing the population: each probably totalled approximately 220,000–230,000. Second, the loss of births during the Famine was only a little less important than mortality or emigration. Had the pre-Famine birth rate (thirty-nine per 1,000) prevailed between 1846 and 1851, births would have totalled 510,000. As it was, actual births seem to have been around 300,000. There was thus a 'loss' of births of 200,000 or more.

We should not assume that the decline in fertility during the Famine was experienced equally throughout the province, but it was probably greatest in those counties most affected by emigration and mortality since both tended to reduce fertility. Famine emigration, we have already noted, was highest in Cavan and Monaghan, followed by Fermanagh and Tyrone; according to Mokyr, mortality followed the same pattern.[7] Hence the south and south-western counties experienced more emigration, more mortality, and, probably, lower fertility in the 1840s than the counties in the north and east, thus explaining their greater losses of population shown in Table 4.2

After 1851 the reduction in population proceeded more slowly. Between 1851 and 1871 the annual rate of decrease was barely a quarter of the rate during the 1840s. Nevertheless the earlier regional differences persisted, with relatively severe losses recorded in Cavan,

Monaghan and Fermanagh and smaller declines in the eastern and north-eastern counties. In some rural areas, indeed, where there was still waste land available for colonisation and capable of supporting old patterns of marriage and fertility, population actually increased.[8] The rate of decline accelerated again in the late 1870s and 1880s following the collapse of agricultural prices after 1877, once more with the south-western counties in the lead. At the end of the century, however, the fall in population slackened considerably and in the east of the province practically ceased.

The proximate cause of the continuing decline in population after the Famine was the interaction of mortality, fertility and emigration. Emigration statistics were gathered from 1851, and registration of births, deaths and marriages was introduced in 1864. Table 4.4 summarises the position for Ulster. None of the series is totally reliable and, in particular, emigration was under-recorded, notably in the western counties.[9]

Table 4.4 *Demographic variables, Ulster, 1851–1911*

	1851–61	1861–71	1871–81	1881–91	1891–01	1901–11
Birth rate (per 1,000)	–	26·7 (a)	26·2	23·6	23·0	24·0
Births per marriage	–	–	5·4	5·0	4·2	4·1
Marriage rate (per 1,000)	–	5·2 (a)	4·8	4·8	5·5	5·6
Death rate (per 1,000)	–	16·3 (a)	18·0	18·0	19·0	18·1
Emigration rate (per 1,000)	17·3	10·7	14·0	13·8	6·6	6·9

Note. (a) 1864–71.
Sources. Vaughan and Fitzpatrick, *Irish Historical Statistics*, pp. 311–32; *Annual Reports of the Registrar General of Marriages, Births and Deaths in Ireland, 1864–1911*; and *Decennial Summaries, 1871–70 – 1901–11* in *British Parliamentary Papers* (full references given in Vaughan and Fitzpatrick, pp. 361–3).

According to Table 4.4 emigration was high during the 1850s – the first four years of the decade caught the end of the Famine exodus[10] – but declined in the 1860s, returning to a high rate in 1871–91. Thereafter it dropped back to pre-Famine levels. However, the recorded figures cannot be taken at face value. For example, the birth, death and emigration rates in the decade 1861–71 imply that the population of Ulster was static, whereas in fact it declined by 81,000. It is, of course, possible that because registration was still new and people were suspicious of officialdom, recorded births and deaths are inaccurate. But the statistics of emigration are much more likely to be defective since they were collected at the ports from persons stating their intention to leave Ireland for good. Temporary migrants were not counted even though, in practice, many of them became permanent.

A method of adjusting published emigration statistics, using age-cohort analysis of census data, has been suggested by Ó Gráda. It assumes that post-Famine emigration was concentrated among the 5–30 age group and that over a ten year period 5 per cent of the cohort will die. In the absence of migration, 95 per cent of the cohort will be present ten years later aged 15–40 years. If, however, the census shows fewer people in the 15–40 year cohort the shortfall can be attributed to migration. Similarly, a larger than expected figure indicates in-migration.[11]

Table 4.5 compares recorded and estimated emigration rates for Ulster counties (excluding Antrim) between 1851 and 1911. In the

Table 4.5 *Recorded and estimated emigration rates from Ulster counties, 1851–1911 (per 1,000)* (excluding Antrim)

		1851–61	*1861–71*	*1871–81*	*1881–91*	*1891–01*	*1901–11*
Armagh	R.	15·3	9·6	11·5	13·4	5·4	6·9
	E.	13·5	13·8	13·4	15·2	13·6	9·2
Cavan	R.	22·2	15·0	14·4	18·0	12·5	9·9
	E.	20·1	16·8	14·7	17·4	15·2	12·0
Donegal	R.	15·6	5·2	14·2	15·7	7·2	7·2
	E.	16·7	16·6	13·0	15·2	14·0	11·8
Down	R.	15·5	9·8	11·9	10·0	3·6	7·7
	E.	14·4	13·7	13·4	12·6	10·3	6·3
Fermanagh	R.	15·7	10·0	11·8	12·8	7·8	5·6
	E.	16·8	16·9	12·9	14·2	12·4	10·2
Londonderry	R.	14·8	9·4	15·9	14·6	5·2	6·5
	E.	13·0	18·4	10·6	11·9	8·5	8·7
Monaghan	R.	20·0	12·4	12·4	14·2	6·7	5·9
	E.	17·7	15·1	14·0	16·9	13·7	8·7
Tyrone	R.	15·9	10·4	14·3	15·7	7·8	7·2
	E.	15·1	15·1	12·6	14·8	12·3	9·2

decade 1851–61 the two sets of figures are very close; presumably most emigrants intended to leave Ireland permanently and were recorded as such. In the next decade the estimated rates exceed the recorded rates in all counties. There were two reasons for this. First, permanent emigration declined in the 1860s from the high levels of the previous decade. Seasonal emigration persisted, however, and constituted a greater proportion of the total outflow than previously, but by definition it went unrecorded. Second, the estimated rates reflect inter-county (and inter-provincial) migration as well as movement out of Ireland. It is for this reason that Antrim has been omitted from the table. According to official emigration returns, the county experienced emigration at a level that would have reduced the population in the 1860s; in fact the population increased as people poured into Belfast. To a smaller degree the city of Derry had a similar effect in County Londonderry, particular in the 1870s and 1880s. The estimated and recorded rates throughout Ulster come close together again in the 1870s and '80s, but diverge quite sharply once more in the period 1891–1911. In the latter period inter-county population movements were at high levels, especially during the '90s when the population of Belfast grew by 36 per cent.

It is noticeable that the adjusted emigration rates display narrower regional differences than the official statistics, although counties Cavan, Fermanagh, Monaghan and Tyrone continue to have the highest rates of emigration. The narrowing is significant, nevertheless, for it implies that differences in rates of emigration cannot, by themselves, account for the relatively greater losses of population in the west and south-west of the province; some of the burden of explanation must rest on regional differences, either of mortality or of fertility.

When the Famine abated the death rate in Ulster returned to its pre-1841 level and remained virtually unchanged for the rest of the century. However, death rates were generally higher in the growing towns and since these were concentrated in the eastern counties, Armagh, Antrim and Down had the highest county death rates (see Table 4.6). In particular the increasing proportion of Ulster's population living in Belfast, congested and unhealthy, largely explains why the province-wide death rate did not fall in the later nineteenth century. Compared with Belfast, the rural counties of the west appear remarkably healthy. Indeed, they were even healthier than their crude death rates indicate since emigration removed relatively more of the

Table 4.6 *County and urban death rates in Ulster, 1864–1911 (per 1,000)*

	1864–71	1871–81	1881–91	1891–01	1901–11
County					
Antrim	19·1	20·7	21·0	21·9	17·1 (a)
Armagh	20·4	18·9	19·1	19·9	19·6
Cavan	15·2	16·1	14·5	16·2	15·5
Donegal	11·6	15·2	14·5	15·0	15·5
Down	16·3	19·4	19·1	19·4	18·0 (a)
Fermanagh	12·4	15·7	15·3	16·8	16·3
Londonderry	17·0	17·7	17·7	18·3	18·0
Monaghan	16·0	16·5	16·7	18·4	18·7
Tyrone	15·3	16·4	16·6	17·9	18·2

Note. (a) Excluding Belfast.

Urban (towns of 10,000 plus)

	1864–71	1871–81	1881–91	1891–01	1901–11
Armagh	–	19·1	19·2	–	–
Ballymena	–	–	–	17·3	16·9
Belfast	–	24·1	23·5	23·4	20·0
Lisburn	–	20·2	20·2	20·7	19·1
Derry	–	18·6	18·5	18·5	17·6
Lurgan	–	19·1	19·3	19·6	18·2
Newry	–	18·6	18·7	19·6	19·2

Source. As for Table 4.4.

younger members of the population, leaving behind the elderly with the highest age-specific mortalities.

What then of fertility? Table 4.7 shows the crude birth rates for the Ulster counties and larger towns between 1864 and 1911. Three points should be noted. First, birth rates did not return to pre-Famine levels after 1851; in this respect the Famine inaugurated a new era in demographic history. Second, urban birth rates were higher than rural birth rates, and birth rates in the east were higher than in the west. Finally, birth rates everywhere declined over time. The Ulster average fell from 26·7 in the 1860s to 20 in 1901–11; but the fall was most pronounced in counties Armagh, Cavan, Monaghan and Tyrone.

Crude birth rates are sensitive to changes in the age and sex structure of the population, both of which are affected by emigration. Counties with the highest levels of emigration experienced the greatest falls in birth rates because emigration removed those most likely to marry. Emigration also strengthened those forces in society leading

Table 4.6 *County and urban birth rates in Ulster, 1864–1911 (per 1,000)*

	1864–71	*1871–81*	*1881–91*	*1891–01*	*1901–11*
County					
Antrim	30·2	30·6	27·9	29·1	23·6 (*a*)
Armagh	33·1	25·8	23·6	23·3	22·8
Cavan	27·8	25·4	20·4	19·4	19·2
Donegal	21·5	24·1	21·5	21·1	22·3
Down	24·8	26·2	25·4	26·6	22·7 (*a*)
Fermanagh	21·0	23·6	19·8	19·4	20·8
Londonderry	26·9	25·5	22·9	23·1	23·5
Monaghan	26·2	23·6	19·4	19·0	20·0
Tyrone	25·0	23·9	20·0	20·2	20·5

Note. (a) Excluding Belfast.

Urban					
Armagh	–	23·4	21·6	–	–
Belfast	–	33·1	30·7	32·9	30·6
Lisburn	–	27·2	25·1	24·7	22·7
Derry	–	26·2	25·1	24·9	25·7
Lurgan	–	28·6	27·6	26·3	24·8
Newry	–	25·6	22·7	22·4	22·5

Source. As for Table 4.4.

to the high levels of celibacy that were characteristic of late-nineteenth century Ireland. The proportion of the male population aged 45–54 which was unmarried in 1911 exceeded one-third in counties Cavan, Fermanagh, Monaghan and Tyrone. In Belfast, by contrast, where there were plenty of jobs and a surplus of women, the proportion was only 13 per cent. Celibacy also increased among women in rural areas in the later nineteenth century, although to a smaller extent than among men.

The consequence of emigration, therefore, was to reduce birth rates sharply in the west and south-west. Nevertheless marital fertility remained high especially in the west. Marital fertility is defined as the number of births per 1,000 married women aged 15–44. In 1871 – the first year for which the calculation is possible – the figure was 299 for Ulster; by 1911 it had fallen to 270, still a high level by international standards.[12] But, as Table 4.8 shows, the east-west contrast was very considerable. Over time marital fertility declined in six of the nine Ulster counties. The most obvious exception was Donegal, where marital fertility actually rose by 23 per cent between 1871 and

1911, possibly because of a decline in seasonal emigration that had once been an important feature of the social life of the county.[13] The small increases in marital fertility in counties Down and Fermanagh occurred, one suspects, mainly after 1901 when emigration declined, thus resulting in more of the most fertile age groups remaining at home.[14]

Table 4.8 *Births per 1,000 married women aged 15−44*

	1871	1911	1911 as a % of 1871
Antrim	299	252	84
Armagh	354	272	77
Cavan	327	291	89
Donegal	273	336	123
Down	238	253	106
Fermanagh	280	292	104
Londonderry	326	287	88
Monaghan	301	286	95
Tyrone	317	291	92

Source. Censuses of Ireland, 1871 and 1911.

The most important cause of the fall in marital fertility was a rise in the age at first marriage. Marriage ages are difficult to ascertain from published data, but one indicator is that the proportion of single women in Ulster aged 25−29 rose from 54 to 59 per cent between the 1870s and the early twentieth century. The proportions were higher in the western counties of the province. However, this is not the whole story since marital fertility was high in precisely those counties where marriages were most delayed. It follows, therefore, that once marriages were contracted in the west, age-specific marital fertility must have been higher. This raises the suspicion that in east Ulster, and especially in Belfast, married couples were using contraception to a greater extent than in the west.

III

Behind the demographic variables discussed above lay a complex set of economic and social influences, analysis of which would take us beyond the confines of this chapter. It is worth considering briefly, however, why it was that the western and south-western counties of

Ulster, after gaining population more rapidly than the east before the Famine — with the notable exception of Belfast — lost it more rapidly in the second half of the century; and also why the urban population of Ulster grew both relatively and absolutely throughout the period.

Population growth before 1841 had been made possibly by sub-division of land into tiny holdings and extensive cultivation of potatoes as a food crop. In some parts of the province, too, the linen industry had provided supplementary incomes which supported and encouraged increasing population. From the end of the Napoleonic wars market conditions turned against this form of rural economy. Emigration increased, marriages were delayed and so the growth of population slowed down in the decade before the Famine.

The failure of the potato in 1845–49 was serious throughout Ulster but, as noted earlier, it affected the south-western counties most severely. After 1851 these same counties continued to shed population more rapidly since their economies offered little employment outside farming. For a decade or two, vestiges of the old population patterns lingered on where sub-division of land persisted; but from the 1870s economic pressures created by collapsing agricultural prices and — at the end of the decade — by renewed potato failure, emphatically made counties Cavan, Fermanagh, Monaghan and Tyrone places of exodus. By contrast, counties such as Down, Antrim and London-derry possessed more diversified economies which restricted the outflow of people. Above all, the east had towns which offered employment for some of the displaced agricultural population.

The urban history of Ulster has yet to be written. However, the expanding towns can provisionally be grouped into four kinds. Most obviously there were manufacturing towns, of which Belfast was the exemplar. From the 1820s to the 1860s the driving force of its development was the mechanised flax spinning industry. From small beginnings in 1828–29, the number of spindles in the city had grown to nearly 500,000 by 1862. During the cotton famine, owing to the American civil war, the total soared by 724,000 by 1868. Power-loom weaving developed more slowly; in 1862 there were fewer than 3,000 power looms in Belfast, but by 1868 there were 9,000. The linen industry created employment for women especially, and so Belfast became a city with a substantial surplus of females, in marked contrast to most of Ulster society in the late nineteenth century. The linen industry in Belfast reached its pinnacle during the cotton famine, but the city's economy continued to expand thereafter on the basis of shipbuilding, engineering, tobacco, commerce and finance, as well as on the trade of its port.[15] Other manufacturing towns included Lurgan and Gilford in the south of the province, Ballyclare and Ballymena to the north, and Derry in the north-west. Lurgan presents an interesting case, growing rapidly from under 3,000 to over 10,000 between 1821 and 1871, but thereafter stagnating. It was primarily a linen town, and once the great boom of the 1860s was over there was little economic diversification to sustain further development. We may contrast it with two other towns in County Armagh. The city of Armagh had been one of the leading inland towns of Ireland in the eighteenth century, a centre of trade and administration, and possessing an important linen market. In the nineteenth century the world passed Armagh by: it lost many of its marketing functions, gained few new industries; even the possession of one – and later two – cathedrals could not ensure material, as opposed to spiritual growth. By 1871 Armagh had been surpassed in size by Lurgan, and in the 1890s even by the upstart Portadown which had hardly existed in 1821.

Portadown is an example of a second type of developing town in nineteenth-century Ulster: the transport centre. The railway, penetrating from Belfast and Lisburn, reached Portadown in 1842 and it became one of the most important railway junctions in Ulster with lines pushing south-eastwards to Newry and Dundalk, south-westwards to Armagh, Monaghan and Cavan, and west and north-west to Dungannon, Omagh, Strabane and Derry. Portadown consequently developed as a prosperous market for the whole of south Ulster; unlike Lurgan its expansion did not rest narrowly on one industry.

The railway also aided the growth of other towns, including Cookstown and Omagh – two of only five growing urban communities west of the Bann – and the market towns of Ballymena and Ballymoney. It also contributed to the development of Larne, although the major stimulus there was the introduction of the steamship and the subsequent establishment of a sea route between Larne and Stranraer at the expense of the older sailing ship link between Donaghadee and Portapatrick.[16]

A third class of town which owed much to the railway was the resort town. The incongruous presence on the south-west coast of Donegal of Bundoran, with the most spectacular rate of population growth in the whole of Ulster, is explained by the arrival of the railway and the opening of the Great Northern Hotel. Its mushroom growth, in fact, occurred mostly in the first decade of the twentieth century, for the population increased from under 900 in 1901 to over 2,000 in 1911. By then Bundoran was roughly the size of Portrush which had developed as a holiday resort from the 1880s. Closer to Belfast was the even bigger and more popular resort of Bangor. Its population had actually fallen between 1841 and 1861, but the railway link with Belfast *via* Holywood was completed in 1865: thereafter the population grew from 2,500 to 7,800 in 1911. None of the resorts, of course, was solely the creation of the railway. They were the product also of the rising prosperity of the commercial and industrial classes of Ulster who had money to spend and time in which to spend it on day trips and summer holidays by the sea.

By the end of the nineteenth century the same combination of convenient travel and modest affluence was beginning to stimulate the development of the dormitory town, housing the better-off workers of Belfast. Holywood is perhaps the best example, linked by rail to Belfast in 1848, and with a population of over 4,000 in 1911. Lisburn, too, was beginning to add the role of a commuter town to its older functions as a market town and manufacturing centre.

All urban growth in Ulster was subordinate to the burgeoning of Belfast. After the Famine it was the one place in Ulster − indeed in the whole of Ireland − that attracted people in large and continuing numbers. It is Belfast that directly explains two of the three features of the population history of Ulster identified at the beginning of this chapter: the rising share of Ireland's population living in the province; and the fact that the Ulsterman became increasingly an urban creature. The third feature − the loss of 800,000 people between 1841 and 1911 − was caused by conditions in the countryside, but Belfast had an influence here too. The greater part of this loss was from the west and south-west of the province and the shedding of population from counties Cavan and Monaghan was as severe as anywhere in Ireland. But in the east, Belfast acted as a dam holding back the outflow. Many men and women from the west, of course, streamed towards new hopes or new desolations in Britain, America and Australasia; but some remained to populate the last great urban creation of the Industrial Revolution.

The influence of Belfast also largely explains the fourth characteristic of Ulster's population change noted in the introduction: the declining proportion of Roman Catholics. The only region of Ulster which experienced a substantial change in the ratio of Catholics to non-Catholics was the city of Belfast (see Table 4.9). The table, in fact, does not reveal the full extent of the change, for the proportion of Catholics had risen from about 10 per cent at the beginning of the nineteenth century to its peak of 34 per cent in 1861 and had then fallen back to less than one-quarter at the end of the century.[17] Thus, although Catholics had migrated to Belfast in larger numbers than Protestants before and during the Famine, the position was reversed from the 1860s. The most likely explanation is that the labour market was less able, or less willing, to absorb Catholics than Protestants. Up to and including the 1860s, the linen industry had been the main stimulus to Belfast's growth, creating jobs for the unskilled. From the 1860s, although unskilled occupations continued to multiply, there was a relatively greater growth of skilled and semi-skilled jobs in commerce and industry. For a complex of reasons Catholics found it more difficult to obtain employment in these occupations.[18] Part of the problem was, doubtless, discrimination by employers. But it was probably also a reflection of the way in which workers were recruited. In the linen industry, for example, in the early years of the present century, children coming up to employment were 'spoken for' by relatives already employed.[19] The barrier of Belfast against emigration, therefore, was a selective one, restraining skilled and semi-skilled Protestants more effectively than unskilled Catholics. In this way the new industrial city became the setting for old sectarian battles.

Table 4.9 *Proportion of Roman Catholics and other denominations, 1861–1911 (%)*

County/town		1861	1871	1881	1891	1901	1911
Co. Antrim	R.C.	24·8	23·5	22·7	21·8	20·6	20·5
	O.D.	75·2	76·5	77·3	78·2	79·4	79·5
Co. Armagh	R.C.	48·8	47·5	46·4	46·1	45·2	45·3
	O.D.	51·2	52·5	53·6	53·9	54·8	54·7
Belfast	R.C.	33·9	31·9	28·8	26·3	24·3	24·1
	O.D.	66·1	68·1	71·2	73·7	75·7	75·9
Co. Cavan	R.C.	80·5	80·4	80·9	80·9	81·0	81·5
	O.D.	19·5	19·6	19·1	19·1	19·0	18·5
Co. Donegal	R.C.	75·1	75·7	75·6	77·0	77·7	78·9
	O.D.	24·9	24·3	24·4	23·0	22·3	21·1
Down	R.C.	32·5	31·7	30·9	29·8	31·3	31·6
	O.D.	67·5	68·3	69·1	71·2	68·7	68·4
Fermanagh	R.C.	56·5	55·9	55·8	55·4	55·3	56·2
	O.D.	43·5	44·1	44·2	44·6	44·7	44·8
Co. Londonderry	R.C.	45·3	44·4	44·4	44·6	41·4	41·5
	O.D.	54·7	55·6	55·6	55·4	58·6	58·5
Co. Monaghan	R.C.	73·4	73·4	73·7	73·3	73·4	74·7
	O.D.	26·6	26·6	26·3	26·7	26·6	25·3
Tyrone	R.C.	56·5	55·6	55·5	54·6	54·7	55·4
	O.D.	44·5	44·4	44·5	45·4	45·3	44·6
Ulster	R.C.	50·5	48·9	47·8	46·0	44·2	43·7
	O.D.	49·5	51·1	52·2	54·0	55·8	57·3

Source. Vaughan and Fitzpatrick eds., *Irish Historical Statistics*, pp. 49–68.

Appendix

Table 4.10 *Components of population change in Ulster, 1841–1851 ('000)*

	Census population, 1841	2,386
A	Estimated emigration, 1841–45	−108
B	Estimated emigration, 1846–51	−224
C	Estimated normal mortality, 1841–51	−527
D	Estimated famine mortality, 1846–51	−238
E	Estimated births, 1841–45	+449
F	Estimated births, 1846–51	+340
G	Estimated births, 1846–51, calculated as a balancing item	+254
H	Census population, 1851	2,012
I	Computed population, 1851	2,098
J	Excess of computed population over census population, 1851	+86

Notes

A Emigration, 1841–45. Estimated by asuming that the emigration rate of 9 per 1000 calculated by Mokyr for 1821–41 ('The Deadly Fungus', p. 243) continued to 1845. The population between 1841 and 1845 is assumed to be growing at 0·4 per cent per annum (the 1831–41 rate).

B Famine emigration, 1846–51. Calculated from Cousens, 'Regional Pattern of Emigration ... 1846–51', p. 121. Cousens presents emigration rates for all Irish counties in grouped frequencies. The rates for the individual Ulster counties are assumed to be the median of the relevant group frequency.

C Normal mortality, 1841–51. The normal death rate is assumed to be twenty-one per 1000 (Mokyr, 'Deadly Fungus', p. 243). The population 1841–45 is assumed to be increasing at 0·4 per cent per annum (see note A); between 1846 and 1851 it is calculated as declining at 3·15 per cent per annum.

D Famine mortality, 1846–51. The mean of Mokyr's six lower-bound estimates of Famine mortality (Mokyr, 'The Deadly Fungus', pp. 248–9).

E Estimated births, 1841–45. Based on an assumed birth rate of thirty-nine per 1000 (Mokyr, 'Deadly Fungus', p. 243). The population 1841–45 is assumed to be growing at 0·4 per cent per annum (see note A).

F and G Estimated births, 1846–51. There are two ways of approaching the problem: (a) to estimate the number of births using an assumed birth rate of 26 per 1,000, calculated from the formula given by Mokyr ('Deadly Fungus', p. 247) and making use of age cohort data taken from the census of 1841 and 1851; (b) to compute births as a balancing item necessary to bring the 1841 population less mortality and emigration but plus births 1841–45 to the 1851 population. The total thus established (254,000) implies a birth rate of 19 per 1,000.

I and J Computed population 1851 and excess over census population 1851. The computed population is 86,000 greater than the census population. Two possible reasons are: (a) estimated births 1846–51 (F) are too large. But the alternative estimate (G) with its implied birth rate of 19 per 1,000, is implausibly low; (b) estimate of famine emigration (B) and/or famine mortality (D) are too low. Cousens' estimates of the former range from 188,000 to 260,000; and Mokyr's of the latter from 192,000 to 289,000.

Notes

1. Excluding Ligoniel and Bessbrook. The former appears as an independent community only between 1851 and 1891; and the latter for the first time in 1861 (Vaughan and Fitzpatrick, *Irish Historical Statistics*, pp. 36–7.

2. L. A. Clarkson, 'Marriage and fertility in nineteenth-century Ireland', in R. B. Outhwaite ed., *Marriage and Society: Studies in the Social History of Marriage*, London, 1981, pp. 244–5.

3. Joel Mokyr, 'The deadly fungus: an econometric investigation into the short-term impact of the Irish famine, 1846–1851', *Research in Population Economics*, 2, 1980, p. 243.

4. S. H. Cousens, 'The restriction of population growth in pre-famine Ireland', *Proceedings of the Royal Irish Academy*, LXIV, section C, no. 4, 1966, pp. 85–99.

5. Mokyr, op. cit., pp. 243, 251–73.

6. S. H. Cousens, 'The regional pattern of emigration during the great Irish famine, 1846–51', *Transactions and Papers of the Institute of British Geographers*, no. 33, 1963, pp. 145–62.

7. Mokyr, op. cit.

8. S. H. Cousens, 'Emigration and demographic change in Ireland, 1851–1861', *Economic History Review*, 2nd ser. XIV, 1961, pp. 275–88.

9. S. H. Cousens, 'The regional variations in population changes in Ireland, 1801–1881', *Economic History Review*, 2nd ser. XVII, 1964, pp. 305–13.

10. Cousens, 'Emigration and demographic change', p. 274.

11. C. Ó Gráda, 'Some aspects of nineteenth-century Irish emigration', in L. M. Cullen and T. C. Smout eds., *Comparative Aspects of Scottish and Irish Social History, 1600–1900*, Edinburgh, 1977, pp. 68–71.

12. R. E. Kennedy Jr., *The Irish: Emigration, Marriage, and Fertility*, London, 1973, pp. 176–82.

13. C. Ó Gráda, 'Seasonal Migration and Post-Famine Adjustment in the West of Ireland', *Studia Hibernica*, XIII, pp. 48–76.

14. For a general discussion of the relationship between emigration and marital fertility see Kennedy, *The Irish*, pp. 195–99.

15. Ulster business history is relatively underdeveloped, but for a recent brief survey of the textile industry see Emily Boyle, 'Linenopolis': the rise of the textile industry', in J. C. Beckett *et al.*, *Belfast: The Making of the City, 1800–1914*, Belfast, 1983, pp. 41–56.

16. W. H. Crawford, 'The evolution of Ulster towns, 1750–1850', in Peter Roebuck ed., *Plantation to Partition: Essays in Ulster History in Honour of J. L. McCracken*, Belfast, 1981, p. 150.

17. A. C. Hepburn, 'Belfast 1871–1911: work, class and religion', *Irish Economic and Social History*, X, 1983, p. 34.

18. Hepburn, 'Belfast', pp. 36–50.

19. Betty Messenger, *Picking Up the Linen Threads: A study in Industrial Folklore*, Austin, Texas and London, 1975, p. 34.

CHAPTER FIVE

INDUSTRIAL LABOUR AND THE LABOUR MOVEMENT,

1820–1914

Henry Patterson

Throughout the nineteenth century Ulster was the most industrially developed province in Ireland. However, during this period the structure of industry and the nature of its labour force were transformed. The relationship between the industrial north east and economic tendencies elsewhere on the island also changed radically. Urbanisation was an integral aspect of these changes. In 1926 the six counties of the newly created Northern Ireland state held half of its population in urban centres.[1] This degree of urbanisation, while high by Irish standards, was lower than in England and Wales (where the urban proportion of the population in 1911 was 79 per cent).[2] Belfast with its phenomenal rate of growth from 37,000 in 1821 to 387,000 in 1911 clearly dominates the story of urbanisation (see Chapter Four), though there was also substantial urban development in other parts of eastern Ulster. By the late nineteenth century sharp contrasts in occupational structure had emerged between north-east Ireland and the rest of the island. These are summarised in Table 5.1.

Textiles
General indices of change tell us little about the specific economic relationships in which working people were involved. In 1841 more than one-third of a million persons were classified by the Census as 'ministering to clothing', though most were female spinners, working in their own homes in rural areas. Similarly, despite the fact that it was by this stage possible to weave coarse linen by power loom, most linen weavers were male handloom weavers. By the end of the century although the vestiges of domestic linen production remained, the industry was carried on in spinning mills and weaving factories. In his classic history of the industry, Conrad Gill wrote that 'the chief interest in the industrial history of Ulster after 1750 is the growth of

Table 5.1 *Proportionate distribution of population by general occupational category, northern and southern Ireland, 1881 (%)*

Class	26 counties	6 counties
Professional	9	5
Domestic	19	13
Commercial	3	4
Agricultural	45	34
Industrial	24	44
	100	100

Source. Peter Gibbon, *The Origins of Ulster Unionism*, Manchester, 1975, p. 10.

new groups of producers and new social relationships'.[3] At the end of the eighteenth century, although the industry was organised on a domestic basis, there had been a fundamental change in the position of the majority of linen weavers. Most had moved from the position of being petty-commodity producers, earning a living by a combination of agricultural work and the selling of the produce of their loom on the open (brown) linen markets, to that of full time proletarians employed by a bleacher or linen manufacturer and selling, not a product, but their own labour power. Gill estimated that by 1820 only a third of weavers in Ulster were still independent.[4]

The capitalist organisation of the industry thus preceded its factory organisation. There was a considerable regional variation in the organisation and structure of the industry. The most capitalistically developed section was in north Armagh, west Down and south Antrim. The west and north-west of the province were more backward and in the latter areas households concentrated on the spinning of yarn for the cloth-producing counties of central and south-east Ulster. In these areas yarn production and flax cultivation were crucial in obtaining cash incomes for paying the rent.[5] In Donegal, for example, according to the 1841 Census, over 37,000 females were classified as spinners, in counties Tyrone and Londonderry the figures were respectively 42,000 and 26,000. The lower production cost of machine-spun cotton yarn and its increasing substitution for handspun linen yarn in Lancashire and Scotland, led to a rapid and sustained fall in linen yarn exports from Derry from 1813.[6] In the mid-1820s the development of the wet-spinning process which enabled linen yarn of as fine

159

a quality to be produced by machinery as by hand, spelt the end for the hand spinners in the north-west and west and for the small farm economy which relied on their incomes. As a result there was a substantial increase in emigration.[7]

Concentration of flax spinning in the south and east of Ulster in factories also undermined weaving in the peripheral areas as mill-spun yarn now tended to be supplied by mill owners and putting-out manufacturers. Machine-spun yarn was more even in quality and reliable and it therefore required less skill and strength in weaving. Increasingly women switched from spinning to weaving and boys and girls could now compete with men.[8] The combination of weaving and subsistence agriculture provided a large reservoir of cheap labour for the industrialists who controlled the supply of machine-spun yarn. Thus although the technique for the power weaving of yarn was available from before the Famine, the large supply of cheap weaving labour ensured that employers had no incentive to turn over to powerlooms. The Famine decade which saw a drop of nearly 17 per cent in the province's population − a decrease most marked amongst labourers and cottiers − and in which thousands of linen workers emigrated, led to a labour shortage and, as noted in Chapter Two, wages increased by about a quarter in five years.[9] The 1850s saw the beginning of the mechanisation of weaving, a process accelerated in the next decade during the Cotton Famine.

In contrast to the handloom weavers who were predominantly male, the labour force of the weaving factories was largely female.[10] As noted earlier, mechanisation allowed an influx of women and young workers into weaving. This meant that the weaving trade began to suffer a lowering of status as it became defined as 'women's work'.[11] Already male workers regarded the factory with aversion, associated as it was with the massed ranks of low paid female spinners. A related reason was the harsh discipline, long hours of work and monotony. In her recent reconstruction of the working world of linen workers at the beginning of this century, Betty Messenger refers to the hostile attitude to their work displayed by male weavers in comparison to females:[12]

> While individual personality factors undoubtedly accounted for some of the negative attitudes, equally important was the sense of confinement and frustration which seemed to overwhelm them at their looms, and the realisation that they, often the primary wage earners for a family, were undercompensated when compared with men labouring at other jobs ...

Being called in the city 'old ladies' for undertaking what was there considered to be women's work, did not improve their self-image.

The social effects of the transition from domestic production to the factory was at the heart of the traditional 'pessimistic' view of the industrial revolution. A recent critic of this approach has suggested however, that migrants may often have been resentful of both the monotony and the oppressions of rural life, placing a premium on higher wages, excitement and greater independence of town life.[13]

Many male handloom weavers were much less enthusiastic. Clearly, important values of independence and relative freedom from the discipline of the factory were involved. John Hewitt has uncovered the activities and writings of independent weavers in south-east and mid-Antrim, and north Down in the late eighteenth and early nineteenth century. These men had read Sterne, Smollett and Tom Paine; they supported lending libraries and reading societies. Most important for the historian, they supported a number of local vernacular poets whose poetry reflected increasingly the strains brought about by mechanisation and competition with the powerloom. One poet looked nostalgically backwards in 1853:[14]

> Oh, had I the power to restore,
> The reel would still crack and the spinning wheel snore,
> Mill yarn would sink down as it never had been,
> Trade flourish as fair as it ever was seen,
> A swab with a steam loom would never appear
> Our country to steep in affliction and fear.

A short term boost for the handloom weavers had come at the end of the eighteenth century with the development of the Belfast cotton industry. For three decades at the beginning of the nineteenth century cotton challenged linen as the dominant form of textile production in the Belfast area, where, by 1825, it employed 3,600 workers in spinning mills.[15] It was a high-wage industry with the gross wage of a cotton spinner in 1811 at £2 7s out of which up to 6s a week went to pay each of three juvenile helpers.[16] Weavers' wages were lower and there was a considerable variation between weavers of different sorts of cloth, but they were still high in comparison to linen. In the last brief period of expansion in the early 1820s, a skilled weaver could earn as much as 24s a week. The decline of the industry in the late 1820s left a large and skilled labour force. In 1835 it was estimated that there were 10,000 cotton weavers in Belfast and its neighbourhood.[17] They were earning very low wages. A first class weaver would be on 6s to 8s per week while muslin and calico weavers were on 5s 6d and 3s 6d respectively.[18] Already in the mid-1820s there was a growing tendency for the muslin weaving sector to pass into the hands of Scottish agents who put out local and Scottish yarn.[19] Wages were so low that Scottish firms could afford to send yarn to Ireland, have it woven there, bleach it and send it to Ireland once more for sale.[20]

The extinction of the cotton weavers as a class did not, in fact, come until the outbreak of the American Civil War and the subsequent Cotton Famine. The final agony of the class is sympathetically described in Rodney Green's fine essay. He showed that up until the 1860s their number was, if anything increasing; in 1860 there were 20,000 within a ten mile radius of Belfast.[21] During the Cotton Famine of the mid-1860s great numbers got no work at all and those who did had to labour up to sixteen hours a day to earn a mere eight pence.

The plight of the handloom weavers is a reminder to avoid a one-dimensional view of the industrial revolution as bringing universal improvement. Also it reminds us not to exaggerate the income-generating capacity of the factory-based linen industry. Adult male workers constituted a relatively small minority of the workforce. Between 1835 and 1895 women, young persons and children made up between 78 and 88 per cent of the workforce.[22] By the end of a short-lived period of expansion in the 1860s the industry had almost reached its nineteenth-century peak in terms of employment and towards the end of the century there were periods of stagnation (see Chapter Two). Apart from the core processes of the industry it is important to remember that the linen industry was linked to certain cognate low-paid industries, in particular dress-making and 'making up'. According to the 1901 Census there were 7,978 female dressmakers in Tyrone, 10,530 in Donegal, 6,388 in Antrim, 13,283 in Down and 14,961 in Belfast. Derry grew rapidly in the second half of the century but on the precarious base of shirt-making. By the beginning of the twentieth century even this low-wage industry began to feel the effects of competition from cheaper foreign imports, and the problems for which the city was to become notorious later in the century, in particular the lack of employment for male workers, were emerging.[23]

Another low-wage industry was the making of handkerchiefs, where both linen and cotton cloths were used. The trade combined factory and home work.[24] In Bangor, Co. Down for example, out-work in the preparation of handkerchiefs was the main industry in' the later nineteenth century. The centre of the industry was around Lurgan and Portadown. Here, in the 1880s, its predominantly female factory labour force earned wages ranging from between 5*s* and 11*s* for hand sewers to between 12*s* and 16*s* for veiners. There was also a large domestic industry 'where mothers of families and children are able to get handkerchiefs from the factories to take home ...'[25] The local Medical Officer noted the effects of the use of young children in the Lurgan area in 1906:[26]

> In the poorest and most unhealthy of our dwellings this variety of homework is carried on to an inconceivable extent, and in some streets one could hardly enter a house without seeing 2, 3, 4 or more children, varying in age from 6 to 12 years sitting around a table all intensely busy trying to earn a miserable pittance ... these children are kept close at work from the time they return from school until late ...

The effects of the making up and associated trades on the health of workers became an issue in the first decade of this century when the Superintendent Officer of Health for Belfast made various reports to the Public Health Committee of the Corporation linking 'sweated trades' to the high death rate in the city. As a result of a campaign by the local Labour movement with the support of the Nationalist MP for West Belfast, Joe Devlin, a committee of inquiry into con-ditions of employment in linen and other making-up trades in the north of Ireland was set up by the government. In its report the committee calculated that there were 22,000 young women employed in factories and workshops and probably in excess of that number in outwork.[27] The report recognised the intrinsic vulnerability of out-workers who 'furnish the employer with a supply of labour on which in time of pressure he can make demands, unrestricted by the Factory Acts, whilst in time of slackness he can turn them off, without incurring the standing charges involved in the case of factory workers'.[28] The characteristic types of outworkers were identified as widows and spinsters dependent on this work for their livelihood, married women whose husbands were unemployed and women whose husbands were labourers and earned 'small pay'.[29] Some women actually took work home after their day in the factory. The committee concluded that outworkers' wages were so low as to constitute underpayment.[30]

Together, the linen and related trades were by far the largest industrial employers of labour, both in the province and in Belfast itself. In 1907 according to official figures 61,000 people were employed in the linen industry in Belfast.[31] But it was in the engineering and later the shipbuilding industries that adult male workers, in particular skilled workers, found the most rapidly expanding sources of employment.

The metal trades

The modest development of the metal trades in Ulster before the 1840s has been described in Chapter Two. The thirty years or so after the Great Exhibition was, however, a period of massive expansion in the capital goods industries througout the United Kingdom. The number of workers in engineering, machine building and shipbuilding doubled between 1851 and 1881.[32] In Belfast if we compare the 1851, 1881 and 1911 Census reports for certain key occupations there is similar evidence of impressive expansion.

For shipbuilding the period of most rapid expansion did not begin until after Harland and Wolff employed about 5,000 in the early 1880s. In 1879 a second important yard, Workman and Clark, was established. By 1900 the two yards were employing 12,000 and the combined labour force had grown to 20,000 by 1914.[33]

Although at least one-third of the workers in these industries were labourers earning wages of less than half those of skilled workers, it was the fact that they were the main sources of employment for adult male skilled and semi-skilled workers that gave them a disproportionate influence on the history of the labour movement.

Other industries

Two industries which benefited from the growth and centralisation of population in the greater Belfast area were building and transport.

Table 5.2 *Employment in certain Belfast metal trades, 1851–1911*

	1851	1881	1911
Turners	93	539	2,633
Boilermakers	59	240	1,528
Machine makers	89	385	1,650
Iron manufacturers	135	1,309	3,778
Shipbuilders	297	1,307	6,932

Source. Census of Ireland, relevant years.

In the 1851 Census for Belfast 2,376 were classified in 'transport and storage' and 2,032 in 'building'. By 1911 there were 1,266 railway workers, 563 in the local tramway company, 1,565 in 'harbour and docks' and 3,244 'carmen, carriers and carters'. Building must have accounted for many of the 3,250 carpenters, although some of these would have been employed in the fitting-out trades of the shipyards. It would have employed all of the 912 bricklayers and most of the 1,900 painters.

As a major port and consumption centre Belfast had by the end of the century developed a group of consumer goods industries – mineral waters, soap and candles, matches, and the tobacco industry. The last had a number of factories employing between 400 and 500 workers, the most famous of which was Gallahers.[34] The Belfast Ropeworks established at the end of the 1870s was already employing over 1,000 a decade later.

Wages and standards of living

Wage statistics are patchy before the 1880s and we lack detailed studies of changes in the retail prices of the main consumption articles of the working class. Data on movements in house rents are also lacking. It is, therefore, difficult to be precise about trends in working class living standards in the period. It is, however, certain that linen was the lowest paid of all the textile industries in the United Kingdom.

The calculations of Emily Boyle suggest that, although there was an upward movement in wages in the linen industry between 1833 and 1905, only a small minority of the labour force, primarily skilled men and overlookers, could have consistently earned enough to support

Table 5.3 *Average earnings of operatives working full time in the last pay week of September 1906*

	Men		Lads		Women		Girls		All workers	
	s	d	s	d	s	d	s	d	s	d
Linen	22	4	7	8	10	9	6	7	12	0
Cotton	29	6	11	6	18	8	10	1	19	7
Wool	26	10	8	10	13	10	8	4	15	9
Silk	25	8	8	2	11	2	6	4	13	2

Source. Report of Board of Trade Enquiry into earnings and hours of labour in ... the textile trades, BPP, 1909, LXXX, p. xxii.

a family of four at a 'minimum comfort' level.[35] It is only in the period 1883–1905 that she detects a substantial improvement in real wages of linen workers and this is largely attributable to a fall in the cost of living rather than a rise in money wages. The wages of women workers, girls, and juveniles – the bulk of the workforce – were still pitiably low at the beginning of the twentieth century.

It is also important to remember that official figures *exaggerate* the level of disposable income. 'Even if the average wage per week for women over 18 years of age ... was as indicated by the wage census, about 12*s* 11*d*', explained Adelaide Anderson, one of the first women factory inspectors, 'those of an immense number of women ... did not rise above 7 or 8*s* out of which came deductions for disciplinary fines, charges for damage or purchase of damaged articles, so that for many young women 5–6*s* per week was nearer the mark.'[36]

A government report published in the 1890s detailed the structure of the elaborate system of fines imposed in Ulster's linen industry: 1*d* to 6*d* for late attendance, from 4*d* to 2*s* 6*d* for damaged cloth, from 6*d* to 1*s* for talking, and similar fines for singing or leaving one's place of work without permission.[37] If workers objected they were often dismissed and refused a 'certificate of discharge' – a statement that the worker had been employed by the firm for a period of time and that all wages due had been paid. The practice in Belfast was to refuse it in such cases and this made it extremely difficult to get another job.[38]

Whereas in linen there was only a minority of workers who earned wages over £1 per week at the end of the nineteenth century, ship-building and engineering employed large numbers of skilled and relatively well-paid workers. At the beginning of the nineteenth century when engineering skills were scarce, earnings were high in Belfast. At the Lagan Foundry in 1812 skilled workers could earn as much as £2 per week. By 1836 the level of earnings appears to have fallen and 'the better sort of artisan' could only earn approximately £1 per week.[39] In the 1880s skilled workers in Belfast engineering plants were earning rates comparable to the United Kingdom average whilst labourers as Table 5.4 shows were clearly on a much lower rate.

By 1910 the fitter's rate in Belfast was exceeded only by rates in London, South Wales and Sheffield, and in general the rates of skilled workers in shipbuilding, engineering and building were closely comparable with those in the main centres in the rest of the United Kingdom.[40] In provincial Ulster towns wages rates were lower than

Table 5.4 *Some weekly wage rates in Belfast, 1886*

	United Kingdom		Belfast	
	s	d	s	d
Patternmakers	30	8	29	1
Ironmoulders	30	9	29	10
Brassfounders	30	8	27	7
Turners	29	6	27	1
Fitters and Erectors	29	2	27	1
Labourers	23	1	13	0

Source. Average rates of wages of workpeople employed in engineering and machinery
works at 1 October 1886, BPP, 1893–4, LXXXII, part II, pp. 20–4, 74–5.

in Belfast but by no means the lowest in the United Kingdom. It was symptomatic of their well-being that in their evidence to the *Royal Commission on Labour*, the Belfast representatives of the Amalgamated Society of Engineers and the Boilermakers, two of the most important skilled unions, shared a tone of complacency. The District Agent of the Boilermakers, with 1800 Belfast members, claimed: 'We are getting on very nicely and amicably as far as our members are concerned with our employers.' The President of Belfast No. 2 branch of the ASE amplified: 'We have nothing to complain of in the city of Belfast with regard to our position as a society of workmen, with regard to wages, overtime or piecework. Our wages would stand comparison wtih any in the U.K.'[41]

In terms of wages, therefore, there were two important divides. First there was the division between high- and low-wage industries, as in the cases of shipbuilding and engineering on the one hand and linen on the other. Second there was the divide within industries between the skilled and often unionised men and the unskilled and often non-unionised labourers and women. The distinction between the 'labour aristocrat' and the 'labourer' was one which originated in the language of the period itself, although it has since been taken up by historians as a concept with a certain explanatory power in the analysis of the development of the working class movement in nineteenth-century Britain.[42] The classical use of the concept relies on a contrast between those workers who were normally able to enforce a restriction on the supply of particular forms of labour power, thus forcing up its market price, and those who had no marketable skill and who operated in labour markets which were usually over-supplied.

In Ulster, the post-Famine decline in population did not result in a tight labour market except for relatively brief periods and then only in particular areas and for specific groups of workers. Thus to take the case of agricultural labourers, betwen 1841 and 1912 there was a process described by Fitzpatrick as a 'social revolution'; the virtual disappearance of the hired labourer from Irish agriculture, due in large part to general tendencies towards the concentration of holdings and a move towards cattle farming.[43] However, in many parts of Ulster where the decline occurred there was no subsequent diversification of employment opportunities and so those who remained were in no position to bargain for higher wages. It was only in those areas where alternative sources of employment existed that wage rates moved upwards. In Ulster only two counties had wage rates of more than the Irish average of 10s 9d which, as Fitzpatrick puts it, 'was much less than his English counterpart and absurdly less than his relatives employed in foreign cities. Thus even if real wages had been increasing labourers would have remained discontented with their unaltered state of relative deprivation'.[44]

The extremely low rate of pay for engineering labourers was noted above and this was a general phenomenon amongst the unskilled. In 1894 the average wage for an unskilled labourer in the shipyard was 15s per week, 7s lower than on the Tyne or the Clyde.[45] The position of employers situated in an agricultural hinterland dominated by the decline of small and medium scale agriculture and rural industry was, except in periods of exceptional expansion, a favourable one. They were guaranteed a continuing supply of rural immigrants to employ in unskilled and semi-skilled industrial processes.

The weaknesses of the labourers' bargaining position due to oversupply was reflected in the rigid and antagonistic attitude of employers to any attempts to unionise their labourers. In 1907 at a time of much unrest amongst non-unionised workers, labourers in the Sirocco works, an important engineering firm, went on strike and set up a branch of the National Amalgamated Union of Labour (NAUL). They were locked out and the managing director stated that no worker would be accepted back until he had signed the 'document' committing himself not to join a union. In a revealing interview with the *Belfast Newletter* he commented, 'I have received numerous applications for employment so that at any moment we can go full steam ahead. In the meantime a weeding out process will go on, or to change the metaphor, we have had a sort of spring cleaning and when the dust is shaken out of the carpet, the microbes will not come back.'[46]

It was not until the First World War that there was a substantial improvement in the relative position of the unskilled workers. Labourers benefited from the expansionary economic conditions during the war and there was a very rapid increase in unionisation. Thus if the Belfast membership figures for the ASE are compared with those for the two unions which organised labourers, the relative increase in organisational strength of the latter is evident. By the end of the war, the NAUL, until then really a Belfast organisation, had branches throughout the province including one that gave as its address Macosquin Orange Hall, County Londonderry.[47] In July 1914, a labourer's weekly rate of pay in shipbuilding and engineering was 51 per cent of a plater's and 54 per cent of a fitter's. By 1918, the corresponding ratios were 67 per cent and 69 per cent.[48]

Working conditions

As far as working conditions were concerned there was considerable variation both within and between industries. In linen the internal status hierarchy which placed female spinners at the bottom and the wareroom workers at the top, reflected, in part at least, real differences in the conditions under which the various groups worked.[49] Weavers regarded themselves as superior: 'We were the "elite". We were the "swanks". They (spinners) were the "down".'[50] Nonetheless, conditions in the weaving sheds were also harsh. As well as the deafening noise made by the power belts of the machines and the racing of the shuttles, the weaver also faced heat and dampness, the latter as a result of the induced humidity necessary for weaving linen yarn. A female weaver who started work in a Belfast factory at the age of thirteen in 1904 describes her first day, 'Well, that first day that I went to the weaving ... was desperate. ... Its what you call the fever you take ... its the awful blundering (noise) of the looms. ... Well, coming out, an awful feel over you ... I was very sick. ... That sickness was on me nearly a fortnight.'[51]

Male workers had various roles. Some were weavers, and men practically monopolised all supervisory roles like that of tenter (the overlooker in charge of a number of looms), and they were dominant in the preparatory stages of the linen process. Here, as hacklers and roughers, they were involved in processes with extremely high health risks. In hackling and roughing flax, dust known as 'pouce' filled the air. It irritated and dried up the throat after which it attacked the lungs causing violent spasms of coughing, producing the condition known as 'poucey', which was the forerunner of the killer disease mechanical phthisis.[52] In the preparation and carding rooms working life was short and mortality rates high. In 1872 the average working life of a carder before he became unfit for work was seventeen years and out of every 1,000 at work thirty-eight died. The Belfast death rate at the time was only fourteen per 1,000.

The 1894 *Royal Commission on Labour* contained a report on the employment of women in Ireland which was dominated by discussion of conditions in the spinning mills and weaving factories of Belfast. It included evidence from the physician in charge of the local consumption hospital on the relationship between the unhealthiness of many of the occupations in the linen industry and the high mortality rate from consumption.[53]

In 1894 many of the processes carried on in flax mills and linen factories were declared to be dangerous within the terms of the Factory and Workshop Act and a set of special rules and regulations were published by the Home Office in that year. The main regulations governed ventilation, primarily for the introduction of extractor fans in weaving sheds and in roughing, sorting and hackling rooms. In the wet spinning rooms splash boards were to be erected to cut down on the constant stream of spray which soaked the clothes of workers. Other rules provided for the insulation of steampipes to keep temperatures down, humidity regulations, and the drainage of the floors of the spinning rooms. However, the means of enforcing these regulations were only weakly developed as the local courts were notoriously unsympathetic to prosecutions.[54] Between 1894 and 1914 two more reports were published which demonstrated the degree to which the dangers of dust had been reduced although the problems of heat, damp and humidity remained.[55]

Peter Gibbon has compared the working conditions of the linen workers with those in shipbuilding in an attempt to locate a basis for differing social and political attitudes inside the working class:

> Workers in the linen trade were interchangeable, lacked any choice of work technique, were subject to constant work pressure and were forbidden free physical movement. For employment opportunities they were entirely dependent on local conditions.

Gibbon contrasts these workers with the shipyard men:

> Possessing trade qualifications as they did, they were generally free from reliance upon conditions of purely local prosperity to find work. ... They

were not tied to the mechanical indefinite repetition of the same tasks, but had a fair discretion of job selection, freedom of movement and could work more or less in their own time.[56]

While it is certainly the case that in terms of wage rates and working conditions, the skilled worker in shipbuilding and engineering was in a relatively superior position to the mass of the linen workers, this should not be allowed to obscure the specific hardships that they faced. In the shipyards those men who worked outside on the hulls in all weather conditions were involved in tough and dangerous work. More generally shipbuilding was a capital goods industry subject to severe fluctuations. In its periods of depression large numbers of workers would be laid off. Between 1902 and 1920, for example, the quarterly figures for registered unemployment of trade unionists in Belfast shipbuilding averaged 6 per cent, in eighteen of the quarters it was above 10 per cent, and in the serious depressions of 1903–5 and 1908–9 it shot up to over 20 per cent. This was in a period of general prosperity for the industry. As Alastair Reid comments on the wages of the shipyard labour aristocrats: 'These high earnings have to be evened out over periods of lower rates, under-employment and unemployment. Thus skilled workers' overall earnings may not have been significantly greater than those of unskilled workers, as has normally been assumed.'[57]

Whilst acknowledging the importance of Reid's argument, it is still difficult to escape the impression of the substantial difference in condition and status between, for example, a plater in the shipyard and one of the myriad labourers who were trying to get work on the building sites, docks and in the city's commercial traffic. That the skilled worker's life was hard and insecure can be accepted but this only serves to increase our awareness of the straits to which labourers were so often reduced. The contempt with which many employers regarded labourers is one indication of the difference. In the case of skilled men, for instance, most employers in Ulster had accepted their right to join unions by the end of the century. Another indication of difference is the long hours of work and irregularity of employment of many unskilled workers. Thus whereas by the 1870s the hours of work in linen factories were reduced to fifty-six per week (ten hours a day and not more than six on Saturday), and fifty-four in shipbuilding and engineering, a worker on the tramways at the end of the century could be working up to seventy-two hours a week.[58] But at least tramway workers were guaranteed a fairly regular wage. This was not the case for labourers in other transport occupations or in the building industry. The latter was strongly affected by seasonal fluctuations, as well as by population movements and the movement of interest rates. Although such fluctuations affected craftsman and labourer alike, the former was more likely to have been able to accumulate some savings which, together with union benefits, made it easier to get through a lean period. Dock work and the associated carting trade were subject to severe seasonal fluctuations and as far as the docks were concerned, was organised on a predominantly casual basis. At the time of the famous 1907 strike only one-third of Belfast dockers were 'permanent men'.[59]

Of course the category of labourer was as heterogenous as that of skilled worker. Specialised labourers like coal carters and dockers were paid more than general labourers, and a labourer who worked along-side a craftsman acquired a little of his status, including greater job security and a small pay differential.[60] But of the just under 19,000 workers classified as general labourers in the 1911 Belfast census, not many would have been in this position. For most, unemployment for long spells during the year and low wages while in work made sup-porting a family impossible unless wives and children also worked.

When the factory inspectors carried out a series of investigations into various aspects of female employment in linen in the period 1906–10, they found much evidence of the intense financial pressures on women and children workers because of the lack of opportunities for adequately paid male work. Many families relied on sending their children into the mill as early as was legally possible, and often earlier. By the beginning of this century the half-time system, under which young children of school age alternated work and a rudimentary schooling, was in decline. However, there were widespread attempts to evade the minimum age regulations which determined when a child could leave school and start work. In 1874 the minimum age at which children could be employed was raised from eight to ten, in 1891 to eleven, and in 1901 to twelve.[61] School leaving certificates which had to be presented to employers were forged and under-age children would attempt to impersonate their older brothers and sisters. The effects of the work on the children's health was noted. The poverty of their backgrounds was poor preparation for the rigours of work. In many cases mill children were 'delicate' through undernourishment, tea and white bread, potato bread and oatmeal bread being the principal food. As a result, it was noticed that 'children of mill workers are rather degenerating than improving in physical makeup'.[62] In explaining such circumstances a factory inspector linked them directly to the general problem faced by the unskilled labourer in the city:[63]

> It must be admitted that in a town where there is so much destitution and ill health amongst the poor, opportunities of a family securing 10s paid by utilising the services of a child form a powerful temptation. Again unskilled labourers make very poor wages indeed and a smart boy of thirteen will earn at times almost the same amount as his father ... .

The labour movement

Organisation amongst groups of workers in Ulster to protect and improve their wages and conditions predated the nineteenth century. Gill records the weavers' strike of 1762 as, in part at least, an instance of organisation and resultant class conflict.[64] The first urban manifestation of organisation was amongst the cotton workers. Organisation was sufficiently effective amongst weavers to allow them to negotiate wage scales with employers in 1792, 1810 and 1818. A major strike in Belfast occurred in 1802 and the magistrates issued a public notice that they were determined to suppress all unlawful combinations. In 1816 two men were hanged following an attempt to blow up the house of an unpopular employer, and in 1817 the president of the Muslin Weavers' Society was murdered on Belfast's Malone Road and his employer was accused of the crime. A cotton spinners' society also existed from 1810.[65]

After the decline of the cotton industry in the later 1820s, trade union organisation amongst textile workers disappeared and it only resurfaced later in the century in an extremely weak form. In linen there were no unions at all until the boom years of the early 1870s when unions were established amongst the minority of male workers. The flax-dressers and tenters had unions from that time, the linen-lappers from 1890, and the flax roughers from the same year. From 1889 until 1893 Belfast, like many other industrial centres in the United Kingdom, experienced the upsurge of trade union organisation among hitherto unorganised groups. This was the 'new unionism'. A result of this brief period of militancy was an attempt by the local trades council to organise the mass of female workers in linen. A union, The Textile Operatives Society of Ireland was established, but by 1910 it had only managed to unionise a small section of potential recruits, and in 1914 only about 10 per cent of the labour force in linen was organised.[66]

The weakness of organisation amongst this large group of workers can be explained by a number of factors. First, there was the relative ease with which the basic tasks could be learned. This, together with the large reservoir of potential competitors for work and the frequent depressions in the industry itself during the period from 1873 to 1914, meant that the market position of the linen worker was not a strong one. Second, there was the complex of factors related to a predominantly female labour force. There was the traditional assumption, shared by men of all classes and, no doubt, by many women, that women ought to earn less than men, as the women's earnings were a supplement to a family income based predominantly on a male's earning capacity. Throughout the United Kingdom before 1888 the attitude of male trade unionists to women workers was one of indifference or hostility.[67] Certainly many of the younger women did regard work as a temporary halt on the road to marriage, and those who did not had to struggle hard against formidable obstacles of ingrained submissiveness.[68]

The third factor was the broader 'cultural' aspect of factory life. There was a high degree of localism in the mills' workforces with daughters following mothers and older sisters into the same mill.[69] This was a process often encouraged by the employers. Such family traditions, and the age at which most workers entered mills, created a naturalness about the whole process that served to perpetuate restricted horizons. As the managing director of a large mill explained to a factory inspector, '... it would be useless to employ girls of seventeen and eighteen years who had not previously worked in a spinning mill as they would not put up with the heat and the damp, whereas the children are eager to work and quick at it and do not complain of the conditions ... it would be the ruin of the trade if children could not be employed ...'[70]

There was a positive aspect to all this. Messenger in a wide-ranging set of interviews with retired spinners noted that the camaraderie of the workplace, expressed in practical jokes, songs, occasional outings and celebration of birthdays and other events, were all remembered.[71] Factory inspectors, more imbued with the values of domesticity and maternal responsibility, were more likely to view the same things negatively, and sometimes lamented the lack of interest of many married textile workers in hearth and home. Some workers even went as far as Mrs F, a weaver aged thirty-seven with six children, who 'admitted she knew nothing of housework or the rearing of children and preferred work in a factory'.[72] From this perspective, factory work clearly had its liberating aspect and this, together with the localism mentioned above, would have served to weaken the impulse for unionisation.

A related factor was the intense awareness of status differences; reelers looked down on spinners, weavers regarded themselves as superior to both, and female wareroom workers considered themselves to be the real aristocrats. Status differences were given physical expression in difference in dress with reelers getting 'dressed up terrible', in blouses made of satin and crepe de Chine, and wearing a coat, not a shawl to work.[73] Similarly it was considered a major solecism to say to a weaver that she worked in a 'mill'; 'remember spinning is a mill, weaving is a factory, and stitching is a wareroom.'[74] The airs adopted by the other grades reinforced a strong in-group solidarity amongst the spinners, but this was more likely to be expressed in jibes at other workers than antagonism towards employers.

Fourth, there was the brute reality of employers' power and resources. Much has recently been written of the role of paternalism among Lancashire cotton employers in producing class peace in that area.[75] There is evidence of paternalistic practices in Ulster. Most important were the industrial villages created by industrialists for their labour force. Thus the Barbour family who were the world's largest manufacturers of linen thread, erected a model village at Hilden, near Lisburn, with 350 houses, a primary school and the E. Milne Barbour Memorial Hall 'to minister to the intellectual requirements of the district', with a lecture room and reading and recreation rooms.[76] In Belfast there was also a considerable amount of mill housing. A good example was the village of Ligoniel, effectively controlled by the Ewart family, one of the largest linen firms. In a celebration of the firm's history it was claimed that the 'spirit of achievement flows throughout the entire staff, who favour old traditions by unswerving loyalty. In many cases sons and daughters of employees enter the service of the Company and continue the tradition. ...'[77]

The Ewart's control not untypically extended into the sphere of politics where they encouraged a loyalty to Belfast conservatism amongst their workforce.[78] The negative aspects of paternalism were also clear when an employee came into conflict with the firm, for to lose one's employment could also mean the loss of one's home. In 1909 the British-based Workers' Union organised bleachgreen workers employed by the York Street Flax Spinning Company at its works in Clady, County Antrim. When the men went on strike they were dismissed and asked to hand in the keys of their houses.[79]

Attempts to start unions were often met by lock-outs and in the case of male linen lappers their replacement by machinery and women.[80] Linen workers' appreciation of the weakness of their position and fears of victimisation must therefore be placed alongside recollections of paternalistic employers.

The final factor in weakening unionisation in linen, and indeed in many other sections of industry, is often considered to have been the sectarian division inside the working class. Alexander Moncrieffe in his evidence to the Select Committee of Handloom Weavers in 1835 said of Ulster, there was 'so much political difference between the men, that they cannot permanently co-operate together'.[81] The notion that religious differences, encouraged by employers, were at the heart of many of the problems of the labour movement in Ulster has been at the centre of a traditional view of the province's labour history.[82] However, if we wish to deal with the structural reasons for the weaknesses of union organisation amongst linen workers, then the factors outlined above are of fundamental importance. Sectarianism would, at most, have exacerbated these problems at particular times of heightened political tension. But it is important to remember that the majority of employers wanted a disciplined workforce and production unhindered by sectarian outbursts. Those employers who, like the Ewarts, encouraged an almost completely Protestant labour force were in a minority.[83]

In contrast to linen, shipbuilding and engineering had a labour force with large groups of workers in categories with relatively high levels of trade union organisation throughout the United Kingdom. Metal workers had been unionised from the first half of the century; the iron moulders had a branch from 1826; the boilermakers from 1841; and when the Amalgamated Society of Engineers was established in 1851, there were already branches of its constituent unions in Belfast.[84] A key characteristic of these groups of workers was their intense sectionalism; the degree to which they were concerned with the protection of their own place in the labour market and the work process. Because of this, conflicts with other workers, skilled and unskilled, were frequent.

There was a complex differentiation in the shipbuilding labour force which went far beyond the simple division between 'tradesman' and 'labourer', comprising a hierarchy of more or less 'advantaged' trades as well as an internal hierarchy within each trade. By the end of the century there were over twenty major unions in United Kingdom shipbuilding and up to 200 if all the local and short-lived societies are included. The complex division of labour resulted in an overlap in the applicability of skills which led to conflict between different unions – the demarcation disputes for which the shipbuilding industry has long been famous. The most persistent disputes were between boilermakers and shipwrights, boilermakers and drillers, engineers and plumbers, shipwrights and joiners, and iron moulders and brass moulders. There was also competition between the unions to increase membership and funds. This could lead to bitter conflicts. One of the most long running was between the ASE and the United Patternmakers Association. It climaxed in a dispute in Belfast in 1892 when the ASE refused to support a Patternmakers' wage claim and encouraged its Belfast members to blackleg.[85] Of the forty strikes recorded in the reports of the Board of Trade labour correspondents, between 1888 and 1913, in which skilled shipbuilding and engineering workers were involved, fourteen arose from demarcation issues.[86]

Some of the most bitter sectional disputes arose between skilled men and labourers. The boilermakers in the United Kingdom as a whole responded to attempts by their assistants to organise with complaints of the need 'to get the labourers to keep their places ... the helper ought to be subservient and do as the mechanic tells him'.[87] Initial unionisation amongst workers like this would often be directed more against the craftsmen than the common capitalist employer. In Belfast during the upsurge of new unionism in the early 1890s, the National Amalgamated Union of Labour began to organise labourers in the shipyards for the first time. The first demand was for a wage increase and the end of the system by which platers' helpers were paid by the boilermakers they assisted.[88] On the trades council, hitherto dominated by delegates of the craft unions of the skilled workers, the appearance at this time of what was regarded as an excessive number of delegates from the new unions of the unskilled, led to the resignation of some prominent members.

These divisions amongst the trade unionists, together with the fact that such a high proportion of the working class in the largest industry was not unionised at all, were two of the major problems facing those who in the last decade of the century began the struggle to develop a labourist political consciousness. In Belfast, by far the most important centre of activity, the local trades council, established in 1881, and made up of delegates from most of the industries in the city, played a prominent part in the attempt to develop a political movement. But the problems members of the council faced were immense. William Walker, a founder member of the Belfast branch of the Independent Labour Party, and perhaps the most important figure to emerge in the Belfast movement before 1914, in his annual report on the trades council's activities in 1899 clearly described the limits of trade union consciousness at the time:[89]

> ... the average trade unionist, it is to be deplored, interests himself very little in labour problems, except insofar as they affect his own trade, hence the difficulty of getting him to realise the immense influence the trades council would exert if loyally supported by those whose interest it was formed to defend.

The organised section of the working class was disproportionately Protestant and this has often led commentators to claim that the weakness of class consciousness in Belfast and the other main centres of industry in Ulster was a reflection of the 'privileges' which Protestant workers enjoyed over their Catholic counterparts.[90] It is clear that Catholics were under-represented in skilled occupations throughout the nineteenth century. Thus in Belfast, according to the 1901 Census, whilst 24 per cent of the population were Catholic, they made up only 8 per cent of ship, boat and barge builders, 6 per cent of shipwrights, 10 per cent of engine and machine workers, 11 per cent of fitters and turners, and 10 per cent of boilermakers. They constituted 15 per cent of carpenters, 27 per cent of bricklayers and 12 per cent of plumbers. In contrast they accounted for almost half of female linen spinners, a third of general labourers and 41 per cent of dockers.[91]

But if Protestant privilege existed, it did so for only a minority of the Protestant working class, as clearly the majority of unskilled workers was Protestant and their politics cannot easily be explained by reference to privilege. Another problem with this argument is that it was precisely from the so-called 'privileged' section of the working class that the movement towards a form of labourist politics was most pronounced both before and after the war. Concomitantly it was often from the least privileged sections of the working class that manifestations of sectarianism came; the role of rivet boys and other unskilled labourers in the periodic shipyard expulsions is only one example.[92]

In fact the 'problem' as far as the politics of the labour movement in Ulster is concerned is, in part, in the eyes of the beholders. It is based on an implicit overestimation of the degree to which the labour movement in the rest of the United Kingdom had developed a political class consciousness. At least before 1914, it is easy to exaggerate the extent of class consciousness and support for socialist politics. As Hunt has written: 'Despite industrialisation, urbanisation and the widening gulf between employers and workers, the persistence of harmonious class relations and the remarkably slow development of working class consciousness are two of the major themes of nineteenth century British labour history.'[93]

When it is remembered that the formative years of the labour movement, from the 1880s onwards, were also the years when Irish politics were dominated by the conflicts between what Gibbon has called 'the two most spectacular popular class alliances in the political history of the British Isles'[94] (Irish nationalism and Ulster unionism), then it is the existence at any level of a labour movement which is worthy of notice, not its lack of development.

Belfast at the turn of the century was the dominant centre of trade unionism and labour politics in Ireland. Its trades council was active politically at both municipal and, from the Edwardian period, at parliamentary level. It was active in the creation of the city's Labour Representation Committee in 1903, and the Committee's candidate, William Walker, came within a few hundred votes of winning a seat in 1905 and 1906. In the same period two of Belfast's four parliamentary seats were held by MPs who, if their bitterly contrasting positions on the future government of Ireland are put to one side, could quite easily have fitted into the Labour group at Westminster.[95]

For too long historians of nationalist sympathies have tended to exaggerate the dismal side of the labour history of Ulster. They have tended to reproduce the type of blinkered view so clearly articulated by William O'Brien, a close associate of the one outstanding Irish marxist of the period, James Connolly. O'Brien later wrote of the attitudes of himself and other members of the small Socialist Party of Ireland who, in the first decade of this century, sought to implement Connolly's thesis of the necessity of fusing Irish socialist and nationalist traditions: 'There was very little connection between the labour movement in Belfast and the rest of Ireland. We thought the majority of workers and employers being in the same political camp there was little likelihood of antagonism in the industrial field.'[96]

179

In fact there was a long tradition of conflict between capital and labour in Ulster. That this did not lead to a similar history of political class conflict was a consequence, in part at least, of the tendency of many socialists to link socialism to demands for an independent and unitary thirty-two county state. Whatever the appropriateness of this strategy for the rest of the island of Ireland, it was incapable of coming to terms with that enigma − central to the problems of labour politics in Ulster − the active trade unionist who was also a Unionist in political loyalties.[97]

Notes

1. W. E. Vaughan and A. J. Fitzpatrick eds., *Irish Historical Statistics: Population, 1821–1971*, Dublin, 1978, p. 27.
2. Francois Bedarida, *A Social History of England 1851–1975*, London, 1979, p. 17.
3. Conrad Gill, *The Rise of the Irish Linen Industry*, Oxford, 1925, p. 138.
4. *Ibid.*, p. 274.
5. Brenda Collins, 'Protoindustrialisation and pre-famine emigration', *Social History*, 7, 1982, pp. 136–7.
6. *Ibid.*, p. 138.
7. *Ibid.*, p. 139.
8. *Ibid.*, p. 140.
9. See also Gill, *Irish Linen*, p. 328.
10. D. L. Armstrong, 'Social and economic conditions in the Belfast linen industry', *Irish Historical Studies*, VII, 1951, p. 241.
11. Betty Messenger, *Picking up the Linen Threads*, Belfast, 1982, p. 160 and Mary E. Daly, 'Women in the Irish workforce from pre-industrial to modern times', *Saothar*, VII, 1981, p. 77.
12. Messenger, *Linen Threads*, p. 158.
13. E. H. Hunt, *British Labour History 1815–1914*, London, 1981, p. 67.
14. See John Hewitt, *Ulster Poets 1800–1870*, M.A. thesis, Queen's University of Belfast, 1951, p. 113.
15. F. Geary, 'The rise and fall of the Belfast cotton industry: some problems', *Irish Economic and Social History*, VIII, 1981, p. 35.
16. *Ibid.*, p. 42.
17. M. G. Doyle, *The development of Industrial Organisations Amongst Skilled Artisans in Ireland, 1780–1838*, M. Phil. thesis, Southampton, 1973, p. 172.
18. *Ibid.*, p. 177.
19. David Dickson, 'Aspects of the rise and decline of the Irish cotton industry', in L. M. Cullen and T. C. Smout eds., *Comparative Aspects of Scottish and Irish Economic History*, Edinburgh, 1977, p. 110.
20. Doyle, *Skilled Artisans*, p. 177.
21. E. R. R. Green, 'Cotton handloom weavers in the north-east of Ireland', *Ulster Journal of Archaeology*, 3rd ser. VII, 1944, pp. 32, 40.

22. Emily Boyle, *The Economic Development of the Irish Linen Industry*, unpublished Ph.D. thesis, The Queen's University of Belfast, 1979, p. 147.
23. Desmond Murphy, *Derry, Donegal and Modern Ulster, 1790–1921*, Derry, 1981, p. 174.
24. *Factory Inspector's Report, 1887*, BPP, 1888, XXVI, p. 417.
25. *Ibid.*, p. 417.
26. *Factory Inspector's Report for 1906*, BPP, 1907, X, p. 190.
27. *Committee of Inquiry into the Conditions of Employment in the Linen and Other Making-Up Trades of the North of Ireland*, BPP, 1912–13, XXIV, p. v.
28. *Ibid.*, p. v.
29. *Ibid.*, p. vi.
30. *Ibid.*, p. 418.
31. *Summary of Returns of Persons Employed in Textile Factories in U.K. in 1907*, BPP, 1909, LXXIX, p. 856.
32. E. J. Hobsbawm, *Industry and Empire*, London, 1969, p. 17.
33. Henry Patterson, *Class Conflict and Sectarianism*, Belfast, 1980, p. 88.
34. *Factory Inspector's Report for 1889*, BPP, 1890, XX.
35. Emily Boyle, *Economic Development*, p. 166.
36. Adelaide Anderson, *Women in the Factory: An Administrative Adventure 1893–1921*, London, 1922, p. 84.
37. *Report Upon the Conditions of Work in Flax Mills and Linen Factories*, BPP, 1893–94, XVII.
38. *Ibid.*
39. Coe, *Engineering Industry*, p. 173.
40. Coe, *Engineering Industry*, p. 177.
41. *Third Report of the Royal Commission on Labour*, BPP, 1893–94, XXXII, Q.23310.
42. The classic statement is Hobsbawm's 'The labour aristocracy in nineteenth century Britain' in *Labouring Men*, London, 1964.
43. David Fitzpatrick, 'The disappearance of the Irish agricultural labourer, 1841–1912', *Irish Economic and Social History*, VII, 1980.
44. Fitzpatrick, 'Agricultural labourers', p. 81.
45. Minutes of Belfast Trades Council, 9 March 1894.
46. R. M. Fox, *Jim Larkin: The Rise of the Underman*, London, 1957, p. 30.
47. In June 1914 the ASE, the NAUL, and The Workers' Union had 3,405, 3,566 and 3,483 members respectively. By June 1918 the corresponding totals were 5,224, 12,767 and 7,705. (These data are derived from monthly and annual reports published by the three unions.)
48. Patterson, *Class Conflict*, p. 95.
49. Messenger, *Linen Threads*, p. 61.
50. *Ibid.*, p. 121.
51. *Ibid.*, p. 122.
52. Boyle, *Economic Development*, p. 161.
53. *Report Upon the Conditions of Work in Flax Mills and Linen Factories*, BPP, 1893–94, XVII, p. 12.
54. *Factory Inspector's Report* for 1900, BPP, 1901, X, p. 340.

55. *Report Upon the Conditions of Work in Flax and Linen Mills as Affecting the Health of Operatives Employed Therein*, BPP, 1904, X; *Report of the Departmental Committee on Humidity and Ventilation in Flax Mills and Linen Factories*, BPP, 1914, XXXVI.
56. Gibbon, *Ulster Unionism*, pp. 83–85.
57. Alastair Reid, 'Skilled workers in the shipbuilding industry 1880–1920' in Austen Morgan and Bob Purdie eds., *Ireland: Divided Nation Divided Class*, London, 1980, pp. 117–18.
58. Robert McElborough, *Memoirs of a Belfast Working Man*, Belfast, 1974.
59. Henry Patterson, 'James Larkin and the Belfast dockers and carters strike of 1907', *Saothar*, IV, 1978, p. 10, *et seq.*
60. Hunt, *Labour History*, p. 90.
61. Armstrong, *'Belfast Linen'*, p. 269.
62. *Factory Inspector's Report for 1906*, BPP, 1907, X, p. 248.
63. *Ibid.*, p. 248.
64. Gill, *Irish Linen*, p. 147.
65. Doyle, *Skilled Artisans*, p. 169 and pp. 173–5. The Westminster Parliament passed a Special Combinations Act for Ireland which was in some respects even harsher than the British Combinations Acts. See J. D. Clarkson, *Labour and Nationalism in Ireland*, New York, 1978, p. 55.
66. Boyle, *Economic Development*, pp. 154–5.
67. Hunt, *Labour History*, p. 258.
68. Messenger, *Linen Threads*, p. 207.
69. *Ibid.*, p. 31 and p. 205.
70. *Factory Inspector's Report for 1908*, BPP, 1909, XXI, p. 533.
71. Messenger, *Linen Threads*, p. 73.
72. *Factory Inspector's Report for 1906*, BPP, 1907, XI.
73. Messenger, *Linen Threads*, p. 72.
74. *Ibid.*, p. 162.
75. Patrick Joyce, *Work, Society and Politics*, Hassocks, Brighton, 1980.
76. 'Century old Northern Ireland firms supplement', *Belfast Newsletter*, 24 May 1932.
77. *Belfast Newsletter*, 24 May 1932. See also D. S. Macneice, 'Industrial villages in Ulster 1800–1900' in Peter Roebuck ed., *Plantation to Partition*, Belfast, 1981.
78. See evidence of Sir William Ewart to *Select Committee to whom the Belfast Corporation Bill was referred*, BPP, 1896, VIII.
79. *Annual Report of the Workers Union for 1909*, p. 221.
80. Patterson, *Class Conflict*, pp. 37–8.
81. Doyle, *Skilled Artisans*, p. 174.
82. See for example Andrew Boyd, *The Rise of the Irish Trade Unions 1729–1970*, Tralee, 1972.
83. Gibbon mentions one Sandy Row mill owner who in the mid-Victorian period drew his workforce entirely from local Orangemen and their families. It was known as the 'Orange Cage' (*Ulster Unionism*, p. 85). A Catholic priest who gave evidence to the inquiry on the 1886 riots, whilst criticising some firms, Harland and Wolff and Ewarts in particular, for not adequately protecting their Catholic workers, added,

'the heads of many firms acted firmly and suppressed all intimidation and annoyance inside their works with the best results', *Report*, Q.14, 457.

84. Patterson, *Class Conflict*, p.xiii.

85. This paragraph relies heavily on Reid, 'Workers in shipbuilding', pp. 119–120.

86. Austen Morgan, *Politics, the Labour Movement and the Working Class in Belfast 1905–23*, unpublished Ph.D. thesis, Queen's University, Belfast, 1978, pp.54–5.

87. Quoted in Hunt, *Labour History*, p.260.

88. Patterson, *Class Conflict*, p.73.

89. Belfast Trades Council, *Biannual Report for 1899–1900*.

90. See Geoff Bell, *The Protestants of Ulster*, London, 1976, and Paddy Devlin, *Yes We Have No Bananas*, Belfast, 1982.

91. J.W. Boyle, *The Rise of the Irish Labour Movement 1888–1907*, unpublished Ph.D. thesis, Trinity College, Dublin, 1961, p.54.

92. See Patterson, *Class Conflict*, ch.6.

93. Hunt, *Labour History*, p.340.

94. Gibbon, *Ulster Unionism*, p.3.

95. The MPs were Joe Devlin, first elected in 1905 for West Belfast and the Protestant populist, Tom Sloan, 1902–1910 for South Belfast. For a more detailed treatment of the politics of this period see Patterson, *Class Conflict* and 'Independent orangeism and class conflict in Edwardian Belfast – a reinterpretation' in *Proceedings of the Royal Irish Academy*, LXXX, Dublin, 1980.

96. Morgan, *Labour Movement*, p.329.

97. For an analysis of the weaknesses of traditional Irish socialist thinking on Ulster see Paul Bew, Peter Gibbon and Henry Patterson, *The State in Northern Ireland 1921–72*, Manchester, 1979, ch.1.

CHAPTER SIX

THE NORTHERN IRELAND ECONOMY, 1914–39

D. S. Johnson

The Great War which began in August 1914 was to have a considerable and long lasting effect on Ulster as it had for the whole of Ireland. In demographic terms it was a disaster second only to the Famine of the late 1840s. By Armistice Day 1918, 49,000 Irishmen had lost their lives in the hostilities, of whom probably around 24,000 came from the six Ulster counties which in 1920 were to become Northern Ireland.[1] This represents 12·6 per cent of males aged 18–40 at the time of the 1911 census. Yet despite the human misery that lies behind these bare statistics, the war brought considerable economic prosperity to the whole of Ireland, north and south – indeed it is ironic that the most affluent years of the Union were those immediately prior to its ending. Nowhere was this boom more marked than in the six north-eastern counties. The cause of this upsurge in activity was simply that the war effort made heavy demands on those goods which had traditionally been produced within the province, namely textiles, foodstuffs and shipping.

After a period of rapid expansion in the 1860s and early 1870s, the linen industry, at least in terms of the numbers it employed, stagnated down to the turn of the century. During the years immediately prior to the war, the industry showed signs of resurgence, based largely on the growth of exports, particularly to the United States; numbers employed increased from 67,000 in 1907 to 76,000 in 1912. The expansion was maintained during the war, when employment rose to 90,000.[2] This was a direct result of the increased demand for linen goods for military purposes, notably tents, haversacks, hospital equipment and aeroplane fabric, which more than offset the losses in overseas markets. As *The Economist* noted: 'During the war the linen industry was almost entirely devoted to providing war supplies and enjoyed prosperity, even though it was entirely government controlled from the raw supplies through every stage to the final disposal of the products.'[3] Initial problems resulting from the German invasion of Belgium, a traditional source of the raw materials for Ulster's mills, were overcome in two ways. The acreage under flax within Ireland was doubled, thus helping to spread the benefits of the boom to the agricultural community and increased use was made of other fibres, particularly cotton. The second main branch of the province's textile sector, the Derry shirtmaking trade, also benefited from military demands. In 1907 the industry's total output was £1·04 million, while during the hostilities, War Office contracts alone annually averaged nearly £830,000, though admittedly the general price level had risen over the intervening period.[4]

Like linen, agriculture had also experienced a period that was in general one of stagnation from the late 1870s to the turn of the century, after which prices began to rise particularly from the end of 1904. It was still by far the largest employer of labour, accounting for nearly a third of the labour force in the six north-eastern counties in 1911, thus its fortunes were important in determining the prosperity of the province as a whole. War brought unprecedented affluence. Naval hostilities, in particular the German U-boat campaign, greatly increased shipping rates and made certain sea routes, notably the Atlantic and the North Sea, physically hazardous. The result was that the United Kingdom (which, of course, included Ireland) had to rely much more on her own producers than before 1914. In beef, for example, by 1917 British and Irish farmers supplied 90 per cent of the country's needs compared to 60 per cent before the war; imports of butter fell from 4·0 million lb in 1914 to 1·6 million in 1918.[5] The result was that Ulster's farmers, like those in the rest of the country, were operating in a seller's market. Agriculture in Ireland generally prospered even more than in Britain as governmental attempts to control prices were less successful in the former, largely because of the numerical strength of the farming community and their general resistance to state intervention. In beef the regulation scheme broke down completely while for pigs it was estimated that by 1918 between 90 and 95 per cent were being sold above the prices fixed by the government.[6] As can be seen from Table 6.1 agricultural prices generally rose substantially faster than the cost of living in both the wartime and immediate post war years. It is true that the volume of foodstuffs exported fell during the period, but this is not indicative of agricultural stagnation. First, the imports to Ireland of both butter and pork fell in the war, particularly after 1916, so domestic suppliers were simply filling this gap. Second and even more important, falling exports were a sign that

185

Table 6.1 *Prices and the cost of living in Ireland, 1914–29 (1914 = 100)*

Year	Butter	Pork	Eggs	Beef	Flax	Cost of living
1915	126	124	128	133	191	123
1916	148	149	155	152	249	146
1917	189	210	213	195	286	176
1918	220	256	359	211	331	203
1919	261	269	341	221	396	215
1920	296	314	314	250	423	249

Source. B. R. Mitchell and P. Deane, *Abstract of British Historical Statistics*, Cambridge, 1962, p. 478; T. M. Barrington, 'A review of Irish agricultural prices', *Journal of the Statistical and Social Inquiry Society of Ireland*, XV, 1926–27, pp. 249–80.

home consumption was increasing: not only were prices rising, but the real burden of the annuity payments owed under the Land Acts was being eroded by inflation, thus the agricultural community could afford to consume more of the foodstuffs it produced. Some farmers found their incomes further increased by the encouragement given to arable production, both cereals and flax. The ploughed area in Ulster (six counties) increased from 637,681 acres in 1910 to 856,719 in 1918, the highest level since the collapse of grain prices in the early 1880s.[7]

The effect of the war on the province's third major sector, shipbuilding and its ancillary industries, is less easy to assess because of the absence of information relating to government contract work. Certainly war created a demand for new shipping; the U-boat campaign ensured that. The problems came on the supply side. There were shortages of steel and other raw materials and the number of skilled workers was inadequate. Many of them had volunteered at the outbreak of war and such was their value as engineers that the armed forces were reluctant to release them. The trade unions exacerbated the situation by their reluctance either to allow the 'dilution' of the labour force with unskilled workers or to agree to changes in traditional working practices. After 1916 however, the problem was tackled more vigorously as by then U-boats were each month sinking three times more tonnage than was being replaced. The government's response was to accord shipbuilding a higher priority than previously and to bring the yards, including those of Belfast, under direct control; work was diverted away from commercial production towards admiralty projects and other war materials. During the wartime period, Harland and Wolff launched approximately 400,000 tons of mercantile and naval vessels. The latter comprised largely destroyers, monitors and light cruisers, but it also constructed hospital ships such as the 50,000 ton *Britannic* and troop carriers like the 33,000 ton *Justicia*. Workman Clark launched vessels totalling 260,000 tons, mostly small ships, boom defence vessels, sloops, patrol boats and cargo carriers. In addition to the work provided in the shipyards, Admiralty contracts were also important for the adjacent ropeworks; 50 per cent of the total cordage made for the navy was produced in Belfast. By the end of the war, not only had capacity increased, but the labour force in Harland and Wolff, and Workman Clark had risen from 20,000 in 1914 to over 29,000 five years later.[8]

Thus during the war the province's three largest sectors saw considerable prosperity, though not all sections of the community benefited equally. Down to 1916 wage rates tended to lag behind rising prices with a consequent deterioration in workers' living standards. Even so, this relative fall may well have been offset by the low levels of unemployment, overtime working, and the greater opportunity for more members of the family to find work. In any case, from 1917 wage rates rose faster than prices, so that by 1919 they equalled and sometimes exceeded those prevalent before the war.[9]

The high level of economic activity experienced in the province during the war continued into peace. The boom of 1919–20 occurred in most of the developed world with the exception of certain areas of Europe which remained battle-scarred or wracked by political disorder. It was caused partly by the deprivation that had existed over the previous five years, and partly by the destruction the war had brought about. The boom was financed by the large volume of liquid assets which had been accumulated between 1914 and 1919 but which people had been unable to spend because of wartime restrictions on investment and consumption.[10] For consumer goods, like linen, there was a considerable 'pent up' demand which had remained unsatisfied during the hostilities when 80 per cent of the industry's productive capacity had been devoted to military rather than civilian needs. Between 1918 and 1920 the numbers of both spindles and looms in the province reached their historical peak. In 1919 the *Belfast Newsletter* noted with considerable prescience in view of the later decline, that 'in the long history of the linen industry, 1919 may in future be called the *annus mirabilis*.'[11] The paper went on to describe shipbuilding in the city as having had 'a most successful year'. This was a consequence of the attempt to replace the losses incurred by the world's merchant fleets which had been impossible during the war because of shortages of steel and skilled labour, and the diversion of production to military purposes. In 1919 employment in Belfast shipbuilding rose to a peak of nearly 30,000, a figure never exceeded before or subsequently. Harland and Wolff and Workman Clark were respectively first and second of all United Kingdom yards in terms of tonnage launched and the Queen's Island also built the largest ship, the *Arundel Castle*. The demand for agricultural goods also remained buoyant immediately after the war. Prices were still rising as the supply situation in parts of Europe had not returned to its normal peace time condition and in areas of the centre and east of the continent there were famine conditions. As Table 6.1 shows, the price of agricultural commodities, already high in 1918, largely kept pace with the rise in the cost of living into 1920. The *Northern Whig* in its review of 1919 noted that as a result of the sustained prosperity experienced over a five year period, 'the price of land had soared to a remarkable degree.'[12]

The first half of 1920, then, saw the culmination of a boom in the province that had lasted more than a decade. But within just over a year, the economic situation had changed beyond recognition as depression of a most persistent and unyielding nature replaced prosperity. For the next twenty years unemployment was rarely below 20 per cent and the province's main industries were always operating at well below capacity. For farmers the income levels achieved in 1919–20 were not regained for over a decade and not markedly surpassed until the Second World War.

Partition

We will examine the causes and consequences of the depression in the province's staple industries later but, first, there is another aspect of the Ulster economy in the inter-war period that merits attention; namely the partition of Ireland after 1922. How did the existence of a Land Boundary in the island affect the development of the six northeastern counties? Did it, as one polemicist has suggested, worsen the province's economic position by cutting it off from southern markets, so that 'Unemployment followed Dismemberment'?[13] Before answering the question it is necessary to specify what the alternatives to partition were. The first was an economically united Ireland within the United Kingdom. This would certainly have benefited Northern Ireland as the region would have enjoyed all the advantages of the British link with none of the drawbacks. It was not, however, a realistic possibility as the twenty-six county provisional government wanted both political and fiscal independence from the United Kingdom. The second alternative to partition was an Ireland united, but economically separate from Britain. This gives rise to further questions, admittedly both hypothetical and unanswerable. Would an independent united Ireland have embarked on protection? Would the 'economic war' of 1932–38 have taken place?[14] Or would a combination of northerners and conservative southern elements have prevented both these developments and set up some sort of free trade area which comprised Britain and Ireland? We raise these questions only to indicate the complexity of the issues involved. If we imagine, however, that in a united Ireland, the same economic policies would have been undertaken, as those actually pursued in the Irish Free State after 1922, then there is little doubt that the north-east would have suffered economic damage.

First, as we shall see below, the province received certain subsidies both to its unemployment fund and its agriculture which a poorer government in Dublin might have been unable to provide. Furthermore by 1930 Northern Ireland was receiving certain benefits, including army, navy and consular services virtually free. Second, its economy undoubtedly would have suffered from a diminution of exports to the British market. Tobacco, for example, would have been subject to prohibitive duties from 1923 and after 1931 many of the province's textile and engineering goods would have been affected by British protective measures. The total of Northern Ireland's exports to Britain of these commodities alone exceeded the *whole* of its exports to the Irish Free State: in 1931, for example, they were approximately £10 million compared to cross-border exports of just over £5 million.[15] It is very doubtful therefore if gains in the southern market could have compensated the province's industries for the losses that economic separation from Britain would have entailed. Third, the Northern Irish farming community would have suffered from the 'economic war' as did that in the Irish Free State. Largely as a result of the 'war' Free State agricultural exports to Britain halved between 1931 and 1935 while those from Northern Ireland rose by 20 per cent. Indeed it could be argued that in some measure the province benefited from the duties on southern produce as they gave Ulster farmers a superior competitive position on the British market. True, partition had certain drawbacks, particularly after 1932 when de Valera transformed the Irish Free State from among the least to one of the most protected countries in the world. Exports across the Land Boundary fell from approximately £5 million in 1931 to £1·68 million five years later: nonetheless not all this decline was attributable to partition. Two-thirds of Northern Ireland's exports to the South consisted of goods previously imported from Britain and overseas. As the Free State reduced its imports from *all* sources in the 1930s it was only natural that less should enter by way of Belfast, Derry and the Land Boundary, just as fewer goods came in through southern ports like Dublin and Cork. Furthermore it is well known that as a result of partition a substantial border smuggling trade came into existence and consequently official trade statistics considerably underestimate the true level of economic intercourse between north and south. Indeed it was the very geographic irrationality of the Land Boundary winding its way over the Irish countryside bisecting villages, farms, fields and even on occasions shops and houses, that made it less of an economic reality. Thus although partition inflicted some harm on the six counties, it was probably slight compared to the losses a fiscal boundary between Northern Ireland and Britain would have entailed. It was certainly much less than the damage caused to the province's industries by developments within the international economy.[16]

As for the three Ulster counties transferred to the Irish Free State in 1921, Cavan, Monaghan and Donegal, they remained extremely poor throughout the inter-war period, even by Irish standards. This poverty, however, was of long standing: Cavan and Monaghan had experienced higher rates of population decline in the period 1841–1922 than virtually all other Irish counties, and West Donegal was one of the most impoverished areas in Ireland. Until 1932 the border had little effect on their main economic activity, agriculture, as farming products could cross the Land Boundary freely. With the beginning of the 'economic war' farmers in these three counties were adversely affected in common with those in the rest of the Free State. Paradoxically, though, they may well have suffered less than other areas of the country because of the prevalence of cross-border smuggling.

Industry and employment

During the period from 1920 to 1939 the Northern Ireland economy experienced persistently high rates of unemployment, 19 per cent of the insured labour force on average between 1923 and 1930 and 27 per cent between 1931 and 1939. In terms of the proportion of the population out of work, of all the regions of the United Kingdom only Wales had a worse record. These high rates largely stemmed from the problems experienced by Northern Ireland's three staples, shipbuilding, linen and agriculture which during the period account for between 40 and 50 per cent of the working population. Additionally there was a failure to attract 'new' rapidly growing industries which would have created fresh employment. Finally, and of much less significance, there is the possibility that the level of insurance benefits, much higher in relation to incomes than in Britain, may have led to greater unemployment, partly through reducing emigration. Why did Northern Ireland's three main sectors of employment experience such difficulties between the wars? All three were adversely affected by worldwide economic developments which, to a large extent, local industrialists, farmers, and government ministers were powerless to control. As we shall see, given the unpromising environment in which they were operating, both industry and agriculture in Northern Ireland, despite depression, in many respects performed creditably.

The main problem for the Belfast shipyards was worldwide over capacity. The volume of international trade in primary products did not regain the level of 1913 until 1925; over the same period world tonnage expanded by a third.[17] Although world trade rose after 1925, in the peak inter-war year, 1929, it was still only 20 per cent above its pre-war level, after which it fell once more. Furthermore not only did the boom of 1919–20 reduce the need for new vessels by greatly increasing the mercantile marine but it also reduced replacement demand. By 1921 the world's shipping stock was much newer than before the war, so a smaller proportion needed to be built each year as substitutes for older ships retired from service and scrapped. Thus shipbuilding throughout the world was in difficulty during the interwar period and in the United Kingdom the industry was hit especially hard. Between 1914 and 1919 because of the domestic demands made upon them, British yards had been unable to fulfil their traditional role of 'shipbuilders to the world' (prior to 1914 they had supplied nearly 60 per cent of all new tonnage). The result was that, during the war, other countries (notably the United States, Japan, Scandinavia and Holland) fostered, largely by subsidies, the development of their own industries, which they were reluctant to see disappear after 1919.[18] Thus in the interwar period Britain's relative position had worsened within a highly competitive market.

Given these underlying difficulties the Belfast yards performed creditably, particularly down to 1930. Between 1909 and 1913 the proportion of United Kingdom merchant shipping launched from the city was approximately 9·5 per cent. In the period 1922–30 it was 9·7 per cent, virtually the same, and Harland and Wolff retained its traditional place as one of the world's great shipyards.[19] In 1929 for example, it launched both the largest tonnage in the world and the biggest ship, the *Britannic*.[20] This relatively successful performance was based on three main elements. First, largely due to the foresight of Lord Pirrie before the war, Harland and Wolff had been closely involved with the development of the diesel engine: particularly important were the links it established with the Scandinavian firm of Burmeister and Wain.[21] As diesel-powered shipping became increasingly important – in the inter-war period its share of United Kingdom output more than doubled – Harland and Wolff were well placed to benefit from the trend.[22] Second, before the war the firm had specialised in liners and large merchant vessels; this market was more buoyant in the 1920s than that for the smaller tramp ships. Third, though probably of less significance, the Northern Ireland yards benefited from certain advantages connected with its governmental institutions. As we shall see below, after 1920 the Northern Ireland parliament was granted a limited amount of economic independence from Westminster. The shipbuilding industry benefited from this in two ways. First, the government guaranteed against default any loans made to the yards by banks and insurance companies. In England this policy applied only until 1927, after which date Northern Irish shipbuilders may have found it easier to obtain finance than their mainland competitors. Second, though this may reflect geographical remoteness as much as the existence of devolved government, both Belfast yards were able to use cheaper steel than their British counterparts, as they did not feel bound by the voluntary embargo placed by the latter on imports of foreign metal.[23]

After 1930 the province's shipbuilders suffered, like those throughout the rest of the world, from the slump in world trade. By the winter of 1932–33 employment in the industry fell to only a tenth of its 1929–30 level, and for a period unemployment was over 80 per cent.[24] In the spring of 1935 Workman Clark ceased operations. Smaller than Harland and Wolff – though the epithet 'the wee yard' hardly describes accurately a firm that on two occasions before 1914 launched more tonnage in a year than any other in the world – Workman Clark had been in financial difficulties since 1920, essentially the result of a piece of sharp financial practice undertaken, at that time, by the firm's management. In February 1920, at the height of the boom and with order books full, the company was acquired in its entirety by the Northumberland Shipping Company, and a new debenture loan for £3 million at 7 per cent was launched, ostensibly to extend the activities of Workman Clark. In fact the proceeds of the loan were used to repay a loan of the Northumberland Shipping Company to Kleinwort's Bank. Although this manoeuvre left both Workman and Clark very rich men (at their deaths they left £800,000 and £1·5 million respectively), the firm was saddled with a huge burden of fixed interest debt which made it financially very vulnerable to the onset of depression. In 1927 the firm was sued in the courts and the directors accused of misrepresentation, fraud, conspiracy, breach of trust and breach of contract, with respect to the prospectus it had issued in 1920 relating to the debenture issue. Effectively it lost and the firm went into temporary liquidation. Meanwhile orders were drying up; in 1928 it launched only one ship, a 360 ton sludge vessel for the Belfast Corporation. The same year the company was financially reorganised as Workman Clark (1928) Ltd., but it could not survive the economic downturn of the early 1930s. Six years later it again found itself without orders and began to lay off men. In April/May 1935 it was acquired by the National Shipbuilders Security Ltd., the syndicate set up by the industry, in co-operation with the banks, to purchase and close redundant yards. However, the closure of Workman Clark had elements of merger as well. Although the larger north yard was shut, the south yard, the engineering factory and part of the labour force were taken over by Harland and Wolff, and William Strachan, the former chairman of the smaller company, was brought on to the board. (Sir Frederick Rebbeck, chairman of the larger Belfast yard, was incidentally a member of the board of the National Shipbuilders Security which had recommended closure.)[25]

Yet in spite of the difficulties experienced in the early 1930s, by 1935 Belfast's share of the British market, 12·8 per cent, was actually higher than the 9·7 per cent average of the 1920s. Furthermore, Harland and Wolff made valiant efforts to diversify; it built, for the Belfast and County Down Railway, the first diesel electric train in the British Isles, as well as more conventional locomotives for companies in Canada, Australia and Latin America; it constructed engines for use in the oil pipeline from Haditha to Haifa; it installed the steelwork for large shops and cinemas, built grain silos and even tendered for work on the Belfast Corporation trams.[26] In the late 1930s, however, for two reasons the company did not recover as well as British yards. First, it did not benefit from the 'scrap and build' scheme for trampship owners introduced by the British government simply because it had never specialised in this area of the market. Second, there was a suspicion, probably justified, that Belfast was receiving less than its fair share of Admiralty contracts. In 1938, for example, the Northern Ireland government drew the attention of Westminster to the current situation with respect to naval vessels under construction at privately owned yards. Of the five battleships and thirty destroyers under construction none was in Belfast, and Harland and Wolff's contracts were limited to one cruiser (out of fifteen) and one aircraft carrier (out of five).[27] It is true that this lack of orders may partly be because the province's shipbuilders had never specialised in naval vessels, but it is also probable that in time of difficulty throughout the United Kingdom industry, Westminster gave preference in placing contracts to the area for which it was primarily responsible (i.e. Great Britain) rather than to one for which its responsibility was indirect.

As with shipbuilding it could be argued that the Ulster linen industry generally performed creditably in difficult economic circumstances. Even discounting for a moment the output figures for 1930, which was a particularly bad year for the industry, Table 6.2 clearly shows that during the interwar period there was a permanent and significant decline in the output and exports of the Northern Ireland linen industry compared to the position before 1914. We have already indicated that during the war and post-war boom labour and capital were drawn into the industry to an extent that could not be sustained in normal peacetime conditions. A comparison with the pre-war period, however, makes it clear that the problems of linen were not simply a consequence of overexpansion between 1914 and 1920 as a major fall in output occurred between 1912 and the early 1920s. The latter point is particularly important as it means that many of the traditional arguments advanced for the industry's decline are beside the point.[28] It cannot have been mainly the result of the competition of new fibres like rayon as these were of little consequence until the 1930s and of no real significance until after the Second World War.

Table 6.2 *Output, exports and employment in the linen industry, 1912–51*

Year	NI output of linen piece goods (million sq. yds.)	UK exports of linen piece goods (million sq. yds.)	NI employment (000)
1912	211	213	76
1924	161	111	75
1930	116	61	56
1935	146	77	57
1951	99	50	56

Source. W. Black, *Variations in employment in the linen industry*, unpublished Ph.D. thesis, Queen's University of Belfast, 1955, pp. 232–5; *Annual Statements the Trade and Navigation of the United Kingdom*, 1912–51.

In any case the industry found little difficulty incorporating them into its production pattern. Nor was overseas competition the main problem. Ulster's main rivals, Belgium, Russia and Czechoslovakia had suffered more, not less from the Great War, with the result that in the early 1920s, the province's industry was in a better relative position than before 1914. In 1923, 68 per cent of the linen imported into the large American market came from the United Kingdom (the vast majority from Ulster) compared to 65 per cent before the war. True, for a time during the late 1920s the industry's competitive position worsened. This was partly a consequence of the return to gold at an overvalued parity in 1925 and partly a result of the nature of American tariffs. These were *ad valorem* (by value) and placed a larger burden on Irish linens which were of higher quality and price than their competitors. Furthermore foreign suppliers were making inroads into the domestic British market. Imports rose from £0·3 million in 1921 to £1·2 million in 1927. Part of this increase was illusory, a result of the Irish Free State being treated as a foreign country after 1923, but it also reflects the overvaluation of sterling from April 1925 onwards. From the 1930s, however, the Ulster manufacturers fought back. The devaluation of the pound in 1931 removed the problem of an overvalued currency, both internally and externally, while the Import Duties Act of 1932 gave the domestic market protection against dumping. By 1935 the proportion of United States imports coming from Ulster had risen to over 60 per cent and by the early 1950s was back to pre-1919 levels. In other important markets, Canada, Brazil and New Zealand, for example, Ulster linen either maintained or increased its share compared to 1924 levels. Domestically, imports declined markedly: by 1938 they were less than a sixth of the 1929 level.

Thus many of the criticisms levelled at the industry, that it was small scale, that there was excessive competition between firms, that it lacked vertical integration and was short of capital, lose their force; comparatively the industry held its own over the inter-war period as a whole.[29] In any case it is doubtful if problems of size, competition, integration and finance were such disadvantages as they sometimes have been painted. Economies of scale were not important. As the *Report of the Linen Industry Post-War Planning Committee* noted in 1944: 'Linen manufacture differs from other industries in that it does not lend itself to the bulk manufacture of standard articles from uniform raw materials.'[30] While competition between firms may have had its disadvantages, theory would suggest that it may have had compensating benefits in stimulating efficiency. As regards vertical integration, it existed in the industry on a much greater scale than is apparent at first glance. Many spinning, weaving and merchanting firms were connected either informally or through interlocking directorships. In his study of the industry in 1953 Dr. Black discovered that approximately two-thirds of spinning capacity was linked with weaving outlets, while a similar proportion of the latter had connections with firms that marketed the final product. Finally there is no direct evidence to suggest a shortage of capital. The lack of investment in the industry is more accurately attributable to the absence of change in technology or optimum size and, most important of all, to the overall diminution in the market for linen.

This brings us to the nub of the industry's problem. The decline in the demand for linen goods was both permanent and world-wide: by the 1930s less than 40 per cent as much flax (the basic raw material for the product) was being processed as before the war. Dr. Black has adumbrated many reasons to account for this; the decline in importance of durability: 'the modern demand is for novelty and few women when they purchase dress goods would be impressed by the fact that the cloth will last a lifetime.' The change in female fashion after the war, particularly the advent of short skirts, no longer required voluminous layers of the material for underwear. The trend towards polished wood surfaces and to the practice of entertaining in restaurants meant that sets of linen tableware were 'no longer an essential accompaniment to gracious living'. The decline in the number of domestic servants during and after the war also reduced demand, as linen is a fabric that requires careful laundering and handling. A further problem was that its price rose in relation to other textiles. It proved difficult either to mechanise flax production or to increase yields per acre, thus it became more expensive compared to other fibres, particularly cotton. Even the increased equality of incomes, which the Great War helped bring about, may have reduced the sales of linen as it increased 'mass demand' at the expense of the market 'for articles of distinction and durability'. In short, then, the fall in linen output between 1912 and 1924 was caused by a permanent reduction in demand. Within the shrinking world market, except for some temporary problems in the 1920s, the Ulster industry held its own, but inevitably suffered from depression and unemployment.[31]

Agriculture, which in 1926 employed a third of the male and a quarter of the total labour force, also experienced economic difficulties between the wars. As in the cases of linen and shipbuilding the problem was international. Relative to industrial goods the prices of agricultural products fell through most of the 1920s and in 1929–30 there was a catastrophic decline. This chronic persistence of over-supply can in part be attributed to the expansion of output during the war in the non-belligerent countries, which failed to contract after 1919 as normal production conditions returned to Europe. To worsen matters the growth in demand was sluggish; world population growth averaged $0 \cdot 9$ per cent per annum in the 1920s compared to $1 \cdot 5$ per cent before the war.[32] At first glance it would appear that the province's agricultural sector was highly vulnerable to this adverse shift in the terms of trade. Holdings were well below optimal size: 70 per cent of them were under thirty acres and 86 per cent under fifty, whereas it has been suggested that Irish farms benefited from economies of scale up to at least 200 acres.[33] Output per head was consequently low, only 46 per cent of the British level in 1924.[34] This is not, however, something for which the province can be blamed. It was a product of its past, and to have changed farming rapidly by con-solidating holdings would have involved enormous social dislocation. It was, in any case, politically impossible such was the strength of the agricultural lobby in the Northern Ireland Parliament. As one disgruntled Belfast MP noted: 'If a farmer wanted somebody to blow his nose some Hon. Member would get up and raise the question ... and a man would be appointed not only to blow the farmer's nose but to wipe it for him.'[35]

On the brighter side the province's agricultural product mix rendered it less vulnerable to world price movements than many other areas of the United Kingdom. Although arable acreage in the province had temporarily increased in the Great War, it was of much less significance than in Britain. In 1924−25 output of cereals accounted for less than 1·5 per cent of Northern Ireland's gross agricultural output compared to 10·3 per cent in England and Wales and 9·5 per cent in Scotland. Conversely 78·4 per cent comprised livestock and livestock products compared to 69·5 per cent in Great Britain.[36]

Table 6.3 *The main farm products in Northern Ireland, 1924−35*

Year	Cattle ('000)	Sheep ('000)	Pigs ('000)	Poultry ('000)	Potatoes (output, '000 cwt)
1924	736	509	140	5,706	480
1930	673	704	216	8,808	430
1935	799	818	458	10,084	548

Source. Ulster Year Books, 1929−38.

During the 1920s, and even more so after 1929, cereal prices generally fell more rapidly than pastoral products; as Edith Whetham has noted: 'Dairying and livestock husbandry were more likely to yield profits than the production of cereals.'[37] Thus we should not be surprised that, relative to Britain, Northern Irish agriculture improved its position during the inter-war period, though in absolute terms it remained far behind. In 1924−25 the province's *per capita* output was 46 per cent of the British; by 1930−31 it was 48 per cent and by 1935, 52 per cent at which level it remained until 1939.[38] The period also saw a growth in the absolute levels of income amongst the Northern Ireland farming community. Output per worker rose in money terms by 28 per cent between 1924 and 1935 (the bulk of the increase coming after 1930) during a period when the cost of living fell by 16 per cent.[39] Part of this increase can be explained by the drift from the land and the consequent rise in the average size of holding, but the growth in livestock numbers also indicates an improvement in output per acre. Although the interwar period saw considerable progress, the province's agricultural community remained miserably poor both in comparison with Britain, and with the industrial sector in Northern Ireland. The living standards of farmers with less than thirty acres were in most cases below those of industrial wage earners, while the income of farm labourers, 25s to 27s 6d per week in the 1930s, was less than the 30s benefit paid to an unemployed married man. This was to create considerable problems after 1936 when agriculture was brought within the scope of the insurance acts, as farm labourers were frequently better off out of work than in.[40]

Despite creditable performances against an unpromising economic background it is undeniable that Ulster's three main employers of labour remained depressed throughout the inter-war period. The question obviously arises as to why the province neither created nor attracted new growth sectors which would have offset this decline. In Britain, despite the depression in many older industries, notably textiles, shipbuilding, coal mining, and iron and steel, other sections of the economy were expanding through most of the inter-war period, motor vehicles, chemicals and electrical engineering, for example. It is clear, though, that these growth industries were not spread uniformly throughout the country, and when Northern Ireland is put in context as a region of the United Kingdom, it is evident that it was not alone in its failure to attract them. As Table 6.4 shows, during the period between 1923 and 1937 only four of the ten regions of the United Kingdom showed increases of employment significantly in excess of that of Northern Ireland. This suggests that the reasons usually given for the province's failure to attract new industries, higher transport costs and the lack of raw materials, particularly coal, are insufficient.[41] Wales suffered from neither of these difficulties, yet its economic performance was markedly worse than that of Northern Ireland. Scotland and the northern areas of England, with an abundance of traditional resources experienced no greater expansion than the province. Similarly, although Northern Ireland's share of total United Kingdom industrial output fell during the period from 1924 to 1935, important areas of Britain, the North East, Lancashire, Cheshire, the West Riding, and Wales experienced a proportionately greater decline.[42]

The Barlow Commission, set up in 1937 to investigate the distribution of the industrial population, explained the shift in the economic centre of gravity in terms of proximity to large markets, which was particularly important for firms producing consumer products. This argument, however, contains an element of circularity: population

Table 6.4 *Indices of numbers of insured persons aged 16–64 in employment, 1923–37 (1923 = 100)*

	June 1929	June 1932	June 1937
London	120	118	145
South-eastern	127	127	159
South-western	117	114	140
Midland	111	101	132
North-eastern	105	92	114
North-western	109	96	112
Northern	99	77	102
Scotland	105	91	112
Wales	85	69	86
Great Britain	110	100	124
Northern Ireland	109	95	112

Source. Aldcroft, *The Inter-war Economy*, p. 49; Isles and Cuthbert, *Economic Survey*, pp. 568–9.

tended to move to areas where new jobs had been created, thereby widening the demand for final goods and services. On the other hand it may best be explained simply by economic inertia. In 1924, perhaps even in 1914, the southern half of Britain contained a larger proportion of those industries which were to expand most rapidly between the wars, building, vehicles, consumer goods and the service sector, for example. With plenty of unemployed labour in all regions, with abundant cheap land and with no substantial government pressure or grants to induce them to do otherwise, firms had little incentive to move; as Professor Alford has put it: 'it was often a case of "J'y suis, j'y augmente".'[43]

If Northern Ireland, therefore, is looked at within its United Kingdom context, it is not surprising that its economic growth was slower than the British average. In 1924, 59 per cent of workers in those firms covered by the Census of Production were in declining industries compared to 41 per cent in Great Britain. Conversely, in the same year, only 11 per cent of the labour force was in the expanding areas of paper and printing, chemicals, electrical and mechanical engineering, motor vehicles and building compared to 22 per cent in Britain. If building is excluded, as it is in some respects a consequence of expansion elsewhere in the economy (as well as a cause), the percentages fall to 6 and 15 per cent respectively.[44] Thus, in 1924, the province, in common with other depressed regions of the United

Kingdom had a very limited base of firms in growing industries; only massive financial inducements, such as have existed since 1945, would have caused them to relocate. For reasons explained below, Stormont was unable, and Westminster was unwilling, to provide the requisite subsidies. Even in Britain itself, it might be noted, the Special Areas legislation, which gave grants to firms willing to set up in depressed regions created at most only 50,000 new jobs before 1939.[45] In the absence of government aid, new industries only located in the province as a result of very special circumstances. There was only one major development along these lines, the establishment of the Short and Harland Ltd. aircraft factory in 1937, and this occurred too late in the inter-war period to have any marked effect on employment until the eve of the Second World War. The origins of this business which by May 1939 employed over 6,000 (and reached a wartime peak of over 20,000) illustrate how important the concatenation of favourable, even chance, circumstances could be in determining the industrial location of new industries. During the 1930s the Belfast Harbour Commissioners embarked on an extension of the port's facilities to accommodate larger ships, in particular the construction of the Herdman Channel and the Pollock Dock and Basin. One by-product was that 400 acres of slob land were reclaimed from the sea.[46] It was decided that part of this area would be used to establish a new city airport for both conventional and amphibious aircraft at Sydenham, close by the Harland and Wolff yards. In 1936 when the RAF placed with Short Bros. of Rochester a large order for Sunderlands, the firm found that their Kent factory could not accommodate the increased demand. Facilities in Belfast were uniquely suitable: there were, in close proximity, a skilled labour force (associated with the shipyards) many of whom were unemployed, a deep water dock, a huge stretch of sheltered water in the Lough suitable for flying boats, and an airport with runways up to 1,500 yards.[47] Although, no doubt, credit should be given to Harland and Wolff, the Belfast Corporation and Harbour Commissioners, and the Government of Northern Ireland for easing the way towards the establishment of Short and Harland, the basic reason for the aircraft industry locating in the city was that it made economic sense. But it was the end result of a series of decisions and events that were only tenuously related: in particular the extension of the city's port facilities and the consequent reclamation of land was decided upon well before Hitler's accession to power and the subsequent decision to build up the RAF.

Although there was an increase in the Northern Ireland labour force of approximately 12 per cent between the wars, this was almost entirely accounted for by two developments, the expansion of the tertiary sector (wholesale and retail distribution, professional services, education, government, etc.) where employment rose from 80,000 in 1926 to 100,000 in 1937 and building, where the rise was from 17,000 in 1923 to 28,000 in 1938.[48] The economy as a whole, however, did not expand sufficiently quickly to accommodate both the shedding of labour in the declining parts of the economy and the growth of the work force. The result was unemployment and emigration to the more prosperous areas of Britain. Nonetheless this does not mean that there was an absence of economic growth in the period although it was slower than in Britain. In the United Kingdom generally, real incomes per head rose by approximately a quarter; in Northern Ireland they rose by 10–15 per cent.[49] Consequently, *per capita* incomes fell even further behind those in the rest of Britain, from 61 per cent of the average in 1924 to 57 per cent in 1937. Even so it is probable that other areas of the United Kingdom, Wales or the North East for example, performed equally badly during the interwar period and that the average figure for the country generally masks considerable regional differences.

The role of the government
Turning to the role of the Northern Ireland government, several questions arise. Could it have done more to attract new industries or sustain the old? Did devolution benefit or hamper the development of the province? Would greater economic powers have been beneficial? Before answering these questions it is necessary to examine the financial relations between Stormont and Westminster and the problems of the provincial exchequer. As this complex subject has been well documented elsewhere we will discuss it only briefly.[50]

Under the Government of Ireland Act, 1920, certain economic powers were devolved to the new Northern Ireland legislature, while others were retained by the imperial parliament in London. Westminster controlled the major forms of taxation, those on customs and excise and incomes, leaving Belfast with powers over less important sources of revenue, motor vehicles, death duties and some relatively minor items like dog licences.[51] All told, imports 'reserved' to the imperial parliament accounted for 80 per cent or more of the total. The revenue accruing to the Northern Ireland government, that is, the total amount of taxation paid by the province's citizens, was determined by the Joint Exchequer Board, a triumvirate 'composed of a chairman appointed by the Crown and one member each of the imperial Treasury and the Northern Ireland Ministry of Finance'.[52] The Government of Ireland Act was, however, passed into law in conditions that were to prove quite untypical of the inter-war period generally.

In 1920 the province's economy was booming, its major industries thriving, and unemployment low. It was envisaged therefore that not only would the Belfast government have ample funds to meet its expenditure within Northern Ireland but also to pay a sizeable 'imperial contribution' to the Treasury to help cover the costs of, for example, the army and navy and the servicing of the United Kingdom national debt. This was to be a first charge on the province's revenue. The economic collapse of 1921 and the subsequent depressed conditions of the whole inter-war period made this impossible, as although it resulted in a fall in revenue (by 1929–30 in per capita terms it was less than half the British level), it led to no corresponding reduction in necessary expenditure, rather the reverse.[53] While the fall in income was largely unavoidable, a result of the depression, maintenance of government spending was partly the consequence of a policy of following Westminster 'step by step' in certain items of social expenditure, unemployment and sickness benefits, old age pensions, and the rate support grant to local and county councils to compensate for the derating of agricultural land.

The motive behind this series of decisions was essentially political: Unionist governments found it difficult to persuade their supporters that they should accept lower standards of social benefits than their fellow British citizens across the water. Whether this was economically sensible is debatable. *Per capita* incomes and government revenue were much lower than in Britain so that it proved more onerous to sustain the same level of social expenditure. Earnings were also less than in the rest of the United Kingdom, which meant that unemployment benefits (the same in the province as in Britain) were much closer to wage levels, particularly for married men with children. This, it was sometimes alleged, mainly by employers, increased the numbers who chose to remain voluntarily unemployed; as early as 1921, for example, one large businessman argued that 'there is no shirking the fact that the "dole" is a potent factor in keeping the percentage [of unemployed] higher, particularly among the thousands who have always taken their work in homoeopathic doses.'[54] The derating of agricultural land was also much more costly in Northern Ireland than in Britain, because of the greater importance of farming; in the 1920s agriculture employed a quarter of the working population compared to seven per cent in Britain.[55] The Health Insurance scheme also proved more expensive in Ulster; in 1930 expenditure per head was £1 14s, as against £1 1s 6d in England and Wales, and £1 0s 1d in Scotland.[56] It was sometimes felt that this was because Northern Irish doctors were more willing to sign 'sick lines' than their colleagues in Britain. More substantial reasons were the generally poorer state of health in the province and the nature of the insurance scheme operating there. In Northern Ireland, unlike Britain, the sick received benefits but no medical treatment, an absurdly false economy as it simply meant they took longer to recuperate.

This commitment to 'parity' in certain social services which involved a heavy financial burden would not have mattered if the Imperial government had been willing to help finance it by a transfer of funds from the Treasury, as has been the case since 1945. In the inter-war period it was not: Westminster was far too concerned with reducing its own expenditure to consider aiding Northern Ireland to anything but a limited extent. This parsimony was largely brought about by the heavy burden of interest payments on the National Debt accumulated during the Great War which in the 1920s accounted for over 40 per cent of total government expenditure. Because retrenchment in this direction was very difficult, the Treasury was niggardly in areas where spending was easier to control. It is true that some aid from central funds was given to the province. The 'imperial contribution' which was supposed to be a first charge on the Northern Ireland revenue became a residual, in other words the Stormont government paid over only what funds remained after it had met its obligatory expenditure. By the early 1930s this was simply a token payment, less than five per cent of the amount originally planned. Some help was given to offset the deficit in the Northern Ireland Unemployment Insurance Fund, separate from that in Britain, and during the 1930s subsidies were given to the province's farmers.[57] Fundamentally, however, unlike the other poorer areas of the United Kingdom, the province was expected to live off the revenue generated within it.

This combination of low revenue and the maintenance of parity in certain areas of expenditure, meant that once the Northern Ireland exchequer had met its commitments, there was little revenue available for positive action in other directions, either in the economy or in other areas of the social services. The lack of funds inevitably limited the effectiveness of government policy, particularly towards industry. We have already noted that actions under the Loans Guarantee Act may have given some aid to shipbuilding, but it was marginal. For linen the government did little and it is unclear what it could have done. To have 'rationalised' the industry by aiding the closure of inefficient firms would simply have added to unemployment. Towards transport its policy of half-heartedly buttressing the railways was misguided. As Greer has convincingly argued, road transport had such economic advantages in most of Northern Ireland that any attempt to reverse the trends towards it was doomed to fail.[58] With respect to the encouragement of 'new' industries the government policy started by being perverse, and ended, through lack of funds, in being derisory. In the early 1920s, a subsidy was given to the mining of coal in the vain belief that the industry would prove viable. To their credit the government swiftly came to terms with reality and withdrew the subvention. The financial inducements provided by the New Industries (Development) Acts of 1932 and 1937 were insufficient to achieve their purpose of attracting new firms to the province. With the exception of Short and Harland, whose establishment, as argued above, was the result of peculiarly favourable circumstances rather than government subsidies, a total of only 279 jobs was created. The poor response to this legislation led one independent Unionist MP to enquire whether 'if the Government set up a few new chip shops they would not give more employment.'[59]

Would Northern Ireland's industrial position have improved if Stormont had possessed greater economic powers, in particular the right to impose tariffs? This matter was carefully investigated in the 1950s by Isles and Cuthbert and their answer was a categorical 'no'. Import duties would simply have raised costs and prices and lowered 'the real earnings of wage-earners, salaried workers, rentiers and others with relatively fixed money incomes.'[60] The Northern Ireland market was small, therefore to benefit fully from economies of scale, industries would have had to export. Yet to be able to do this and compete on world markets presupposes tariffs were unnecessary in the first place. Furthermore was it not possible that Northern Ireland's main market (Great Britain), which was also its chief source of imports, would retaliate to the imposition of duties? Isles and Cuthbert concluded that 'the possibility of using tariff policy as a means of increasing the general level of industry' in the province was 'very slight'.

The government's actions with respect to agriculture were more interventionist, though it had to operate within the general constraints of United Kingdom policy. We have already noted that the farming sector performed rather better than its British counterpart, particularly after 1930, though encouragement by Stormont was only one of the reasons behind the more rapid growth. During the 1920s when Westminster continued its traditional policy of free trade in agricultural produce, the provincial administration could do little more than exhort, encourage, and educate the farming community. Essentially it followed the path pursued between 1899 and 1921 by the Department of Agriculture and Technical Instruction for Ireland, attempting to improve the quality of livestock and livestock products, encouraging diversification into such areas as fruit growing and market gardening, and providing ancillary services in the form of research institutes and education facilities. After 1921 the Belfast government, like that in Dublin, simply extended this policy by using less of the carrot and more of the stick. Whereas the DATI largely operated by rewarding good agricultural practice, new administrations, north and south, outlawed bad. In 1922, for instance, the 'scrub bull' was outlawed by the Livestock Breeding Act which made it an offence to keep an animal not licensed by the Ministry of Agriculture.[61] In 1924 the Ministry regulated the quality of eggs for export by a system of compulsory registration, inspection, grading and packaging. Similar legislation was passed for potatoes (1928), dairy produce (1929), and fruit (1931). Agricultural education was improved. The Ministry organised classes, distributed numerous leaflets and, of the greatest long term significance, established a Faculty of Agriculture at Queen's University. As regards the vexed question of land ownership, over 70 per cent of the transfer from landlord to tenant had been accomplished before 1920. The 1925 Act completed the process by making sales of tenanted land mandatory on landlords.[62]

Valuable as these measures may have been, it was not until the policy of free trade in agricultural produce was reversed by the Westminster government in 1932 that more fundamental change could take place. The Import Duties Act and the Ottawa Agreement Act imposed duties on imported foodstuffs, provided for quantitative restrictions by quotas and gave preference to imperial over foreign suppliers. It was hoped that this legislation would have two effects. First, that United Kingdom farmers would be better able to take advantage of the 1931 Marketing Act which empowered domestic producers of any commodity (providing two-thirds of them could come to an agreement) to organise in compulsory marketing schemes to prevent short run overproduction. Second, British farmers were given a guaranteed share of the market, which was to be gradually increased in an orderly manner through a mixture of improvements in efficiency and the use of subsidies.[63]

The complexities of the legislation governing Northern Ireland agriculture in the 1930s have been well explained elsewhere; only the broad outlines need concern us here.[64] The marketing schemes in the province although based on the same general principles as in Britain, varied in significant details to take account of differing agricultural conditions. The legislation governing milk production, for example, gave a higher level of aid to farmers producing for dairy creameries because of the greater importance of butter manufacture in Northern Ireland. The provincial government became much more directly involved in the pigs' marketing scheme than their Westminster counterparts, largely because the bacon industry had to be completely restructured towards the production of a breed of animal new to Ulster, the lean Wiltshire.[65] In addition to these organisational changes, the Northern Irish farming community benefited from financial subsidies on milk (1934), cattle (1935) and bacon (1938) which were paid for by the Treasury in London, rather than Belfast. Generally speaking the policy of fostering agriculture proved successful in all parts of the United Kingdom. In most agricultural commodities, output in both Britain and Northern Ireland rose very much in line with each other during the 1930s. However, with respect to pigs, the province's performance was markedly superior. By 1938 production was over 300 per cent above that of 1930 both in value and in volume, and accounted for 27 per cent of all agricultural output compared to 14 per cent eight years earlier.[66] The greater involvement of the Northern Ireland government in the marketing scheme may have had something to do with this rapid increase, but it is clear that other factors were also at work. Output was already increasing before the marketing schemes were set up: between 1924 and 1930 production doubled. The Babbington Committee of Enquiry into Agriculture was inclined to give much weight, paradoxically, to the small size of farms in the province which had three advantages. The pig was, according to the report, a beast which responded well 'to the personal care and attention which the smallholder and his family can apply to all branches of livestock production'. It was also an animal which could be used to provide a profitable outlet for by-products such as potatoes and refuse food which were not saleable commercially. Finally the pig's fecundity and rapid maturity was a valuable asset on a small farm as the cash returns came in much more quickly than they did on cattle.[67]

Thus, all in all, the contribution of the Northern Ireland government to economic activity in the province was marginal. The difficulties of the two major manufacturing industries were caused by problems in export markets which Stormont could not solve. Financial penury prevented any lavish subsidies to attract new firms to the province. With respect to agriculture the major forces for change, protection and the provision of subsidies, were instigated by Westminster rather than the provincial government.

Social conditions

We have seen that, during the inter-war period, the prevalence of high unemployment in the towns and the small farms in the countryside meant that the general standard of living in Northern Ireland, though improving, was below the United Kingdom average.[68] Many social indicators confirm this, although to put the province in its proper context it is necessary to make comparisons not only with Britain as a whole, but with other regions.[69] Once this is done then Northern Ireland ceases to appear uniquely disadvantaged.

Let us consider housing for example. It has frequently been pointed out that there was much less housebuilding in the province than in Britain. R.J. Lawrence, for example, has noted that 'during the period 1919 to 1939 only 50,000 dwellings of all types were built. This was in marked contrast to England and Wales where, with a population almost thirty times larger than in Ulster, the number of houses built between the wars was eighty times greater.'[70] The inference is obviously that the province must have been uniquely ill-housed compared to other parts of the United Kingdom. This comparison, however, shows Northern Ireland in too bleak a light, for three reasons. First, the province's population during the period was virtually stable, while that in England and Wales increased by 17 per cent.[71] Second, there was much less internal migration in Northern Ireland. There was a slight movement from rural to urban areas, but nothing compared to the regional shifts from the depressed areas of Britain to the south and midlands. Third, the marriage rate in the province was much lower, less than two-thirds that of England and Wales in the 1930s.[72] These three features of the province's demographic growth, meant that the rate of growth of demand for new housing was lower in Ulster than in Britain. Furthermore, in 1919 Belfast's houses were almost certainly newer than in many British cities, a consequence of its relatively late growth. The level of new housebuilding, therefore, is not the best measure of comparative housing conditions in Northern Ireland and Britain. A far better indicator is the number of persons per room.[73]

As Table 6.5 shows, housing conditions in Northern Ireland were poor, but they were not uniquely so; the situation in Scotland, for example, was worse. Furthermore, if the English regions had been disaggregated to a greater extent than has been possible in Table 6.5, it would have shown that in certain areas, the North East or inner London, containing far larger total populations than the province, overcrowding was worse.[74] Even accepting that housing conditions were generally poorer in Northern Ireland than in most parts of Britain, this cannot be attributed solely to lack of housebuilding. It was also a result of the levels of marital fertility in the province, nearly two-thirds higher than in England and Wales. This simply meant that there was a greater proportion of large families in Northern Ireland. The table further shows that conditions were worse in rural areas of the province than in urban, the reverse of the situation prevailing in Britain. This in part reflects the lower rates of house-building but it also was a consequence of the higher level of marital fertility in the countryside. Nonetheless the table shows that there was a marked improvement in housing conditions between the censal years of 1926 and 1937. Approximately one sixth of the Northern Ireland population moved into new homes during the inter-war period, and there must also have been some upward mobility of the poorer section of the community into houses vacated by the better off.[75] Thus in the years before 1939 housing conditions while poor, were improving. During the war however, they worsened rapidly. Housebuilding virtually ceased while the blitz destroyed over 3,000 houses and damaged many more; others deteriorated, partly through age and partly because of the lack of facilities for proper maintenance. The wartime period also saw an increase in population of 60,000 − the fastest growth rate since the Famine − and a sharp upward movement

209

Table 6.5 *Persons per room in the United Kingdom, 1926–37*

	Average number of persons per room			Population living more than two per room (%)		
	1926	*1931*	*1937*	*1926*	*1931*	*1937*
Northern Ireland	1·01		0·91	18·2		13·3
rural	1·04		0·96	21·6		17·2
urban	0·98		0·87	14·7		9·6
England and Wales		0·83			7·0	
rural		0·75			4·2	
urban		0·85			7·6	
Midlands		0·82			5·6	
North		0·89			9·2	
East		0·71			3·0	
South West		0·71			3·2	
Greater London		0·89			9·4	
Wales		0·82			5·2	
Scotland		1·27			35·0	
Largest provincial cities						
Glasgow		1·57			45·1	
Birmingham		0·83			7·1	
Liverpool		0·93			10·7	
Manchester		0·96			6·7	
Sheffield		0·87			8·2	
Leeds		0·87			8·2	
Edinburgh		1·15			29·8	
Belfast	1·01		0·88	16·8		8·5

Source. Census of Population for England and Wales 1931 Housing Report; Census of Scotland, 1931; Census of Population of Northern Ireland, 1926 and 1937.

in the number of marriages which further exacerbated the situation.[76] The result was that by the end of the war when a survey of housing was undertaken, conditions had deteriorated considerably compared to the late 1930s.[77]

Health conditions in the province were also poor in the inter-war years, at least by present day standards, although when set in their historical context they were far from being abnormal. In 1931 life expectancy at birth in Northern Ireland was 57·1 years compared to 60·8 in England and Wales, 57·8 in Scotland and 58·8 in the Irish Free State. Looked at internationally, however, Ulstermen and women could expect to live longer than most other Europeans with the exception of Scandinavians, Germans, Swiss and Dutch.[78] Furthermore the province's health was generally improving throughout the period: by the late 1930s, life expectancy was eight years longer than in 1911.

While it would be wrong to ignore this improvement, in two respects − infant and maternal mortality and deaths from tuberculosis − Northern Ireland's health record was poor when compared to Britain.[79] During the 1930s 7·8 per cent of children born in Northern Ireland died before reaching the age of one compared to 6·3 per cent in the United Kingdom as a whole, though the figure for Scotland, 8·0 per cent, was even worse. Maternal mortality, though of little significance in terms of its contribution to the overall female death rate, was 50 to 60 per cent higher than in Britain and showed no signs of falling.[80] The death rate from tuberculosis was 20 per cent above that in Britain, although the position was improving rapidly: it fell by more than half during the inter-war period.[81] This relatively bad performance probably stemmed from a combination of poorer standards of nutrition and, to a lesser extent, housing, and also to inferior medical facilities. We have already seen that housing in the province was marginally worse than in most other areas of the United Kingdom. With respect to diet there are unfortunately no statistics which make it possible to examine nutritional levels in the different classes of society. Aggregate data suggest that while meat consumption was significantly (30−40 per cent) below the British level, with respect to other 'quality' foods, fresh milk, butter and eggs, the province's intake was actually greater.[82] In view, however, of the lower income levels prevailing in Northern Ireland, the presupposition must be that malnutrition was more prevalent in the province than in Britain.[83] With respect to tuberculosis the poorer diet and housing are probably sufficient explanations. As McKeown has shown, medical treatment for the disease was ineffective until the 1940s, so that it would be incorrect to blame the higher incidence on inferior facilities in Ulster.[84] The fall in the death rate from tuberculosis was almost certainly the result of the improved housing and rising real incomes that we have noted earlier, and forms part of a trend stretching back into the nineteenth century.

Inferior medical facilities and education were certainly more to blame for infant and maternal mortality, particularly in Belfast. The problem stemmed partly from the division of responsibility for the provision of pre- and ante-natal advice and treatment between the local authorities and the poor law guardians, which led to each group leaving it to the other. But inactivity was also a consequence of the conservative complexion of both bodies, and their general belief that medical care was the responsibility of the parent. A detailed and independent examination of Belfast in 1941 by Dr. Thomas Carnwath concluded: 'In respect to personal medical services, Belfast falls far short of what might reasonably be expected in a city of its size and importance.'[85] Midwifery was poor; no provision of special foods was made for expectant mothers, nor any attempt made to detect anaemia; little effort was put into monitoring problem pregnancies or the education of women as to the value of cleanliness; few health visitors were employed to check on the baby's progress. Carnwath concluded that many of the infant deaths, particularly from measles, whooping cough and gastro-enteritis, could have been avoided by a small increase in expenditure. The same was true of maternal mortality: in 1938 a committee estimated that this could have been halved by better facilities.[86] These blemishes on the province's health record must, however, be seen in perspective. The period between the wars saw in Northern Ireland a substantial improvement in health and an increase in life expectancy. If conditions were poor when compared to the present day, they were similar to those existing in much of the rest of Britain and Europe in the interwar period.

Educational provisions, particularly at secondary level, were also worse in the province than in Britain, especially for children from poorer families, but as in the case of housing and health there were visible improvements, most notably in primary schools.[87] Furthermore, the sectarian division of education, forced upon the government against its will, prevented the most rational use of available resources, particularly in rural areas where it helped sustain the proliferation of small schools. By the end of the 1930s the problems of elementary education had largely been solved. One hundred and thirty eight new schools were built in the interwar period and a further 428 enlarged, improved and reconditioned.[88] The proportion of teachers who had received training in universities and colleges rose from 82 per cent in 1922 to 93 per cent in 1938. School attendance also improved. In 1922 on average a quarter of school children had been absent, partly a consequence, no doubt, of the 'Troubles' of that year; by 1938 this figure had fallen to 14 per cent. In short by 1938 the province's children at elementary level were being taught in better schools, by more qualified teachers, and for a longer period than ever before. The position as regards secondary education remained unsatisfactory. The number of children receiving any sort of instruction past elementary level was low; in 1924 only 8,700 received secondary education (4·3 per cent of the number of pupils in primary schools), and in 1937, 13,700 (7·0 per cent). In England and Wales the corresponding proportions were 6·2 and 9·0 per cent.[89] In the provision of free scholarships the province was even further behind: by the end of the period only 5 per cent of pupils in secondary schools paid no fees compared to 47 per cent in England and Wales.[90] The number of assisted places at university level was derisory, a mere twenty-one a year between 1924 and 1938.[91]

Although social conditions in housing, health and education were undoubtedly improving in the inter-war years, it is clear that more could have been done. The primary responsibility for the failure to do so rests with the local authorities, although it might be argued that the Stormont government should have goaded them into greater activity. As Lawrence has shown, councils were given ample encouragement to subsidise the building of cheap working class housing from local rates, yet only 7,500 were built in the twenty years before 1939 compared to 1·3 million in Britain. Some authorities, like Fermanagh, built none at all. The lack of provision of facilities for pre- and post-natal care, and the scanty funds devoted to free places at secondary schools, can also be blamed largely on the municipal and county councils. Part of the problem stemmed from the smallness and financial weakness of the local government areas, though the record of larger ones like Belfast and Derry was also poor. But the primary cause of the inactivity was, simply, the lack of the necessary desire to improve conditions which stemmed from the conservative nature of public representatives at both governmental and local level.[92]

As we have seen, despite the undoubted persistence of areas of social deprivation in the inter-war period, health, education and housing improved, employment increased, and incomes for the majority of the population rose, so that by 1939 the quality and variety of life in the province was superior to that existing twenty years earlier. Many indicators show this. The number of motor vehicles on the road almost quadrupled over the period while the number of private cars rose tenfold. By 1937 one family in seven possessed an automobile compared to one in sixty two decades earlier. After a slow start during the 1920s when it was confined to the main towns, electrification proceeded more rapidly in the 1930s, particularly after the foundation of the Electricity Board for Northern Ireland in 1932. This was a government appointed non-profit making body whose primary task was to provide a comprehensive system of electricity generation throughout the south and west of the province. Partly as a result of its activities, consumption rose nearly threefold between 1932 and 1938, a faster rate than in the United Kingdom as a whole.[93]

Leisure activities became more varied. The stereotypical Irish pastime, drinking, declined and with it convictions for drunkenness by more than a third. (This, incidentally, was a mixed blessing for the Northern Ireland government, for while Stormont was dedicated to the encouragement of temperance it was financially embarrassed by the loss in revenue the decline in alcohol consumption entailed.)[94] Cinema-going on the other hand increased and with prices as low as threepence at matinees, became common in all social classes. By 1935 Belfast possessed thirty-one cinemas with accommodation for 28,200, one seat for every fifteen of the population compared to one in fourteen in London.[95] After the opening of the BBC transmitter in 1924 radios rapidly became popular and by 1939 nearly 124,000 wireless licences were issued.[96] Given that this probably underestimates the number of receivers as many then, as now, operated unlicensed, this meant that nearly half of Northern Irish families owned a set by 1939 compared to less than one in ten a decade before. Involvement in sport, whether playing it, watching it, or betting on it, became more widespread in all social groups. For the working classes there was Association Football with Irish League grounds full to capacity, and the 'Catholic' team, Belfast Celtic, in the ascendancy. Greyhound racing was started in the city in 1927 at Celtic Park with accommodation for 8,000. This was the second track to be established in the UK and by the 1930s there were four stadia in the province, two in Belfast and the others in Derry and Dungannon. Motor racing became a sport with a widespread following after the beginning of the Ards TT in 1928 when an estimated 500,000 watched the first race. For the middle classes there were rugby – 30,000 at Ravenhill for international matches – golf, yachting and cricket, for example.[97] In short many of the social developments in the province between the wars mirrored those in Britain.[98]

In one notable respect, of course, Northern Irish society differed markedly from that in Britain, viz. its sectarian nature and the occurrence from time to time of violent conflict between the two communities. Both aspects have been well documented by previous writers and need little elaboration here.[99] Discrimination against Catholics existed in many areas.[100] They were under-represented politically, especially in local government; they received less than their fair share of employment, particularly when it was within the patronage of Unionist controlled councils. In Belfast, for example, in 1928 Catholics had only 5 per cent of the 955 corporation jobs, although they constituted a quarter of the city's population.[101] To a lesser extent they were discriminated against educationally and in the administration of justice.[102] The sectarian nature of society revealed itself from time to time in sporadic outbursts of intercommunal violence. The worst of these occurred between December 1921 and May 1922 in which 236 people were killed. The rest of the inter-war period was by comparison much less violent. In 1932 attacks were made on Catholic pilgrims travelling to and from an international Eucharistic Congress in Dublin; riots occurred in Larne after the local priest dressed in full vestments marched his parishioners in procession through the town to the harbour.[103] More serious sectarian conflict occurred in 1935 when there were riots in Belfast. As a result eleven died, the majority Protestant; there were over 500 injured, and more than 300 families, most of them Catholic, were driven from their homes.[104]

Nonetheless these events need to be put into perspective, as it is too easy to let one's picture of inter-war Northern Ireland be coloured by the events of the 1970s, when inter-community violence became both widespread and brutal. In the ten years from 1970 to 1979 there were approximately 2,000 deaths resulting from the 'Troubles', roughly 200 a year.[105] During the whole period from mid-1922 to 1955 (unfortunately no separate statistics have been published for the inter-war period) there were 147 murders of which ninety-seven were political. The majority of the latter category occurred in late 1922 and 1935. Thus in most years during the period there were two or three murders a year. In England and Wales, with a population thirty times greater than Northern Ireland there were on average 150 murders per annum in the period 1920–50.[106] Seen in this light, Ulster society between the wars, while certainly sectarian, was far from being uniquely violent, and to dwell on the exceptional events of one or two years in one or two places undoubtedly creates a distorted image of 'normal' social conditions within the province. Perhaps the following example can serve to illustrate the difference between the 'Troubles' of the 1970s and those of the 1930s. Within a month of the 1935 riots, the Irish Football League programme began. Linfield, from the Protestant Sandy Row/Shankill Road area played Derry

215

City whose ground was in the Catholic Bogside. Celtic, from the Catholic Falls district, played in Protestant Ballymena. There were no incidents of a sectarian nature at either match. Six weeks later Celtic played at home to Linfield. 'Both teams came out together and they got a splendid reception.'[107] This could not have happened in the mid-1970s.

Conclusion

Nearly thirty years ago Isles and Cuthbert wrote of Northern Ireland that it was 'not a separate economy at all, but an undifferentiated part of a single economic system embracing the whole of the United Kingdom'.[108] Although the central accuracy of this statement cannot be denied, with respect to the inter-war period at least, it needs qualifying in two respects. First, that the province was subject to economic forces operating outside the boundaries of the United Kingdom as well as within it. The products of the linen and shipbuilding industries had worldwide markets which were affected by conditions abroad as much as at home. Even agriculture, though not an exporter outside Britain, was affected by international price movements which stemmed from changes overseas. Second, that in some respects it *was* differentiated from the United Kingdom as a whole. Like certain other areas, it possessed more than its share of old declining industries and too few new or expanding ones. Also, unlike other regions it possessed a regional parliament with a separate exchequer; in the inter-war period this was probably a disadvantage. In addition, partly because of the separate government, and partly because of the existence of the Irish Sea, far more statistics exist relating to Northern Ireland, than other regions of the United Kingdom. Separate figures for trade, agricultural and industrial output, national income and mortality rates, either do not exist at all for other areas, or else can only be discovered with considerable difficulty. Thus the tendency has been to compare Northern Ireland with either Britain or the United Kingdom as a whole to the inevitable disadvantage of the province. What we have tried to do is to put Northern Ireland in both a wider (that is international) perspective and into a regional context. The first has shown that essentially the province's economy between the wars was in a hopeless position. With its largest industries adversely affected by worldwide forces quite outside the control of Ulster's businessmen, farmers, workers or politicians, there was little that could be done to remedy the situation in the short and medium terms. It is true that massive government aid might have been a palliative, but this was not forthcoming. This was only in part a result of devolution. Buckland has argued that in certain areas of the social services, rule from Westminster might have benefited Northern Ireland, largely through greater government pressure on local authorities.[109] It is doubtful, however, if integration would have gone far to solve the province's central economic problems, as the London government's regional policy was ineffective, even in Britain.[110]

Given these underlying economic difficulties, we have seen that during the inter-war period Northern Ireland slipped behind the United Kingdom generally, though in many respects its performance was quite comparable to other regions of Britain which had also been adversely affected by declining markets for their products, the North East, Scotland and Wales, for example. But we have also seen that progress did take place. Incomes rose, housing improved, mortality fell, social life became more varied. In short, despite all the province's economic problem, the conditions of life for the vast majority of the Ulster people were better in 1939 than they had been twenty years before.

Notes

1. H. Harris, *The Irish Regiments in the First World War*, Cork, 1968, p. 31. The estimate for the number of war dead in the six Ulster counties is based on the proportion of the army recruited therein; see *Statement giving the particulars as regards men of military age in Ireland*, BPP, 1916, XVII, p. 581.
2. E. J. Riordan, *Modern Irish Trade and Industry*, London, 1920, p. 110; *Third Census of Production 1924, Board of Trade Journal*, 26 January 1938.
3. *The Economist*, 23 August 1919.
4. Riordan, *Modern Irish Trade*, p. 123.
5. J. O'Donovan, *The Economic History of Livestock in Ireland*, Cork, 1940, p. 223. *Annual Statements of the Trade of the United Kingdom*, 1914–18.
6. O'Donovan, op. cit., pp. 223–5. Hansard *Parliamentary Debates: Commons*, CIII, 28 February 1918, Col. 1634, speech of Thomas Lough MP.
7. *Ulster Year Book 1935*, Belfast, 1935, p. xiii.
8. Riordan, *Modern Irish Trade*, pp. 197–8; H. Patterson, *Class Conflict and Sectarianism: The Protestant Working Class and the Belfast Labour Movement 1868–1920*, Belfast, 1980, p. 94; Workman Clark, (1928) Ltd., *Shipbuilding in Belfast 1880–1933*, Belfast, 1934; *The Times*, 4 November 1919 (supplement on Ireland).

H

9. W. Semple, *Wages and Prices in Belfast*, unpublished M. Comm. Sc. thesis, The Queen's University of Belfast, 1923.
10. D. H. Aldcroft, *The Inter-War Economy: Britain 1919–1939*, London, 1970, p. 31.
11. *Belfast Newsletter*, 1 January 1920.
12. *Northern Whig*, 1 January 1920.
13. F. Gallagher, *The Indivisible Island*, London, 1957, pp. 293–4. The title of the relevant chapter is actually 'Unemployment follows Dismemberment'.
14. For an exposition of Irish economic policy in the 1930s see James Meenan, *The Irish Economy Since 1922*, Liverpool, 1970, especially chs. 12 and 13.
15. Figures from *Northern Ireland Trade Statistics: Annual Statement of the Trade of the United Kingdom*; Irish Free State *Trade and Shipping Statistics*.
16. I have explored this in more detail in D. S. Johnson, 'Cattle smuggling on the Irish Border 1932–38', *Irish Economic and Social History*, VI, 1979, pp. 41–63 and D. S. Johnson, 'Partition and cross-border trade in the 1920s', in P. Roebuck, *Plantation to Partition*, Belfast, 1981, pp. 229–46.
17. J. R. Parkinson, 'Shipbuilding' in N. Buxton and D. Aldcroft eds., *British Industry Between the Wars*, London, 1979, pp. 79–102.
18. See E. L. Jones, *Shipbuilding in Britain*, Cardiff, 1957, ch. 111.
19. Calculated from Riordan, op. cit., p. 101 (with downward adjustment to account for other Irish yards), *Ulster Year Books 1926–47*. Parkinson, 'Shipbuilding', p. 82.
20. *Belfast Newsletter*, 1 January 1930.
21. F. Rebbeck, 'Evolution of the liner' in *Belfast Newsletter* (Bicentenary Supplement), 1 September 1937.
22. Jones, *Shipbuilding in Britain*, p. 41.
23. P. Buckland, *The Factory of Grievances: Devolved Government in Northern Ireland 1921–39*, Dublin, 1979, pp. 117–18. Public Record Office of Northern Ireland CAB 4/176/15.
24. Like many of the statistics used in this paper on employment, unemployment and industrial output, the figure is taken from the Statistical Appendix to K. S. Isles and N. Cuthbert, *An Economic Survey of Northern Ireland*, Belfast, 1957. It is calculated by dividing the number of unemployed by the number of insured workers. Unemployment in the shipyards was lower than in shipbuilding because the former also included engineers, amongst whom unemployment was lower.
25. D. S. Johnson, 'Sir Ernest Clark' in L. Hannah and D. Jeremy eds., *Dictionary of Business Biography*, I (forthcoming); *Belfast Telegraph*, 28 May and 14 June 1935.
26. *Belfast Telegraph*, 11 December 1933, 11 December 1937. PRONI CAB 9A 61/2 *Memorandum on Harland and Wolff by F. E. Rebbeck*, 23 November 1936.
27. See PRONI CAB 7R/60/2 *Rearmament work in Northern Ireland*, 30 March 1938, and Public Record Office, London, ADM 209/1 *Blue Lists of Admiralty Ships under Construction*.

28. W. Black, *Variations in Employment in the Linen Industry in Northern Ireland*, unpublished Ph.D. thesis, Queen's University of Belfast, 1955. The following paragraphs draw heavily on this very valuable work. Other figures are taken from the Trade Statistics of Northern Ireland and the United Kingdom cited above.

29. See for example Buckland, *Factory of Grievances*, pp. 53–4. Buckland's analysis follows that of a 1928 Report which almost certainly failed to diagnose the industry's problems with total accuracy.

30. Government of Northern Ireland, *Report on the Linen Industry Post-War Planning Committee*, Belfast, 1944, p. 17.

31. The quotations in this paragraph are taken from W. Black, *Variations in Employment*, pp. 241–51.

32. W. A. Lewis, *Economic Survey 1919–39*, London, 1949, p. 151. (Population growth is for the world excluding Asia and Africa.)

33. *Ulster Year Book 1926*, Belfast, 1926, p. 15; J. Johnston *Irish Agriculture in Transition*, Oxford, 1951, ch. 1.

34. Calculated from *Report ... relating to the output of ... agricultural produce ... of Scotland* Cmd. 3191 1928–29. *The Agricultural Output of Northern Ireland*, 1924–25, N.I. Cmd. 87, 1928.

35. Quoted in Buckland, *Factory of Grievances*, p. 130.

36. Calculated from Agricultural Output Command Papers cited above.

37. E. H. Whetham, *The Agrarian History of England and Wales*, VIII, Cambridge, 1975, p. 148. See also pp. 148–52 and 226–40.

38. Calculated from *Ulster Year Books* 1929–35 and *Agricultural Statistics for England and Wales and Scotland 1935–38*.

39. Assuming (1) that the relationship between gross and net farming income remained constant between 1924 and 1935, and (2) that the cost of living in Northern Ireland moved in accordance with that in the United Kingdom as a whole.

40. See Government of Northern Ireland *Reports of the Agricultural Enquiry Committee* N.I. Cmd. 249, 1947, p. 212.

41. See for example Buckland, *Factory of Grievances*, pp. 53–4.

42. Proportionately the percentage fall in the share of UK industrial output was as follows: Wales 34 per cent, Northumberland and Durham 27·1 per cent, Lancashire and Cheshire 26 per cent, the West Riding 20 per cent, and Northern Ireland 14 per cent. All other regions increased their share. Aldcroft, op. cit., p. 82; Isles and Cuthbert, op. cit., p. 267.

43. B. W. E. Alford, 'New industries for old? British industry between the wars' in R. Floud and D. McCloskey eds., *The Economic History of Britain since 1700*, II, Cambridge, 1981, pp. 308–31; quotation from p. 321. The previous section draws extensively on this source.

44. Calculated from the *Census of Production for Great Britain* and *Census of Production for Northern Ireland for 1924*.

45. Aldcroft, 'New Industries', p. 103.

46. The City of Belfast, *Official Handbook 1936–37*, London, 1936, pp. 32–5.

47. C. Barnes, *Shorts since 1800*, London, 1967, pp. 27–8.

48. W. Black, 'Industrial change in the twentieth century' in J.C. Beckett and R.E. Glasscock eds., *Belfast: Origins and Growth of an Industrial City*, London, 1967, pp. 157–69; Isles and Cuthbert, *Economic Survey*, p. 578.

49. There are no adequate 'national income' statistics for Northern Ireland. The figures in the text are based on my own tentative estimates for 1924–25, 1930–31 and 1935–36 using the data from the Censuses of Production for Industry and Agriculture. An estimate was then made for the output per head of those not covered by the census. Where my own estimates of the province's 'national income' and those of Isles and Cuthbert, (derived from tax data: see Isles and Cuthbert, *Economic Survey*, p. 455) overlap in 1935–36 they show great similarity (£63·9 million and £63·8 million respectively). A major problem is to adjust the figures for price changes. If the cost of living index is used, this produces a more rapid growth rate than the index implicit in C.H. Feinstein, *National Income, Expenditure and Output of the United Kingdom 1855–1965*, Cambridge, 1972, Table 17.

50. Buckland, *Factory of Grievances*, chs. 4–7; R.J. Lawrence, *The Government of Northern Ireland*, Oxford, 1965, chs. 2–3.

51. Technically the Northern Ireland government could have reduced income tax and surtax by compensating those that had paid these duties by giving them rebates. This would simply have had the effect of reducing government revenue and hence expenditure on the social services and was never seriously contemplated. *Government of Ireland Act*, 1920, 10–11 Geo. V, ch. 67, cap 25.

52. Buckland, *Factory of Grievances*, p. 82.

53. *Ibid.*, p. 83.

54. *Northern Whig*, 30 December 1921. This is obviously a contentious subject. However, wartime evidence does suggest that a proportion of the Northern Ireland labour force, 4 or 5 per cent, remained unemployed even when there was a large excess demand for labour in the United Kingdom as a whole and probably also in the province.

55. *Census of Population for Northern Ireland 1926*, Mitchell and Deane, *Abstract*, pp. 60–1.

56. Buckland, *Factory of Grievances*, p. 161.

57. The Unemployment Insurance Schemes, both in Britain and Northern Ireland, were supposed to be self financing, i.e. the contribution of those who were in work should have covered payments to the unemployed. For various reasons they did not, therefore the schemes had to be subsidised from other revenue. Because unemployment in Northern Ireland was higher than in Britain the subsidies per head of the population were generally larger. The problem of government finance is discussed at length by Buckland and Lawrence in the sources cited above.

58. E. Greer, *The Transport Problem in Northern Ireland 1921–43: a Study of Government Policy*, unpublished M.A. thesis, New University of Ulster, 1977, pp. 70–77.

59. Quoted in Buckland, *Factory of Grievances*, p. 126.

60. K. S. Isles and N. Cuthbert, 'Economic policy' in T. Wilson ed., *Ulster under Home Rule*, Oxford, 1955, pp. 137–82. Quotations from pp. 178–80.

61. 'The evolution of agricultural policy' in *Ulster Year Book 1935*, Belfast, 1935, pp. xiii–xxxi. The 'scrub bull', however, stubbornly refused to disappear. Seamus Heaney, in his poem 'The Outlaw', recalls taking a friesian cow to be served by a scrub bull as late as the 1950s. Seamus Heaney, *Door into the Dark*, London, 1969, pp. 16–17.

62. *Ulster Year Book 1929*, Belfast, 1929, pp. 35–6.

63. For further details see Whetham, *Agrarian History of England and Wales*, XIV.

64. Buckland, *Factory of Grievances*, pp. 139–49.

65. *Ulster Year Book 1935*, p. xxii. This was because tastes in the British market had shifted towards a leaner type of bacon.

66. Calculated from *Ulster Year Book 1932* and Northern Ireland Ministry of Agriculture *Sixth Report upon the Agricultural Statistics of Northern Ireland* N.I. Cmd. 371, 1957, pp. 140–1.

67. Government of Northern Ireland *Report of the Agricultural Enquiry Committee* N.I. Cmd. 249, 1948, p. 41.

68. We have suggested above that it was around 60 per cent of the British average. However, it is well known that inter-country comparisons of per capita national income tend to show the country with the *lower* income in too unfavourable a light. Probably in reality living standards in Northern Ireland were about a third lower than in the United Kingdom generally.

69. It is sometimes seen as necessary to apologise for being below average. But if some regions are above average others, normally the majority, will of necessity be below it.

70. Lawrence, *Government of Northern Ireland*, p. 146.

71. Mitchell and Deane, *Abstract*, p. 10.

72. *Ulster Year Books 1932–47*. For women the rate was a third and for men 40 per cent.

73. Ideally we would wish to compare a whole range of items, the proportion of houses with bathrooms, inside toilets, the cubic capacity of each room, for example. Unfortunately this information is unobtainable.

74. In 1931, for example, in Co. Durham 18 per cent and in Co. Northumberland 28 per cent of the population was living more than two per room and in several of the metropolitan boroughs it was between 20 and 30 per cent. *Census of Population 1931: Housing Report*, Table 13.

75. *Ulster Year Book 1947*, Belfast, 1947, p. 206.

76. The number of marriages rose from 8,600 in 1938 to nearly 12,000 in 1941 falling to 10,500 in 1945. *Ibid.*, p. 48.

77. Government of Northern Ireland *Housing in Northern Ireland Housing in Northern Ireland* N.I. Cmd. 224, 1944. The use of this report by historians has almost certainly led to an over-pessimistic appraisal of the housing situation in the 1930s. Conditions were bad in 1939, but by 1943–44 they were markedly worse.

78. N. Keyfitz and W. Flieger, *World Population: An Analysis of Vital Data*,

London, 1968. Northern Ireland figures from *Ulster Year Books 1929–47* are averages of 1936 and 1937.

79. Lawrence, *Government of Northern Ireland*, ch.7, presents an excessively gloomy picture of health in the province.

80. Government of Northern Ireland *Report of Maternity Services Committee*, Cmd. 219, 1938, p.29.

81. *Ulster Year Books 1932–47*.

82. Government of Northern Ireland, *The Agricultural Output of Northern Ireland 1925*, Cmd. 87, 1928, pp.22–35. It is difficult to discover aggregate consumption figures for the 1930s because of the unreliability of the import statistics from the Irish Free State because of cross-border smuggling.

83. And, of course, as the Boyd Orr and Rowntree surveys showed it was still prevalent in Britain in the 1930s.

84. T. McKeown, *The Modern Rise of Population*, London, 1976, pp.92–3.

85. *Report of Dr. Thomas Carnwath to the Special Committee of the Belfast Corporation on its Municipal Health Services of the City*, Manuscript K, Library of Queen's University Belfast, dated 24 December 1941.

86. *Report of Maternity Services Committee*, p.7.

87. See Lawrence, *Government of Northern Ireland*, ch.6, for a fuller account.

88. *Ulster Year Book 1938*, Belfast, 1938, p.127.

89. *Ulster Year Books 1926–37*; B. Simon, *The Politics of Educational Reform 1920–1940*, London, 1974, pp.363–70.

90. *Ibid.*

91. Government of Northern Ireland *Report of the Committee on the Scholarship System in Northern Ireland* N.I. Cmd. 192, 1938, p.14.

92. The reasons for this lie in political and cultural factors which lie outside the scope of this chapter. Obviously, however, it has a great deal to do with the fact that the 'national' question rather than matters of social policy tended to dominate elections at both local and provincial level.

93. In Northern Ireland consumption rose from 77·6 million units in 1932 to 203·1 in 1938. In the United Kingdom it increased from 1946 million to 3355 million over the same period. *Ulster Year Book 1941*, p.101; B.R. Mitchell, *European Historical Statistics 1750–1970*, London, 1975, p.482.

94. Buckland, *Factory of Grievances*, p.83; *Ulster Year Books 1926–47*.

95. *Belfast Newsletter*, 10 June 1935; S. Rouson, 'A statistical survey of the cinema industry in Great Britain in 1934', *Journal of the Royal Statistical Society*, XCIX, 1936, pp.67–119.

96. *Ulster Year Books 1926–47*; A. Briggs, *The History of Broadcasting in the United Kingdom*, I, Oxford, 1961, p.218.

97. See M. Tuohy, *Belfast Celtic*, Belfast, 1978; W. McMaster, *A History of Motorsport in Ireland*, Belfast, 1970, p.16; E. Van Esbeck, *A Hundred Years of Irish Rugby*, Dublin, 1974, p.116.

98. See J. Walvin, *Leisure and Society 1830–1950*, London, 1978, ch.10.

99. See for example P. Buckland, *Factory of Grievances*, chs.9–11; P. Buckland, *A History of Northern Ireland*, Dublin, 1981, ch.4;

M. Farrell, *Northern Ireland: The Orange State*, London, 1980, chs. 4–6.

100. The reasons for the discrimination have been widely discussed. Fears of Catholic 'disloyalty' to the state, the machinations of power-hungry politicians and exploiting capitalists are amongst the many reasons that have been advanced.

101. *Irish News*, 12 October 1928.

102. See Buckland, *Factory of Grievances*, pp. 219–20, 245–6, 264–5 for a summary of the extent of discrimination against Catholics.

103. PRONI CAB 7B/200, W. A. Magill to the Bishop of Down and Connor, 1 July 1932.

104. What precisely happened in 1935 is still confused and likely to remain so as the relevant file has been closed until the middle years of the next century. The figures are taken from Buckland, *A History of Northern Ireland*, p. 71, and from preliminary unchecked notes on CAB 7B/236 (old style) made in the late 1970s. There was also a non-sectarian riot in 1932 relating to Outdoor Relief in Belfast which has been covered in great detail in P. Devlin, *Yes We Have No Bananas*, Belfast, 1981 and P. Bew and C. Norton, 'The unionist state and the outdoor relief riots of 1932', *Economic and Social Review*, X, 1979, pp. 255–65. However, as Buckland has noted, this demonstration of 'working class solidarity' was ephemeral. Buckland, *A History of Northern Ireland*, p. 7.

105. Royal Ulster Constabulary, *Chief Constable's Report 1979*, Belfast, 1980, p. 59.

106. J. Edwards, 'Capital punishment in Northern Ireland', *Criminal Law Review*, 1956, pp. 750–8; *Royal Commission on Capital Punishment*, Cmd. 8932, 1953, pp. 288–90.

107. *Ireland's Saturday Night*, 28 September 1935.

108. In Wilson ed., *Ulster Under Home Rule*, p. 91.

109. Buckland, *Factory of Grievances*, p. 175, p. 279.

110. Alford, 'New industries', p. 321.

CHAPTER SEVEN

THE ECONOMIC HISTORY OF ULSTER: A PERSPECTIVE

John Othick

At its simplest level, economic history entails gathering together the facts of economic and social life in the past. But for the more serious student, the task of economic history is to place interpretations on these facts, and to use them in order to determine whether any general theories might be adduced as to how economic and social change occurred in the past. The attempts which have already been made to provide such a theoretical framework are relevant to the economic history of Ulster, not least because of the emphasis they place on industrialisation. This is commonly recognised to have been the critical process whereby societies have become rich and powerful, though there is profound disagreement as to precisely how and why it occurred. Since Ulster stands out as the one area in Ireland which experienced substantial industrialisation, it could be assumed that its economic history should at the very least provide empirical evidence against which competing theoretical perspectives might be evaluated. Unfortunately, there is only limited scope for making such an evaluation, as most existing theory has focused on the nation-state rather than the region. Because of this, it rests on assumptions which are of dubious validity in a regional context. The first section of this essay has the twin objectives of identifying the shortcomings of approaches that focus on the nation-state, and of proposing several refinements and adaptations that are required in order to provide a theoretical framework for comprehending regional economic history. An attempt is then made in the second part of the essay to locate the economic history of Ulster within this revised framework.

As is pointed out in Chapter Two (p. 62), early industrialisation is increasingly seen as a process that can best be comprehended in a regional context, which reinforces the need for more economic history to be written at this level.[1] Yet this can be effectively accomplished only on the basis of a theoretical approach which recognises the essential differences between a region and a nation. In several ways, existing theory fails to provide an adequate basis for making this vital distinction. Most obviously, this is because many conventional approaches to national industrialisation focus on the origins of the process rather than on its subsequent vicissitudes. Once an initial critical period of transition has been accomplished, a nation is assumed to have embarked on a path which progresses irreversibly upwards towards the ultimate goal of a modern mass consumer society. In a regional context, objections may be raised to such an assumption purely on the basis of historical evidence: it is quite clear, as Professor Pollard has shown, that many European regions started to industrialise only to experience subsequent decline.[2] Existing theory thus fails to explain why some regions succeeded whereas others failed.

On theoretical grounds, too, there are good reasons for believing that complacent assumptions about the self-sustaining character of economic growth look less credible at the regional level. It is generally assumed that, once the initial transition is complete, industrialisation sustains itself through the operation of inter-industry linkages. In some models, these are seen to emanate primarily from a small number of 'leading sector' industries: the demands of the leading sector thus stimulate the growth of other industries supplying it with machinery, raw materials, and services; at the same time, the leading sector itself provides cheaper and more efficient goods and services that are consumed by other industries. Other models place greater emphasis on the 'balanced' nature of industrialisation: several sectors are held to move forwards simultaneously, each one stimulating the others through backward and forward linkages. At the regional level, neither variant of this model is particularly helpful because of two critical and inter-related differences between a region and a nation. One is that a region almost invariably has a narrower industrial base; the other is that a region is relatively 'open', in both economic and political terms, whereas a nation is relatively 'closed'.

The narrowness of a regional industrial base is merely a reflection of the way in which regions are defined and identified: a region is so labelled precisely because it exhibits features which distinguish it from other regions. It therefore follows that its distinctive location and resource endowments equip it to perform an economic function different from that of other regions. In this sense, regionalism signifies specialisation, which is in turn associated with vulnerability. A nation can still progress even when some of its constituent regions and industries are in decline, simply because this is outweighed by the expansion of other regions and industries. At the regional level, there is by contrast rarely any such compensatory process at work, particularly when industrialisation proceeds primarily under the impetus of market forces.

The vulnerability which stems from regional specialisation is partly explained by the relative openness of regions. Specialisation signifies interdependence between regions, and this means that linkages will operate across regional boundaries just as easily as within them. A region, compared with a nation, will draw a greater proportion of its requirements of goods and services from elsewhere; and it will sell a higher proportion of what it produces to outside consumers. So, at the very least, what is required is a theoretical framework which explains the network of linkages which connects a region to others around it, to the national economy of which it is an integral part, and, ultimately, to the world economy in which both region and nation are enmeshed.

Beyond this, it is clearly necessary to consider the impact on regions of the dynamics of national industrialisation. As the national economy experiences fluctuations, so all linkages are periodically weakened, though perhaps with more harmful consequences for some regions than others. Over time, new industries are likely to emerge and older ones to decline, so that different patterns of linkages develop. Unlike a nation, a region might thus be faced with a secular decline in the effectiveness of its external linkages. It is therefore important to understand why and when this is likely to occur, and how it is linked to the fluctuating fortunes of the national economy.

A further inadequacy of much conventional theory is its assumption that linkages can bring only benefits. There is an alternative perspective which suggests that industrialisation in one region can create or reinforce barriers to industrialisation in another. Whether or not this actually happens depends on the relative strength of 'spread' effects, which encourage the diffusion of industrialisation, as against 'backwash' effects, which produce the opposite result. Spread effects encompass the transfer of technology, capital and business enterprise from a more to a less industrialised region, which thus gains access to a wider and cheaper range of goods and services. Backwash effects occur when the less developed region experiences an outflow of capital, or skilled labour, to a more advanced region; or when its local industries succumb to the competition of more efficient rivals elsewhere. If backwash effects are sometimes more

226

powerful than spread effects, so that some regions actually suffer as a result of the progress of others, it is essential that historians should be able to identify the circumstances where this is most likely to occur.

Another difficulty concerns the relationship between short and long term advantages. It is conceivable that a linkage which brings short term benefits can turn out to be less beneficial in the long term. A region can thrive in the short term by exporting foodstuffs, though it may suffer in the longer term because tastes and prices have changed, or alternative sources of supply have emerged. A linkage which sustains an old established industry in a region might in the longer term actually impede the emergence of newer industries. In short, linkages are most likely to produce lasting benefits where they induce, directly or indirectly, the economic diversification of a region. The most appropriate theoretical framework for comprehending regional economic history is one which suggests how, why, and when external linkages are most likely to induce local responses of a type that promote economic diversification.

The foregoing observations are relevant to the economic history of Ulster simply because, by whatever standards, Ulster has to be regarded as a region. Moreover, it was a region whose economic fortunes were in major respects influenced by events in Britain rather than in Ireland.[3] To understand the changing character of the linkages between Ulster and Britain, it is firstly necessary to review the progress of British industrialisation. Yet, because of its preponderant role within the nineteenth-century world economy, Britain's own progress was very much a reaction to, as well as an influence on, broader international fluctuations. It is therefore these fluctuations which must form the basis of our theoretical approach.

There is some support for the view that there were long periods of above average growth and expansion in the nineteenth-century world economy, separated from each other by equally long periods of slower growth. In particular, the years from the 1780s to 1815, from the early 1840s to the early 1870s, and from the late 1890s until the First World War have been identified as periods of upswing in the world economy. By contrast, the two intervening periods have been characterised as times of less spectacular progress, and perhaps even as years of difficulty and depression. A similar cyclical pattern has been identified in the British context: in particular, there is agreement that both the mid-nineteenth century and the early part of the twentieth century were periods of economic boom. Spread effects seem to have been particularly powerful during cyclical upswings, which were thus accompanied by an acceleration in the diffusion of industrialisation, both within and between countries.

The critical issue is of course to understand why, confronted by similar spread effects during the same cyclical upswing, some regions achieved full industrialisation whereas in others it remained an incomplete or ephemeral process. It is never enough merely to observe that some regions possessed advantages for industrialisation, whereas others were beset by obstacles: these advantages and obstacles were themselves consequences of antecedent circumstances generally, and in particular of the interplay of external influences and internal reactions during the preceding downswing. There is some evidence that backwash effects were most acutely felt during cyclical downswings.[4] So it was the strength and character of backwash effects, together with the tensions they generated and the reactions they induced, that either enhanced or impaired a region's capacity for subsequent transformation. Regional industrialisation, and hence the economic history of Ulster, is thus best comprehended as a sequence of challenges and responses: the former emanated from a periodically widening set of production possibilities,[5] which were determined by the rhythms of the world economy and Britain's changing international role; the latter were constrained by the local economic, social and institutional structures that had resulted from the previous interaction of regional, national and international influences.

Ulster's earliest wave of industrialisation, during the Napoleonic wars, was at least partly sustained by the spread effects generated by English industrialisation, then experiencing its first major upswing. Technology, entrepreneurs, and perhaps some capital, crossed the Irish Sea to facilitate the growth of textile production in Ulster. Particularly strong and enduring linkages were established between Ulster and the Scottish Lowlands, and with parts of northern England. It is important not to exaggerate the province's dependence on external assistance, for it is clear that local entrepreneurs responded to new opportunities with a determination and inventiveness similar to that of their British counterparts. In an Irish context, Ulster stood out as the one region to experience a substantial increase in its manufacturing capacity. Yet it would be extravagent to claim that the achievements of these years constituted a major process of industrialisation. The geographical spread of industrial activity remained very limited, whilst agriculture continued to engage the vast bulk of the population. Such industry as did become established tended often to be located in rural areas, or in small towns, so that there was no major urbanisation such as was occurring in parts of Britain. Industries also developed few local linkages, and generally remained extremely vulnerable. Although the cotton industry faced the competition of Lancashire with much greater resilience than is commonly recognised, its ultimate demise suggests that Ulster's more promising opportunities were in areas of industrial activity that were less firmly established in Britain itself.

By comparison with regions elsewhere in Europe, Ulster was favourably placed: its position within the United Kingdom allowed it to benefit from spread effects at a time when war impeded the diffusion of industrialisation between England and the continent. Warfare also encouraged price inflation, thus providing a stimulus to Ulster's agriculture which, in common with agriculture throughout Ireland, was finding a ready market in Britain's rapidly expanding cities. The return of peace marked the beginning of a period when the benefits of incorporation within the United Kingdom were perhaps less obvious. To understand why, it is necessary to consider Britain's position within the world economy.

There can be little doubt that Britain's leading industrial regions were unique in experiencing a major process of structural change in the pre-1815 upswing: although manufacturing output did expand in other parts of the British Isles and Europe, no other regions experienced such a radical inter-sectoral shift of resources. Having attained a hegemonic position in world markets during the wars, British industry was strongly placed to penetrate European markets, which of course became more accessible with the return of peace. In common with regions elsewhere in Europe, Ulster thus stood in an ambivalent relationship with Britain: on the one hand, Britain represented the major potential source of the inputs of capital and technology necessary to revolutionise production; on the other hand, British competition represented a major backwash effect hindering the progress of manufacturing elsewhere. The central paradox of this period is that Britain's success had fostered the growth and diffusion of the will to industrialise − and of the desire to emulate − at a time when the scope for industrialisation was circumscribed, not just by British competition, but also by a relatively slowly expanding range of production possibilities.

The most rational response to the challenge of British competition was for a region to utilise those resources it possessed in greater abundance than Britain. Because Britain led the way in most areas of technology, there was only limited scope for producing goods other than those in which it specialised. An easier alternative was for other regions to employ different combinations of resources to produce goods which were basically similar. The point has already been made that regional specialisation is often regarded as being based on comparative advantage.[6] However, what is being suggested here is that, in the specific context of early nineteenth-century industrialisation, regional specialisation developed initially not as a spontaneous attempt to exploit an obvious advantage, but as a defensive response to a major disadvantage. The response varied from one region to another, not least because they were not all at the same disadvantage.

In the case of Ulster, competitive pressures intensified during the 1820s and 1830s with the disappearance of tariff protection, and with the improvement of cross channel communications that followed the introduction of steamships. The province became more firmly enmeshed within the economy of the world's first and most powerful industrialising nation, though its status remained essentially very different from that of the leading industrial regions in Britain. In many ways, Ulster confronted much the same challenge as other European regions, though it was more restricted in terms of its freedom to respond to the challenge. Because of political incorporation into the United Kingdom, the province's industrialists could not hope to benefit from the sort of protective and promotional government activity that was beginning to occur in parts of Europe.[7] Yet its position must be compared favourably with that of the rest of Ireland, which actually experienced some de-industrialisation in this period.

The evidence, however, is quite clear that Ulster's entrepreneurs were willing to respond positively to changed economic circumstances. The emergence of an enduring framework of locally owned joint stock banks is perhaps the clearest evidence that the business community was prepared to engage in bold new initiatives. The rapid diffusion of the wet-spinning process, and the consequent expansion of the linen industry in the 1830s, again shows that Ulster was able to respond to new production possibilities with perhaps even greater alacrity than other regions. However, even by the 1840s, the province's manufacturing economy still rested primarily on one industry, which had yet to generate substantial local linkages, other than to agriculture, from which it drew its key raw materials. Linen was an industry whose fortunes remained subject to pronounced vicissitudes, as became apparent during the difficult years of the early 1840s. Exogenous factors influenced not just the fluctuations of the industry, but also the character of its growth.

The lines along which the linen industry developed were consistent with a response common in regions striving to industrialise in the face of British competition. Perhaps the most important resource which such regions possessed in greater abundance than Britain was a pool of cheap, underemployed labour located in the agrarian economy. This was of particular significance in Ulster, because of its established role as a supplier of food to the British market. As industrial progress in Britain raised demand for meat and dairy products rather than cereals, so grain prices faltered in the post-Napoleonic period, and there was a check to the rise of the incomes of some groups in agriculture. In these circumstances, rural industry served the interests of both capital and labour: for the former, it meant that lower wages were possible because the workforce produced its own food, compared with an urban proletariat which had to purchase its food; for the latter, even low wages represented a welcome supplement to a meagre income from working in agriculture. The linen industry's strong ties with rural areas have been dealt with in Chapter One. The important point is to view this kind of rural industrialisation as a response to the rise of factory production, and not merely as a potential precursor of full industrialisation. Initially, external competitive pressures induced several branches of the textile industries to minimise costs by locating in rural areas. With the rise of mechanised flax spinning in the 1830s and 1840s, a situation developed where an increasingly urban-based spinning sector stimulated the continued expansion of the weaving sector in rural areas.

The foregoing remarks raise what is perhaps the most fundamental question concerning the economic progress of a region such as Ulster. Although industrialisation is frequently associated with economic development, it can never be sufficient merely to observe that the level of manufacturing output increased over a given period. Growth occurs only when aggregate output expands faster than population. If an increase in output somehow induces a similar, or even greater, increase in population, then industrialisation is occurring without economic growth: the region concerned is caught in what has been termed a low level equilibrium trap.[8] This is not always an insurmountable barrier, and may even be a short term problem which must necessarily be endured in order to obtain longer term benefits. It is therefore of critical importance to assess the demographic consequences of industrial growth.

The pattern of industrialisation that occurred in Ulster in the 1820s and 1830s was, partly because of external influences, one which precluded large scale urbanisation, whilst reinforcing the trend towards a rapidly rising rural population. This trend was apparent everywhere in Ireland, so rural industrialisation was obviously only one of a number of factors encouraging an increase in population. Apart from its links with population growth, proto-industrialisation is often seen as a precursor of industrialisation proper. However, it seems that rural industry in Ulster rarely provided an adequate basis for subsequent transformation, though it was undoubtedly far more resilient than industries elsewhere in Ireland.[9] If anything, it paved the way for a widening of inequalities within the region, as industry migrated towards more attractive locations. Initially, it was the mechanised spinning processes which began gradually to relocate towards the north-east corner of the province, while more peripheral areas continued to expand on the basis of handloom weaving. Ultimately, however, even weaving was destined to decline, so that one part of Ulster became de-industrialised as another industrialised.[10] It is a familiar theme in economic history that regions which were at a disadvantage *vis-à-vis* core industrial areas were often able to compensate by establishing a dominant relationship with regions even less favourably placed than themselves. By monopolising the provision of commercial and other services, and by attracting capital and skills, intermediate regions could sometimes benefit at the expense of their neighbours. Viewed in these terms, the industrial progress of Ulster before the 1840s produced an uneven distribution of benefits, whilst exacerbating the problem of population pressure, particularly in some of the southern areas of the province.[11] The foundations had undoubtedly been laid; but there is only limited evidence that they were yet capable of supporting a more diversified industrial structure.

As Ireland approached its greatest demographic crisis, so the world economy entered another major upswing in the 1840s. This was accompanied by a spread of industrialisation into new regions, including parts of the United States, the expansion of which facilitated the absorption of excess population from the more economically distressed areas of Europe. Although Ulster was less traumatically affected by famine than those parts of Ireland where dependence on agriculture was total, emigration has still to be seen as a vital influence on its economic growth during the mid-nineteenth century. The regional economy was still not remotely capable of generating employment for everyone born there: it thus became considerably easier to accomplish an increase in output per head once emigration began to curb population growth. Apart from helping indirectly to resolve an old economic problem, world economic expansion also confronted the province with new challenges. The technological advances which underpinned the boom allowed Britain to assume a new international role, which in turn provided opportunities for regions such as Ulster to develop new industries. A key factor in the world economic up-swing was the role of steam power in improving communications, first on land, and then over sea. These twin processes and their associated linkages conferred peculiar advantages on Britain which, directly and indirectly, enabled it to assume a unique position in world shipping and shipbuilding.

Railways played a key role in the spread of industrialisation to parts of Europe and the United States. This was just one part of a general widening of the world economy, as new supplies of food and raw materials were opened up in outlying areas of the globe. Britain was at the heart of this process, and came to occupy a position which had no precedent, yet which was destined to be transient. It was the world's major source of finance, technology, expertise, and cheap iron; and it was the world's major consumer of the primary commodities which flowed from the newly opened-up areas. As the world's leading trading nation, it is hardly surprising that Britain emerged also as the leading shipping nation, carrying not only its own rapidly expanding imports and exports but also much of the trade of other nations. As one of the world's major consumers of ships, it was but a short step to becoming the world's major producer: it was merely a question of building on the advantages Britain already possessed in the form of cheap iron and engineering expertise. These circumstances are the background to the rise of the British ship-building industry, specialising in iron-built steamships, to a position of world pre-eminence.

The response of Belfast to this new opportunity has been examined elsewhere.[12] Without wishing to detract from the extraordinary entrepreneurial talents which ensured the long term success of Belfast shipbuilding, it is important that its shorter term contribution to growth is kept in perspective. Compared with other regions in the

United Kingdom, the takeoff of shipbuilding in Ulster came at a relatively late stage of the mid-century upswing. Its growth was not particularly spectacular in the first two decades of its existence, and there must be doubts as to whether it generated substantial local linkages in the period down to the 1870s. Undoubtedly, this new industry represented a much needed addition to the region's manufacturing capacity, but it would be an exaggeration to see it as a dynamic leading sector in its early years. It is also clear that it widened rather than narrowed the spatial imbalance already apparent within the province.

It was in fact the older-established linen trade that provided a more significant source of industrial vitality in the mid-ninteenth century. Heavy dependence on overseas markets still rendered it particularly vulnerable to external shocks such as wars and financial crises. However, it had clearly reached the stage where it could survive even the worst years without ever approaching total collapse; and, in the good years, it could assert its role as a world leader, capable of holding its position in a rapidly expanding international market. During the 1840s and 1850s it began for the first time to stimulate the growth of the Belfast engineering industry, parts of which were also beginning to penetrate overseas markets. It is significant that, as manufacturing spread into new regions, textiles were usually amongst the first industries to become established. The diffusion of industrialisation thus represented a classic case of the potential divergence, previously alluded to, between short and long term interests.[13] Initially, it offered the capital goods industries the opportunity to expand their exports; in the longer term, it meant that textiles had perhaps more to fear than most industries from the emergence of foreign rivals.

Such a situation had not yet arisen, and the linen industry continued to expand as new techniques of production were introduced. As late as 1850, the industry retained strong links with rural areas, even though by then it was also generating expanding employment opportunities in the towns. The spread of powerloom weaving from the 1850s encouraged the beginnings of the relocation of this branch of the industry towards larger urban factories. Behind this process lay the pervasive influence of Ulster's changing demographic experience. Emigration, by reducing the pressure of population on agricultural resources, effectively removed an essential foundation on which rural industry rested: wages began to rise, and businessmen began to look with greater favour on labour-saving innovations. Yet, even with the resultant shift towards mechanised factory production, the links between industry and agriculture were not completely severed. During the period of spectacular growth induced by the American Civil War, linen output was raised partly through an extension of manufacturing into quite remote rural areas. This was only a temporary phenomenon, but it demonstrates how the inter-penetration of industry with agriculture could still serve the interests of business, when the international economic climate was particularly favourable. Moreover, it seems that the survival of such interpen-etration actually retarded the transition from arable farming to livestock, at least in parts of the province. Areas where this occurred tended in the short term to retain more of their population; but, in the longer term, they were more vulnerable to the intensifying com-petitive pressures that were to accompany the world economic down-swing of the 1870s.

Largely because the world economy had been through an upswing which provided unprecedented opportunities for the diffusion of industrialisation, and because there existed within Ulster entrepreneurial talent capable of responding effectively to these opportunities, the province had succeeded in diversifying its industrial base between the 1840s and the early 1870s, whilst at the same time experiencing a check to its population growth. The province generally, and the Belfast area in particular, were beginning to evolve an industrial structure quite distinct from that of the rest of Ireland. At the same time, the emergence of shipbuilding strengthened considerably the ties which already existed with Glasgow and Liverpool. The former for a time provided essential inputs such as marine engines; the latter represented a potentially significant market for ships. But by comparison with Britain's more advanced regions, Ulster's achievements were still modest. The industrial base continued to be precariously narrow, and generated a disproportionately large amount of low-paid female employment. Although earnings were rising for some sections of the population, it seems that these were still often spent on imported con-sumer products. The backwash effects of British competition did not disappear and might even have intensified as railways began to penetrate rural Ulster, allowing products to enter more easily without providing any great stimulus to local manufacturing. The proportion of the population living in towns remained low by British standards, whilst Belfast was much smaller than the major British cities. Intra-regional inequalities survived, and perhaps widened. The spread of branch banking into rural areas was beginning to create a channel whereby capital was transferred from less favoured areas to Belfast, where it was used to finance the expansion of commerce and industry. Paradoxically, the relatively modest response of Ulster's shipbuilding and engineering industries to the opportunities provided by the mid-century boom in some ways mitigated the impact of the ensuing downswing.

The most obvious symptom of the new downswing was a marked downturn in prices which lasted, with minor interruptions, from 1873 to 1896. This trend was the inevitable long term consequence of two processes which had played a central role in the mid-century boom. The first entailed the opening up of new supplies of primary commodities, as a result of the spread of railways and improved transoceanic communications. By the 1870s, European agriculture was having to contend with an influx of cheap overseas food. Although this relatively novel backwash effect was perhaps even more severely felt in other parts of Ireland, it obviously posed greater problems for Ulster than for regions less dependent on agriculture; and, in particular, it affected those parts of the province which continued to engage in the production of cereals, for it was these that suffered the greatest price decline.

The second factor behind the downswing was far more problematic for Britain, though rather less so for Ulster. This involved the growing industrial and commercial power of those regions and nations which had taken off in the 1840s and 1850s. By the 1870s, other nations were beginning to challenge Britain's hegemony for the first time, occasionally bolstering their overseas commercial expansion with policies of aggressive economic nationalism, of a type which the United Kingdom resolutely continued to eschew. It was the old staple industries, with their traditional export orientation, which were the first to feel the impact of foreign competition. Ulster was perhaps less affected than regions where the older industries were more firmly established: hence the observation above that its modest response to the mid-century boom was in some ways an advantage.

The downswing certainly interrupted Ulster's economic progress, at least during the 1870s, when there was a marked deceleration in the growth of Belfast. The linen industry, having over-expanded in the boom years of the 1860s, was again faltering in the face of foreign competition. There was perhaps a further widening of the gap between city and country, because of the depressing effect of world price trends on agricultural areas, many of which experienced in the 1880s their highest rates of outmigration since the Famine. By contrast, the most striking aspect of the manufacturing sector was its resilience: not only did it make a swift recovery from early setbacks, but it was also poised to play a leading role in the subsequent economic upturn.

Global price trends were reversed in the later 1890s as part of another world upswing, which involved both a further spread of industrialisation and the opening up of more regions of primary production. However, Britain's role in this new wave of expansion was much diminished by comparison with the mid-century boom. It had become more closely integrated with its own empire, and with areas in Latin America where it continued to enjoy informal influence. Britain was thus more involved in opening up the resources of these areas than in the spread of industrialisation into parts of Italy, Russia, and Japan. The upswing is usually associated with the growth of new industries, such as electrical engineering, chemicals, and cheap steel. Yet Britain's Edwardian boom was based more on the revival of old industries than on the emergence of new ones. Moreover, this revival was sustained by export demand, which in turn was often dependent, particularly after 1905, on the investment of British capital abroad. This placed additional purchasing power in the hands of overseas trading partners, many of whom were also benefiting from rising export prices. Demand was thus boosted, particularly for the products of the older industries.

Ulster's industrial structure placed it in a strong position to participate in this export-led boom. Britain remained not only a substantial exporter, but also the major importer of the products which flowed from newly opened up regions. Clearly, this expanding trade signified a buoyant demand for shipping, which Belfast was then in a stronger position than ever to provide. Many of Britain's trading partners were poorer countries trying to establish low-technology industries such as textiles; again, the Belfast engineering industry was well placed to meet this growing demand. The more affluent Dominion countries increasingly sought quality products, thus ensuring a market for linen, which was fast attaining the status of a luxury good. However, although external factors strongly favoured the growth of Ulster's industries, it was internal strengths that enabled them to respond so effectively and so soon.

Whereas in the mid-century boom Ulster had lagged behind other regions in responding to widening economic opportunities, it played a more prominent role in the ensuing upswing. If anything, the acceleration in the pace of its industrial progress actually preceded that of other regions. Even by the mid-1880s, the shipbuilding industry was entering on a phase of growth significantly faster than anything previously attained. This resulted in closer economic interdependence with Merseyside, whilst Belfast's economic structure came increasingly to resemble that of Clydeside rather than of anywhere else in Ireland. At a somewhat later date, the linen industry also experienced an upturn, largely because of increasing world demand. New export industries emerged in such fields as drink, tobacco and engineering. For the first time, Ulster's manufacturing had come to encompass a wider range of industries. Belfast doubled in size between 1881 and 1911, becoming in the process an industrial and commercial centre comparable with Britain's major cities. The fortunes of the rural economy also improved with rising prices, and emigration fell to much lower levels. Ulster, it seems, had finally become established as a major industrial region within the United Kingdom economy.

It is one thing to become effectively incorporated within a national economy which enjoys international pre-eminence; it is, however, a rather different matter to become an integral part of a national economy whose fortunes are in decline. Ironically, Ulster having earlier failed to achieve the former, was highly successful in achieving the latter towards the end of the nineteenth century. The province's economic history in the years before 1914 provides valuable insights into two inter-related limitations which commonly afflict regions: one is the extent to which a region's role is circumscribed by national development and its supporting policies; the other is the extent to which the achievements of one generation can become the problems of the next.

With regard to the issue of national development, it has been argued that, particularly after the 1890s, Britain became over-committed to an obsolescent industrial base which depended too heavily on overseas markets. Over-commitment was an easy way out: it was an alternative to the modernisation and diversification of industry, because it allowed Britain to continue to depend on old industries. Although these remained profitable in the short term, their long term prospects already looked uncertain. World demand for the products of these industries was expanding less rapidly than demand for other products. Many of the markets which had traditionally absorbed these exports were already consciously striving for greater economic autonomy: even the Dominion countries were developing a manufacturing base which would make them less dependent on Britain. As industrialisation spread with the world economic upswing, so it was inevitable that Britain would face increasing competition even in the home market, particularly under a regime of free trade. Over-commitment was less a conscious strategy, and more the consequence of an economic system which obdurately adhered to an unshakeable belief in the efficacy of market forces. Ulster's success in winning a place within this system effectively ensured that these same market forces impelled it too along the path of over-commitment. It was this achievement that contributed directly to the structural problems the province was to encounter in the 1920s and 1930s (though in fairness it should be added that the bases of these problems are more obvious in retrospect than they were at the time).

The problems inherited by the inter-war generation have been adequately described elsewhere.[14] In essence, they were the problems of a region too heavily dependent on too narrow a range of industries, which had previously over-expanded in response to a temporarily favourable world-market situation. As the world economy suffered its worst ever downswing, so backwash effects were transmitted to Ulster in the form of a particularly intractable crisis of structural unemployment. The central features of the province's economic history in the twentieth century have thus revolved around the long term decline of its basic industries. In the wake of the world economic crisis, there followed a re-orientation of attitudes towards market forces. It became widely recognised that governments have a responsibility to intervene in order to counteract the disequalising tendencies of market forces. One aspect of this new awareness involved what has come to be known as regional policy.

By any criteria, Ulster has remained a peripheral and disadvantaged region throughout the period since the 1920s. Regional policy has, with varying degrees of success, sought to minimise the disadvantages, not least by creating employment. Yet, even at the peak of the post-war boom, the province lagged far behind the more favoured regions of the United Kingdom: in 1967–68, for example, incomes in Northern Ireland were only 83·6 per cent of the national UK average.[15] The ensuing period has seen the world economy descend into yet another downswing, during which exceptionally heavy job losses have again revealed Ulster's vulnerability. It has been observed that regional inequalities frequently become more pronounced during early industrialisation, though the gap tends to diminish in the later stages of the process. The economic history of Ulster provides much evidence for challenging this complacent assumption: for a disadvantaged region in a declining industrial power, it seems that, diminishing gaps notwithstanding, total convergence looks as unattainable as ever.

Notes

1. ·S. Pollard, 'Industrialistion and the European economy', *Economic History Review*, XXVI, 1973, pp. 636–48.
2. S. Pollard, *Peaceful Conquest*, Oxford, 1981, pp. 29–30.
3. This is not to suggest that Ulster should be regarded as a homogeneous region. Important differences existed within the province at all times, so that there are sound reasons for considering it as a series of inter-dependent sub-regions. This theme is further discussed at p. 000 below; note also the intra-Ulster differences discussed in chapter one in particular.
4. So, for example, contemporaries often attributed Britain's Great Depression of 1873–96 to the harmful effects of foreign competition and hostile trade policies.
5. Cyclical upswings are associated with the introduction of new technologies, the opening up of new resources and markets, and changes in the organisation and structure of business. A widening of production possibilities thus signifies an expanding range of opportunities in one or more of these areas. See for example J. A. Schumpeter, *Business Cycles*, New York, 1939.
6. See above, p. 225.
7. Probably the best example of this was Belgium in the 1830s.
8. See H. Myint, *The Economics of Developing Countries*, London, fifth edn., 1980, ch. 7.
9. According to one school of thought, the more advanced regions within any peripheral society are in a weak, dependent relationship with the nations of the industrialised core; yet, simultaneously, they are in a dominant, exploitative relationship with less favourably placed regions within their own society. See A. G. Frank, *Dependent Accumulation and Under development*, 1978, New York.
10. De-industrialisation generally on the island is dealt with in E. O'Malley, 'The decline of Irish industry in the nineteenth century', *Economic and Social Review*, XIII, 1981, pp. 21–42.
11. See Chapter One, pp. 14–15.
12. See Chapter Two, pp. 86–96.
13. See Chapter Six, pp. 187–8, 191–7, 216.
14. See Chapter Six.
15. C. H. Lee, *Regional Economic Growth in the United Kingdom Since the 1880s*, London, 1971, p. 201.

The rural economy, 1820–1914
W. H. Crawford, *Domestic Industry in Ireland*, Dublin, 1972
James S. Donnelly Jr., *Landlord and Tenant in Nineteenth Century Ireland*,
    Dublin, 1973
T. W. Freeman, *Ireland: A General and Regional Geography*, London, 1972
Conrad Gill, *The Rise of the Irish Linen Industry*, Oxford, 1925
W. A. Maguire, *The Downshire Estates in Ireland, 1801–45*, Oxford, 1972

Industry, 1820–1914
J. C. Beckett and R. E. Glasscock eds., *Belfast: The Origin and Growth of
    an Industrial City*, London, 1967
W. E. Coe, *The Engineering Industry of the North of Ireland*, Newton Abbot,
    1969
E. R. R. Green, *The Lagan Valley, 1800–50*, London, 1949
H. D. Gribbon, *The History of Water Power in Ulster*, Newton Abbot, 1969
Peter Roebuck ed., *Plantation to Partition*, Belfast, 1981
E. J. Riordan, *Modern Irish Trade and Industry*, London, 1920

Transport, 1820–1914
I. J. Herring, 'Ulster Roads on the eve of the railway age', *Irish Historical
    Studies*, 11, 1940
W. A. McCutcheon, *The Canals of the North of Ireland*, Dawlish, 1965
W. A. McCutcheon, *The Industrial Archaeology of Northern Ireland*, Belfast,
    1980
D. B. McNeill, *Irish Passenger Steamship Services*, 1, Newton Abbot, 1969
K. B. Nowlan, 'Communications' in T. W. Moody and J. C. Beckett eds.,
    Ulster Since 1800, London, 1957
K. B. Nowlan, *Travel and Transport in Ireland*, Dublin, 1973

Population and urbanisation, 1821–1911
L. A. Clarkson, 'Marriage and fertility in nineteenth-century Ireland', in
    R. B. Outhwaite ed., *Marriage and Society*, London, 1981
A. C. Hepburn, 'Belfast 1871–1911: work, class and religion', *Irish Economic
    and Social History*, X, 1983
R. E. Kennedy, Jr., *The Irish: Emigration, Marriage and Fertility*, London,
    1973
Joel Mokyr, *Why Ireland Starved*, London, 1983

Cormac Ó Gráda, 'Some aspects of nineteenth-century Irish emigration', in L. M. Cullen and T. C. Smout eds., *Comparative Aspects of Scottish and Irish Economic and Social History*, Edinburgh, 1977
W. E. Vaughan and A. J. Fitzpatrick, *Irish Historical Statistics: Population*, Dublin, 1978

Industrial labour and the labour movement, 1820–1914
D. L. Armstrong, 'Social and economic conditions in the Belfast linen industry, 1850–1900', *Irish Historical Studies*, VII, 1951
Emily Boyle, 'Linenopolis', in J. C. Beckett *et al. Belfast: The Making of the City*, Belfast, 1983
Mary Daly, 'Women in the Irish workforce from pre-industrial to modern times', *Saothar*, VII, 1981
Peter Gibbon, *The Origins of Ulster Unionism*, Manchester, 1975
Betty Messenger, *Picking up the Linen Threads*, Austin, Texas, 1975
Henry Patterson, *Class Conflict and Sectarianism*, Belfast, 1980

The Northern Ireland economy, 1914–39
W. Black, 'Industrial change in the twentieth century' in J. C. Beckett and R. E. Glasscock eds., *Belfast, The Origin and Growth of an Industrial City*, London, 1967
Patrick Buckland, *The Factory of Grievances: Devolved Government in Northern Ireland, 1921–39*, Dublin, 1979
Patrick Buckland, *A History of Northern Ireland*, Dublin, 1981
K. S. Isles and N. Cuthbert, *An Economic Survey of Northern Ireland*, Belfast, 1957
R. J. Lawrence, *The Government of Northern Ireland*, Oxford, 1965
T. Wilson, ed., *Ulster Under Home Rule*, London, 1955

INDEX OF PLACES

INDEX OF SUBJECTS